SONIC REBELLION

MUSIC AS RESISTANCE

DETROIT 1967-2017

TABLE OF CONTENTS

DIRECTOR'S FOREWORD

ELYSIA BOROWY-REEDER

Since opening our doors in 2006, MOCAD has championed artists and disciplines that cross boundaries and foster critical dialogue. The Museum has always looked to artists to help interpret the world and expand our understanding of it. In this moment, when our nation is deeply divided, MOCAD's role as a museum is especially poignant and significant. The exhibition *Sonic Rebellion: Music as Resistance* speaks to the diversity of art and culture both past and present. This country comprises many varied and divergent voices, and I see art as providing a unique lens through which to see our culture and humanity in all its complexity.

First, I would like to acknowledge MOCAD's Chief Curator at Large Jens Hoffmann and Ford Curatorial Fellow Robin K. Williams for their efforts in putting this exhibition together. I also thank all the participating artists for their boundless enthusiasm and imaginative insights. Through all of our exhibitions and programs, MOCAD strives to offer platforms for discussions and debates, and we could not present such ambitious exhibitions as *Sonic Rebellion* without the generous support of the A. Alfred Taubman Foundation. *Sonic Rebellion: Music as Resistance* is generously supported by the John S. and James L. Knight Foundation.

Sonic Rebellion: Music as Resistance is inspired by the vital history of music in Detroit and the legacy of the 1967 Detroit Rebellion. The exhibition continues MOCAD's investigations into the history of Detroit as well as its programmatic focus on the relationships between art, music, and politics. Curators Hoffmann and Williams are thought leaders and experts on convening artists, discovering creativity, engaging the under-represented, and developing deep artist-curator relationships. Their work in the Detroit community and beyond offers audiences opportunities to re-examine accepted histories and newly encounter overlooked artists and historical moments. We owe a thank you to Judith Banham of Middlecott Design for creating the exhibition's graphic identity and catalogue design. We also extend deep thanks to Zeb Smith and Naaman Rosen for their tireless work installing a brilliant-looking exhibition.

The *Sonic Rebellion* Advisory Committee was essential in contributing to conversations during the exhibition's planning that ultimately helped shape the presentation, especially as topics moved beyond art—to music and community activism and beyond. We thank the Committee for their expertise and support: Dan Aldridge, John Collins, Meghan Courtney, Bryce Detroit, Jean Louis Farges, Dameon Gabriel, Oren Goldenberg, Marion Hayden, Shea Howell, Curtis Lipscomb, Cary Loren, Derrick May, Rebecca Mazzei, Michelle McKinney, Marsha Music, Miz Korona, Pirahnahead, Steven Reaume, Tim Retzloff, Karen Hudson Samuels, Tylonn Sawyer, Leni Sinclair, Zana Smith, Sterling Toles, and Patrick Burton.

I hope you visit MOCAD often and we continue to challenge and inspire you. The Museum aims to provide a space for reflection, dialogue, and connection to the world around us.

Elysia Borowy-Reeder
Executive Director
Museum of Contemporary Art Detroit

RIOTS, REBELLIONS, AND REVOLUTIONS

JENS HOFFMANN

What broke out in Detroit on July 23, 1967, has been called a number of things: an uprising, a rebellion, a crisis, a revolt, a civil disturbance, a riot. The available vocabulary splits easily into two general points of view: one that emphasizes the actions of Detroiters responding to the oppressive and unequal systems of their city, and another that casts these same resisters as dangerous lawbreakers. Much of the time, "riot" is the word that emerges most easily—though of course this vocabulary is not without its biases, tending to generate images of persons lashing out violently and without cause. This term links the events of late-July 1967 with a string of other "riots" throughout the United States around that time—in Watts, Harlem, Philadelphia, Cleveland, Newark, and elsewhere—that brought national attention to racial inequalities, economic disparities, police violence, and housing issues throughout the nation's (largely northern) urban centers. This link is appropriate, in many ways, as the conditions facing African Americans in Detroit in the 1960s paralleled those facing African Americans in other cities. But while the term "riot" provides a fitting context within the scheme of national events, it also erases many crucial historical layers of those events: the cities' long-term practices of racially-segregated housing; the cultivation of intimidating, out-of-touch police forces; and, in Detroit, a faltering manufacturing industry that had taken more than a hundred and fifty thousand jobs out of the city and into the suburbs. These things and others, the many facets of the systematized racism of the city of Detroit, provoked its citizens to rebel in the streets.

Whatever terminology is chosen, what happened in the Motor City fifty years ago this summer lasted a little less than a week, rocked the local community, and disturbed the nation. The event started with a rather routine raid on an unlicensed bar in a black neighborhood in Detroit, but quickly became something more than the police had planned for when they found more than eighty—rather than merely dozens—of patrons inside the illegal "joint." A crowd grew on the street to watch the establishment's customers and staff get carted off to jail, and something far less than routine began to bubble. What began with an unlicensed nightclub and a thrown bottle ended with forty-three deaths, one thousand injuries, more than seven thousand arrests, and property damage worth more than $40 million.

The details of this weeklong incursion have been replayed time and again, particularly this year, as the city remembers their fiftieth anniversary. Oral history projects collected at Wayne State University have captured important memories of the time—the realities of living in Detroit at midcentury and the events themselves. Books, journal articles, films, and exhibitions have traced the events, their roots, and their reverberations. But it is not only the minutiae of what occurred fifty years ago that we find ourselves investing this year. Rather, we should turn our investigations to the historical conditions of the city and the nation, the ongoing accumulation of grievances, and the lineages of injustices—where we still find so much relevance for our contemporary moment.

> To understand Detroit and what took place in July 1967, it is important to examine at least the preceding quarter-century and the developments that, on one hand, made the nation's fifth largest city a most unlikely place for the worst civil disorder in the twentieth century, and what, on the other, made such a disorder inevitable.[1]

1 Hubert G. Locke, *The Detroit Riot of 1967* (Detroit: Wayne State University Press, 2017), p. 52.

When writing about riots, their inception, and their proliferation, historians, journalists, and sociologists often use the metaphor of a "spark" to identify a singular event that "ignites" an outburst of action. To borrow and extend this metaphor, we can think about the three elements required for fire: heat, fuel, and oxygen. If the events that took place in the early morning hours of July 23, at the "blind pig" near 12th Street and Clairmount Avenue, acted as the heat, then the city's history was the fuel. While the rebellion was shocking to many, it was but one event in a long history of tense racial relationships in this urban landscape.

The history of racial discrimination is woven into the very fabric of Detroit, as it is in most American cities. Even the names of streets, cities, and counties are subtle reminders of this history, though some of that legacy has faded from collective memory. The Detroit Free Press's Bill McGraw reminds us, in a recent collection published by Wayne State, that slavery was a part of the city's makeup in very early days:

> The Macomb family, whose name lives on in a Detroit street and a suburban county, is one of the numerous southeastern Michigan pioneer families who owned slaves during the French, British, and early American periods of the region's history. Many roads, schools, and communities across metro Detroit carry the name of slave-owning clans: Campau, Beaubien, McDougall, Abbott, Brush, Cass, Couin, Meldrum, Dequindre, Beaufait, Groesbeck, Livernois, and Rivard, among many others.[2]

McGraw goes on to list other familiar examples, for instance John R. Williams, whose name graces John R Street, and Jean-Francois Hamtramck, whose name of course is shared with the city. He summarizes: "Slavery is as much a part of [Detroit] history as Vernor's ginger ale, the automobile history, and the Red Wings."[3] As the city modernized (and slavery faded away, outlawed officially in 1835), this early history of subjugation morphed into different forms of discrimination. Housing was sharply segregated as the city developed, with African Americans barred from moving into the majority of the city's neighborhoods (at times at violent cost), forcing migrating black families into a couple of small areas. Even local businesses, churches, and clubs were segregated in ways reminiscent of the Jim Crow South. The fire department and the police force were predominantly white, and when African Americans did serve, they faced segregation, limited authority, and outright aggression from their white colleagues—conditions that lasted well into the twentieth century, even into the 1960s and the time of the revolt.

Economically, the terrain in Detroit was constantly shifting as the population of the city continued to grow. African Americans settling in Detroit in the late nineteenth century found stable jobs as general laborers, service workers, and domestic workers, but when a wave of European immigrants arrived, these jobs were given over to the newly-arrived whites. This pattern repeated itself as the city grew: in boom times, work was available for all, but as soon as the economy began to contract, African Americans would be the first to lose their jobs. Even when work was plentiful—at the auto manufacturers, in particular—African Americans were given the worst jobs at the plant. During the city's massive growth in the early years of World War II, when the auto companies converted into munitions manufacturers in support of the Allied war effort, an influx of both black and white people seeking jobs stretched already-thin resources to the brink, particularly in black neighborhoods. To accommodate the new residents, some proposed integrated housing developments, but they faced stringent opposition from white Detroiters. The stresses of this boom, and the entrenched racism of the city and the country, exploded in a violent outburst during the summer of 1943, which became a historical precedent for the summer of 1967.

Fleeting but pivotal, the riot of 1943 inspired a measure of change. The author Hubert G. Locke writes, "By the mid-sixties Detroit was beginning to enjoy the reputation of being a model city in race relations in the North; [whereas] in 1943 it was generally considered one of the nation's most segregated, if not bigoted, northern cities."[4] Following the 1943 riots, Detroit's mayor created an interracial committee to deal with the city's problems. Slowly, housing segregation ordinances were rolled back, and segregation in public spaces was also eradicated. Better jobs opened up to the city's African American population through fair employment laws, and black judges began to gain appointments to the city's courts. Progressive (by the measure of the era) politicians, including Mayor Jerome Cavanagh, came into power, and changes at the city level seemed to hold promise for more even-handed treatment of all Detroiters.

Yet, despite some real progress in other sectors of city life, the Detroit police force remained overwhelmingly white and overwhelmingly biased against the city's black residents. Alex Elkins writes:

> Despite this shift from City Hall, the majority of officers in the Detroit Police Department (DPD)—from top

2. Bill McGraw, "Detroit's Forgotten History of Slavery," in *Detroit 1967: Origins, Impacts, and Legacies*, ed. Joel Stone (Detroit: Wayne State University Press, 2017), p. 25.
3. Ibid.
4. Hubert G. Locke, *The Detroit Riot of 1967*, p. 53.

inspectors to the uniformed ranks—rejected the liberal platform of color-blind, equal law enforcement. In African American neighborhoods, police continued to mete out extralegal rough justice on a regular basis. Even middle-class black residents who had long requested greater protection from crime protested the often-unpunished harassment, beatings, and killings.[5]

The long-term police aggression against black Detroiters is well documented. Even black officers working within its ranks were frequently the targets of police violence and intimidation. This open hostility, which hung over the city's black communities like a cloud, provided the oxygen that stoked the fires of July 1967.

Given all of this, not to mention the limited city services, lasting economic inequalities, and poor schools, the fact that one of the biggest civil disturbances in American history arose in Detroit in July 1967 seems far from surprising. What is perhaps more shocking, looking back on these events fifty years on, is how many resonances we can find between Detroit's historical context and our contemporary situation—not just in Detroit but in the United States overall. It is easy to find echoes of 1967 Detroit in the stories of African American men, women, and youths killed at the hands of police in the past several years. Victims like Michael Brown, Eric Garner, Walter Scott, Tamir Rice, and Philando Castile have been killed by American police officers in cities including Ferguson, Missouri; Staten Island, New York; Charleston, South Carolina; Cleveland, Ohio; and St. Paul, Minnesota. Not bound by geography, these deaths are nonetheless linked by the persistent racial biases that still ripple close beneath the surface of American society. Ta-Nehisi Coates writes in his remarkable 2015 text *Between the World and Me*:

> There is nothing uniquely evil in these destroyers or even in this moment. The destroyers are merely men enforcing the whims of our country, correctly interpreting its heritage and legacy. It is hard to face this. But all our phrasing—race relations, racial chasm, racial justice, racial profiling, white privilege, even white supremacy—serves to obscure that racism is a visceral experience, that it dislodges brains, blocks airways, rips muscle, extracts organs, cracks bones, breaks teeth. You must never look away from this. You must always remember that the sociology, the history, the economics, the graphs, the charts, the regressions all land, with great violence, upon the body.[6]

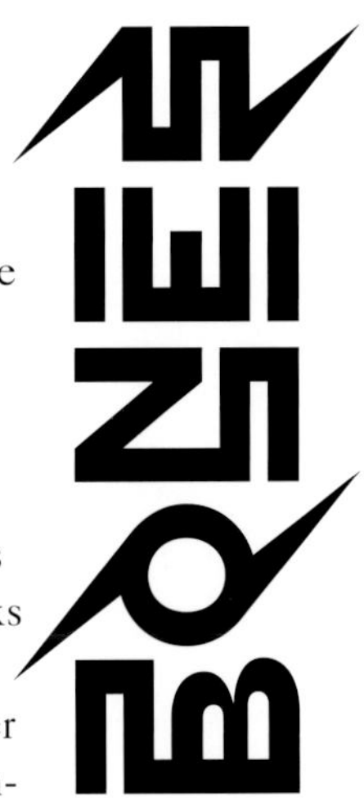

In the city of Detroit, and in the nation overall, the roots of our struggles go deep. It isn't enough to look back fifty years, or even a hundred—the origins of these problems go back much further, to the founding of the nation, to European colonialism before that, and to deeper schisms whose origins are frankly ancient. The same biases that plagued the black community in Detroit in 1967 (and 1943 before that) are evident today in police killings of black citizens and in the increasingly-vocal white supremacist movement once again showing its face in daylight in Trump's America. As before, and as endlessly in the future, we must battle together against these deep-rooted prejudices, face our inescapable history, and accept our shared and individual complicities. Through art, music, action, legislation, personal action, and collective assertions, we must find paths to resistance, rebellion—and, yes, revolution.

5. Alex Elkins, "Liberals and 'Get-Tough' Policing in Postwar Detroit," in *Detroit 1967: Origins, Impacts, and Legacies*, ed. Joel Stone (Detroit: Wayne State University Press, 2017), p. 108.
6. Ta-Nehisi Coates, *Between the World and Me: The Beautiful Struggle* (New York: Spiegel and Grau, 2015), p. 10.

WORKS AND ARTISTS IN THE EXHIBITION

ANDREA BOWERS

Radical Hospitality
2015
Stainless steel, aluminum tubes, wood, chain, 4 neon signs with cable and 2 power sources
118 1/8 x 39 3/8 x 39 3/8 inches
Courtesy KADIST, Paris and San Francisco

Los Angeles-based artist Andrea Bowers works with concepts and figures surrounding social justice movements in the contemporary era. Working directly in and with activist communities and spaces of protest, Bowers aims to reflect and archive the fervent energies of political resistance. Among the issues she addresses in her work are immigration (especially along the U.S. / Mexico border), women's rights, labor rights, and military aggression.

Radical Hospitality sends a mixed message. While the neon blares out an emphatic welcome, the words "radical hospitality" are wrapped in a tangle of barbed wire, making ambiguous or even undermining the implied message of openness. With aluminum wind chimes dangling from the entangled mess, Bowers' sculpture becomes both self-contradictory and gangling.

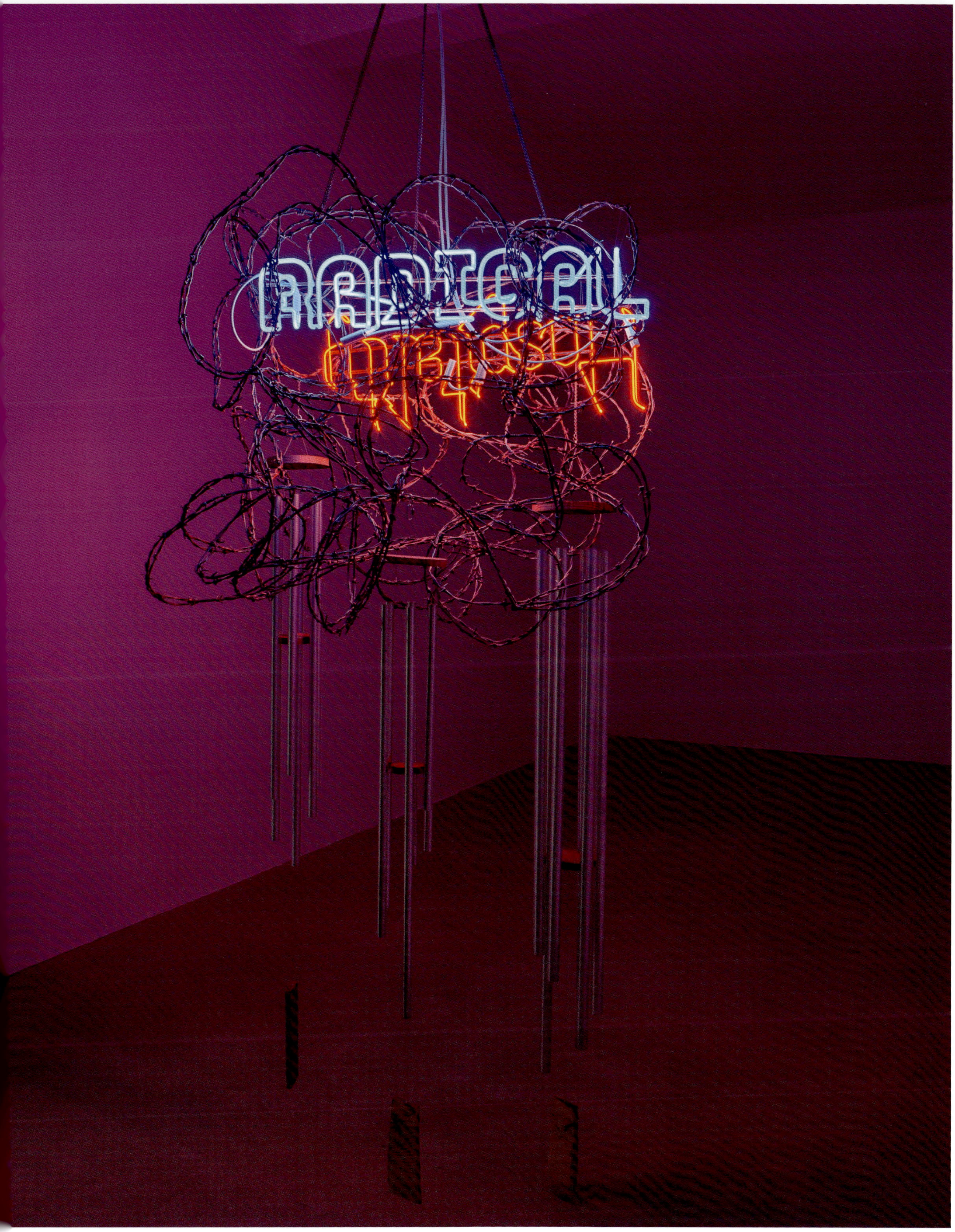

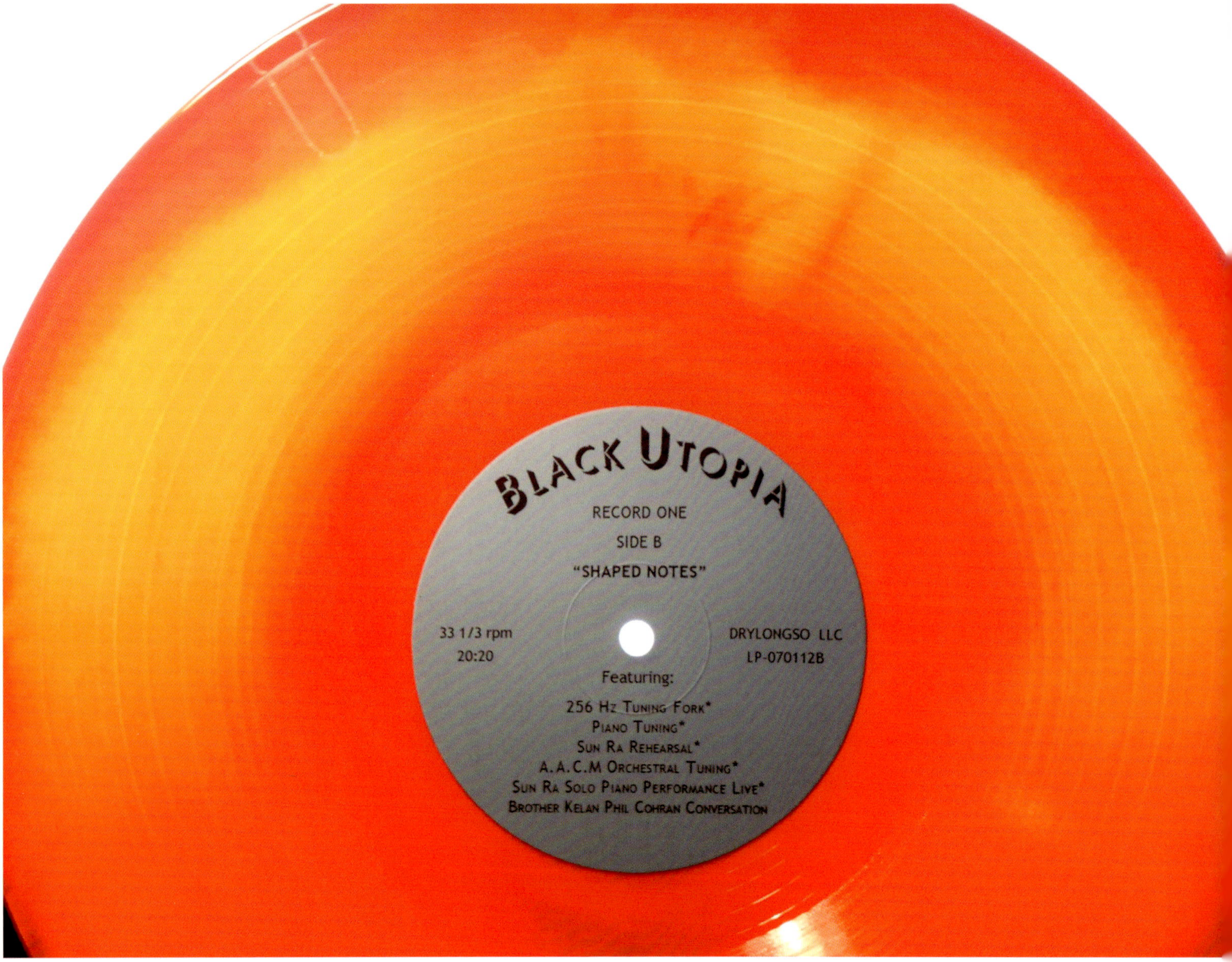
BLACK UTOPIA
RECORD ONE
SIDE B
"SHAPED NOTES"
33 1/3 rpm
20:20
DRYLONGSO LLC
LP-070112B
Featuring:
256 Hz Tuning Fork*
Piano Tuning*
Sun Ra Rehearsal*
A.A.C.M Orchestral Tuning*
Sun Ra Solo Piano Performance Live*
Brother Kelan Phil Cohran Conversation

CAULEEN SMITH

Black Utopia: Rehersal Tapes and Lectures Selected from the Alton Abraham / Sun Ra Audio Archives
2012
Double LP
Courtesy the artist and Corbett vs. Dempsey, Chicago

Cauleen Smith made the double LP *Black Utopia* using audio from the Sun Ra archives at the University of Chicago and mastered at Chicago's Experimental Sound Studio. The record is a collage of original music, rehearsals, lectures, and spoken-word passages. Sun Ra (1914–93) was one of the most influential figures of twentieth-century experimental music, as much for his visionary Afro-Futurist philosophy as for his compositional approach. He played frequently in Detroit and maintained long-standing relationships with many Detroit musicians. Cauleen Smith's installation features a selection of occultist books influential to Sun Ra, in addition to a listening station with the record, which visitors are invited to sit and enjoy.

SADIE BARNETTE

Government Employees from *My Father's FBI File*
2017
Archival pigment prints on archival paper
22 x 17 inches each (5 prints)
Courtesy the artist

Sadie Barnette's ongoing series *My Father's FBI File* reclaims more than 500 pages of documents related to the artist's father, Rodney Barnette, a founder of the Compton, California chapter of the Black Panther Party. Obtained from the FBI through a lengthy Freedom of Information Act request, this extensive dossier reveals a shocking level of government surveillance and interference in Mr. Barnette's life. Beginning in 1969—the same year J. Edgar Hoover declared the Black Panthers the greatest internal threat to the nation—the dossier records personal biographical details as well as misinformation about Mr. Barnette and the Black Panther Party. It also exposes the fact that Barnette's firing from his job at the Post Office, supposedly because of actions deemed unbefitting a government employee, was in fact linked to his involvement with the Black Panthers.

Taking these documents and adding her own graffiti-like interventions—splatters of pink and black spray paint resembling blood stains, glittering adornments, and other personal marks—Barnette inscribes evidence of her own existence. Through reclaiming and selectively redacting the FBI's calculated misrepresentations of her father and the Black Panther Party agenda, she asks viewers to think and evaluate this history for themselves.

FD-263 (Rev. 1-7-72)

FEDERAL BUREAU OF INVESTIGATION

REPORTING OFFICE	OFFICE OF ORIGIN	DATE	INVESTIGATIVE PERIOD
ALEXANDRIA	BUREAU	12/5/73	12/4/73

TITLE OF CASE	REPORT MADE BY	TYPED BY
RODNEY ELLIS BARNETTE Mail Handler U. S. Postal Service San Francisco, California	SA ARTHUR P. ROEHRL/NJA **CHARACTER OF CASE** SGE	pka

REFERENCES: Bureau letter to San Francisco, 11/8/73.
Baltimore teletype to Bureau, 11/29/73

- RUC -

ALEXANDRIA FILE WILL BE DESTROYED IN 90 DAYS

ACCOMPLISHMENTS CLAIMED					ACQUITTALS	CASE HAS BEEN:
CONVIC.	FUG.	FINES	SAVINGS	RECOVERIES		PENDING OVER ONE YEAR ☐ YES ☐ NO PENDING PROSECUTION OVER SIX MONTHS ☐ YES ☐ NO

APPROVED CB SPECIAL AGENT IN CHARGE

DO NOT WRITE IN SPACES BELOW

COPIES MADE:

6 - Bureau (140-37093)
1 - Alexandria (140-RC)

140-37093 - 30 REC-8

RECEIVED DEC 6 1973

EX-117

Dissemination Record of Attached Report

Agency	2 cc CSC		
Request Recd.	1cc Dept.		
Date Fwd.	DEC 18 1973		
How Fwd.			
By			

Notations

FEB 8 1974

A*

COVER PAGE

NATHAN CARTER

Ladies and Gentlemen, Meet the Dramastics
2016
Mixed Media Installation
Dimensions variable
Courtesy the artist and Casey Kaplan Gallery, New York

Created by artist Nathan Carter, The Dramastics is a fictional female punk band imagined through sketches, dioramas, installations, films, and performances. Fronted by lead singer Molly Blowout, the band also includes electric guitar player Crimson Ivy, terminally-anxious bass player Melancholy, and a seven-foot-tall, foul-mouthed drummer from Detroit Rock City named Calamity.

The Dramastics project is a world-building affair. Carter developed each character's distinctive look and persona by constructing ten-inch tall, hand-made figures out of paper, glue, aluminum wire, and paint. He then imagined the characters' contexts and narrative, making dioramas from plywood, plastic, and painted paper to represent places they would inhabit and visit on tour.

Carter has said, "the activity of world-building felt like inventing and playing with punk dolls in their punk dollhouse. The entire process, of improvising and building and recording and filming, was like making a DIY basement recording. All of it looked and sounded immediate, fast, loose, and loud. Meticulous craft took a backseat to enthusiasm."

Channeling a riotous punk rock attitude through four fictional high school girls, Carter's project explores rebellion and empowerment through music.

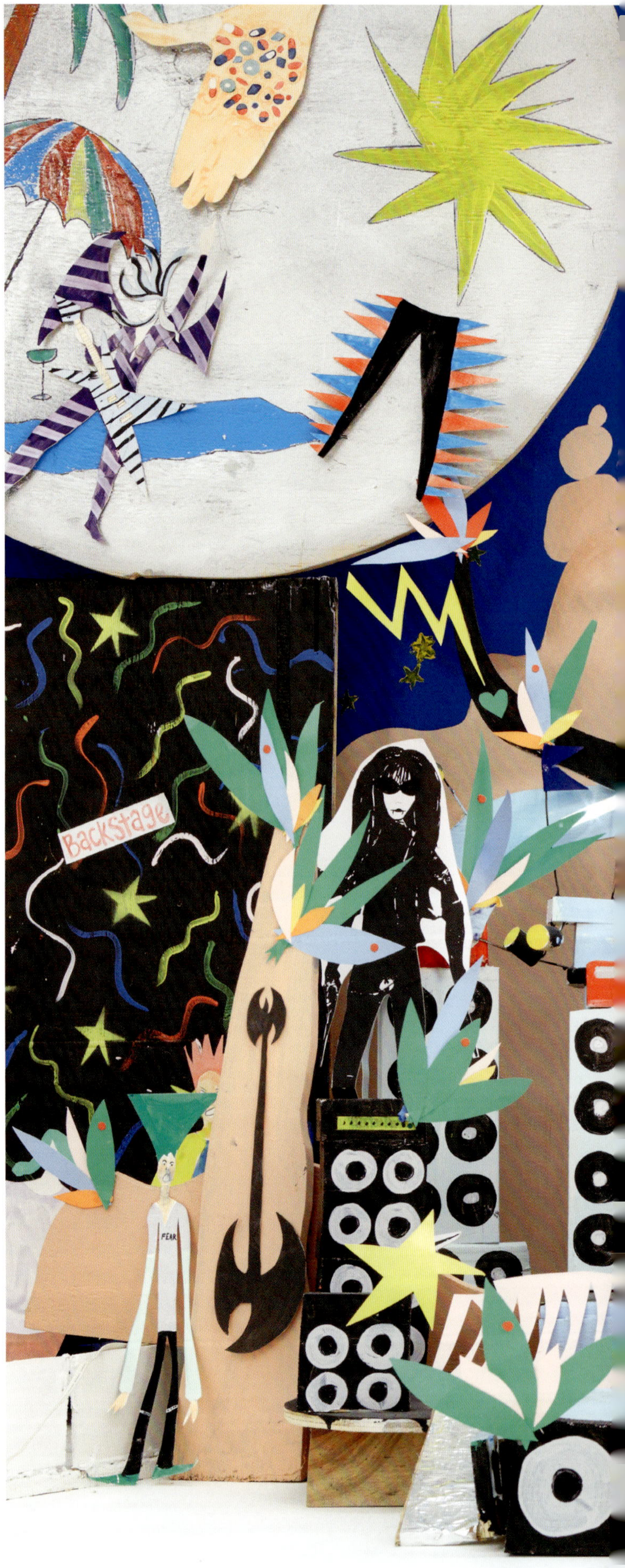

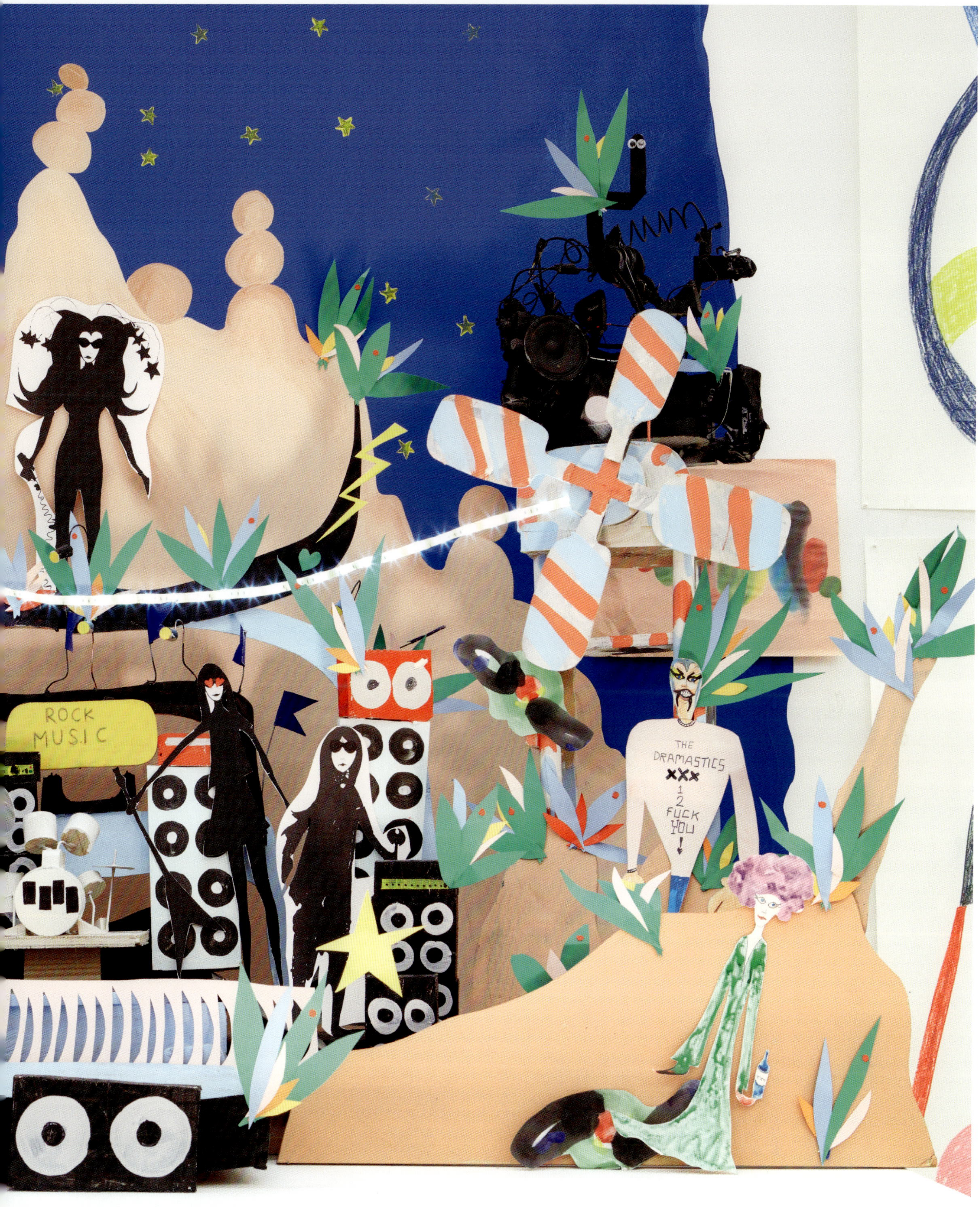
ROCK MUSIC
THE DRAMASTICS
XXX
1 2 FUCK YOU !

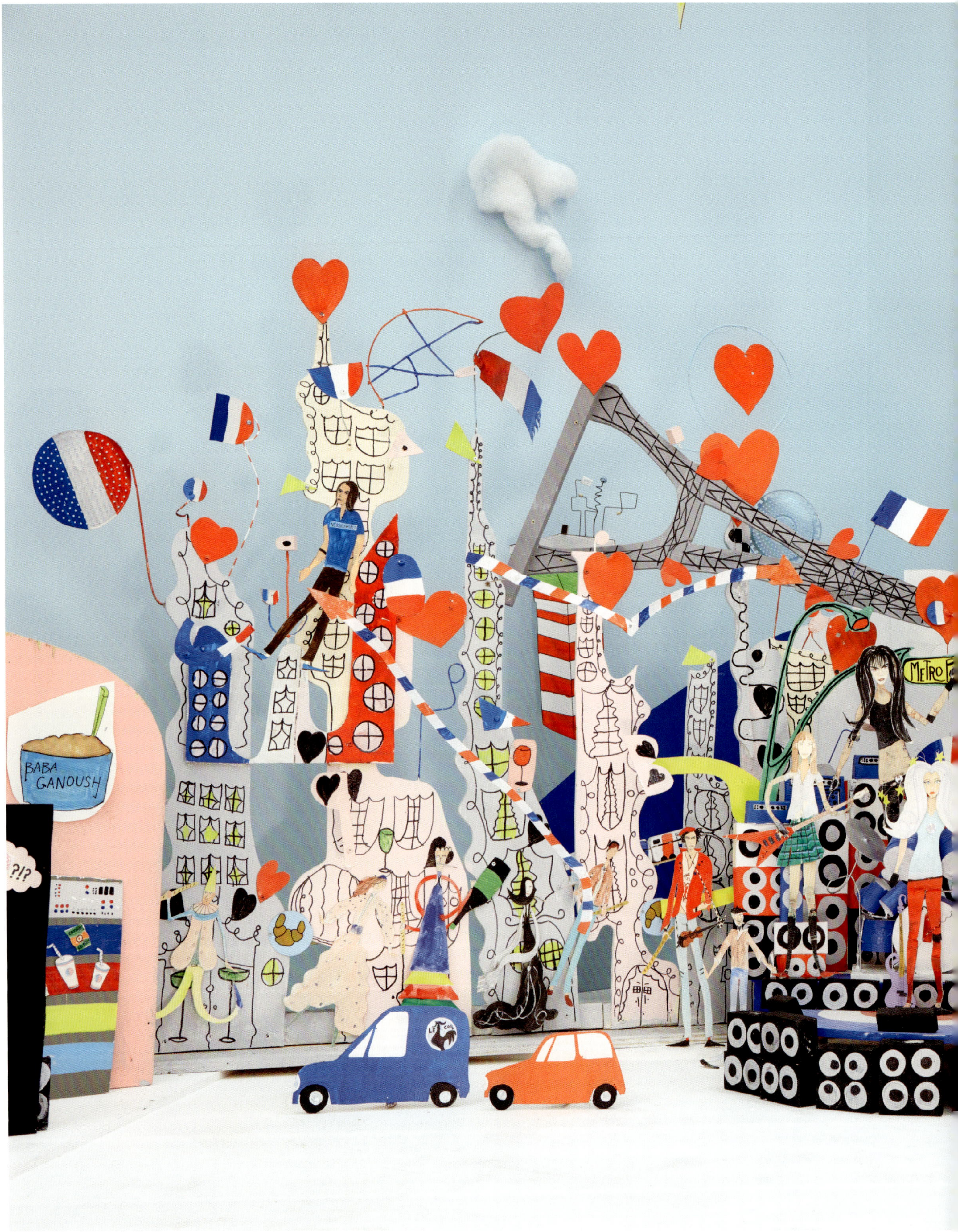
BABA
GANOUSH

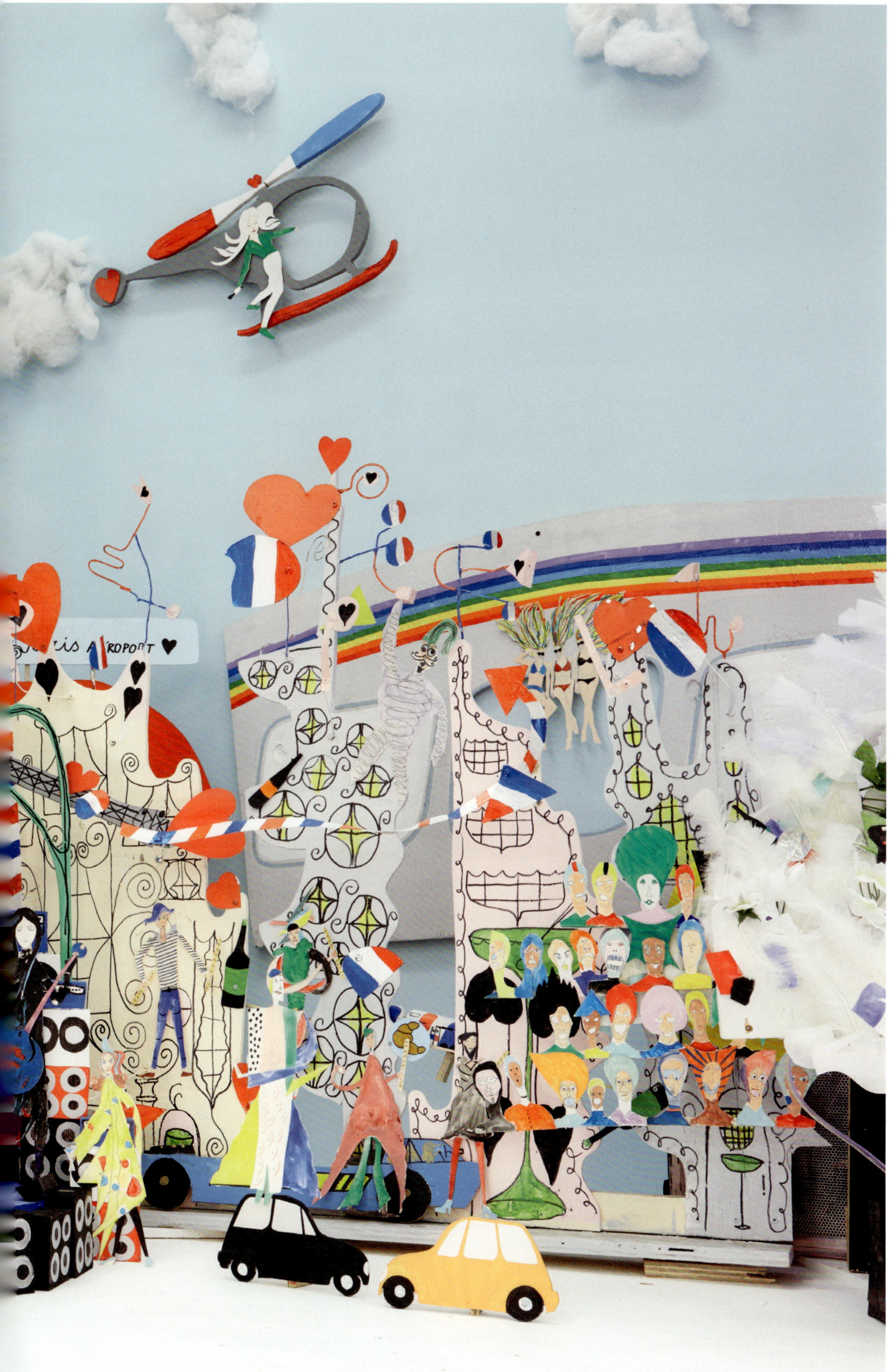

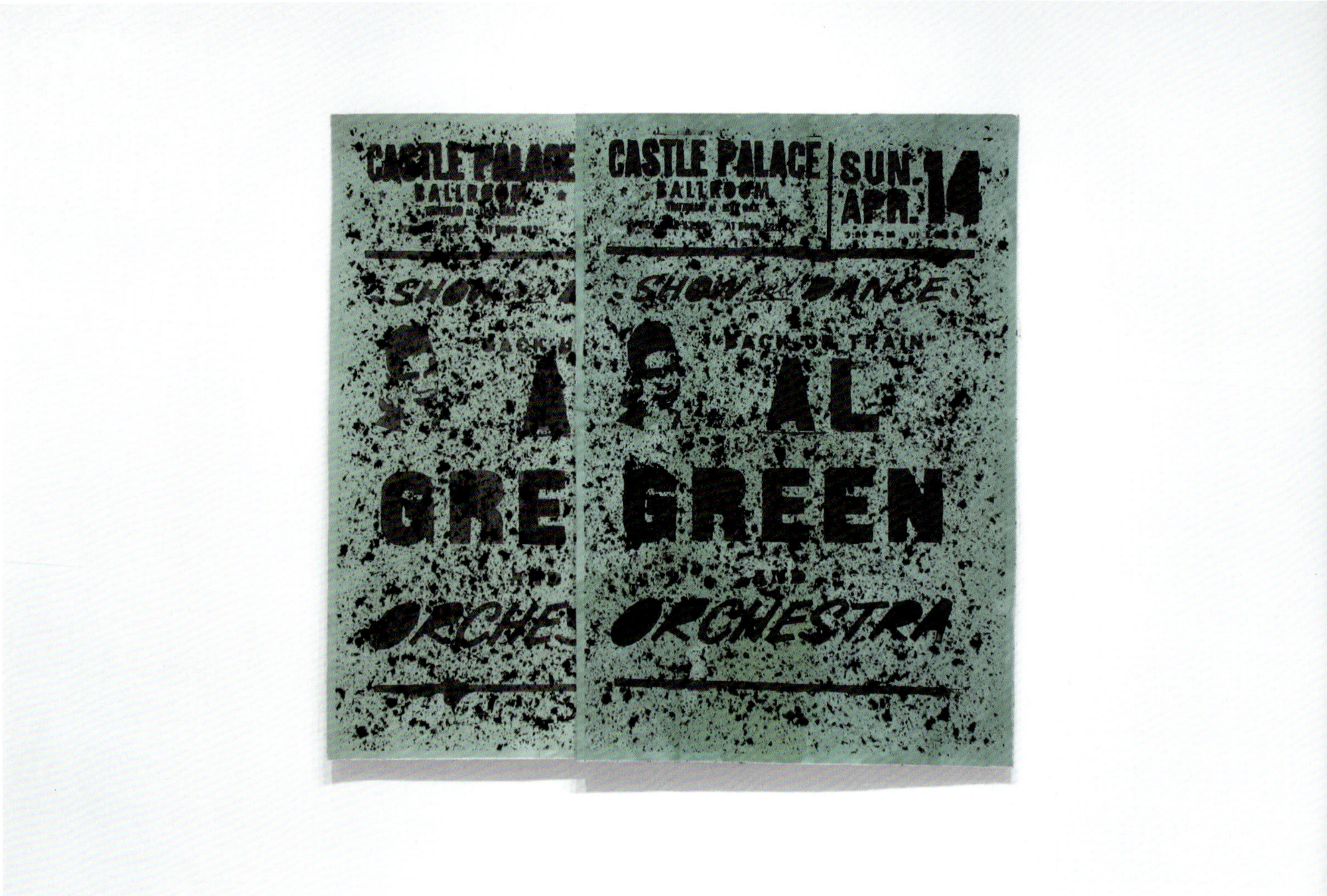

JAMAL CYRUS

Transformation Green
2016
Graphite, wax, vinyl records, grits and gel medium on dyed canvas mounted on styrene
54 × 59 inches each
Courtesy Inman Gallery, Houston

Houston-based artist Jamal Cyrus explores intersections between black identity politics and music in the twentieth century. Through multimedia installations, mixed-media works on canvas, and performances, he reimagines moments of African American life and history. Here, Cyrus uses dyed canvas to create vintage-inspired posters for an Al Green concert. Layered with bits of vinyl, wax, and grits, Cyrus' posters refer to an incident in 1974 when Green's girlfriend, Mary Woodson, threw a pan of hot grits on him before retreating to another room to commit suicide. Some mark this moment as the turning point when Green abandoned popular music to pursue a spiritual path as a minister.

Pride Frieze — Jerry White's Record Shop, Central Avenue, Los Angeles
2017
Record sleeves, digital prints, ink, watercolor, tape, masonite, Golden Gac 100, gesso, acrylic paint, Russian Birch plywood, Golden Fine Pumice Gel, wax, Plexiglass, reclaimed wood
121 ¼ x 126 ½ x 12 inches
Courtesy Inman Gallery, Houston

Jamal Cyrus' interest in the overlapping histories of African American resistance and music finds expression in his projects around "Pride Records," a fictional label he conceived as having emerged from Detroit's 1967 Rebellion. Cyrus's story imagines a record label that initially put out Black Power music, but as the label's influence grew, it attracted the attention of the FBI's Counter Intelligence Program and was forced to abandon its political agenda. As a result, Pride's later releases reflected a mollified, assimilationist point of view. Cyrus' installation presents the façade of the label's imagined storefront, topped with a collection of its releases. The artist-designed record sleeves narrate the label's path from revolutionary record company to coopted black business.

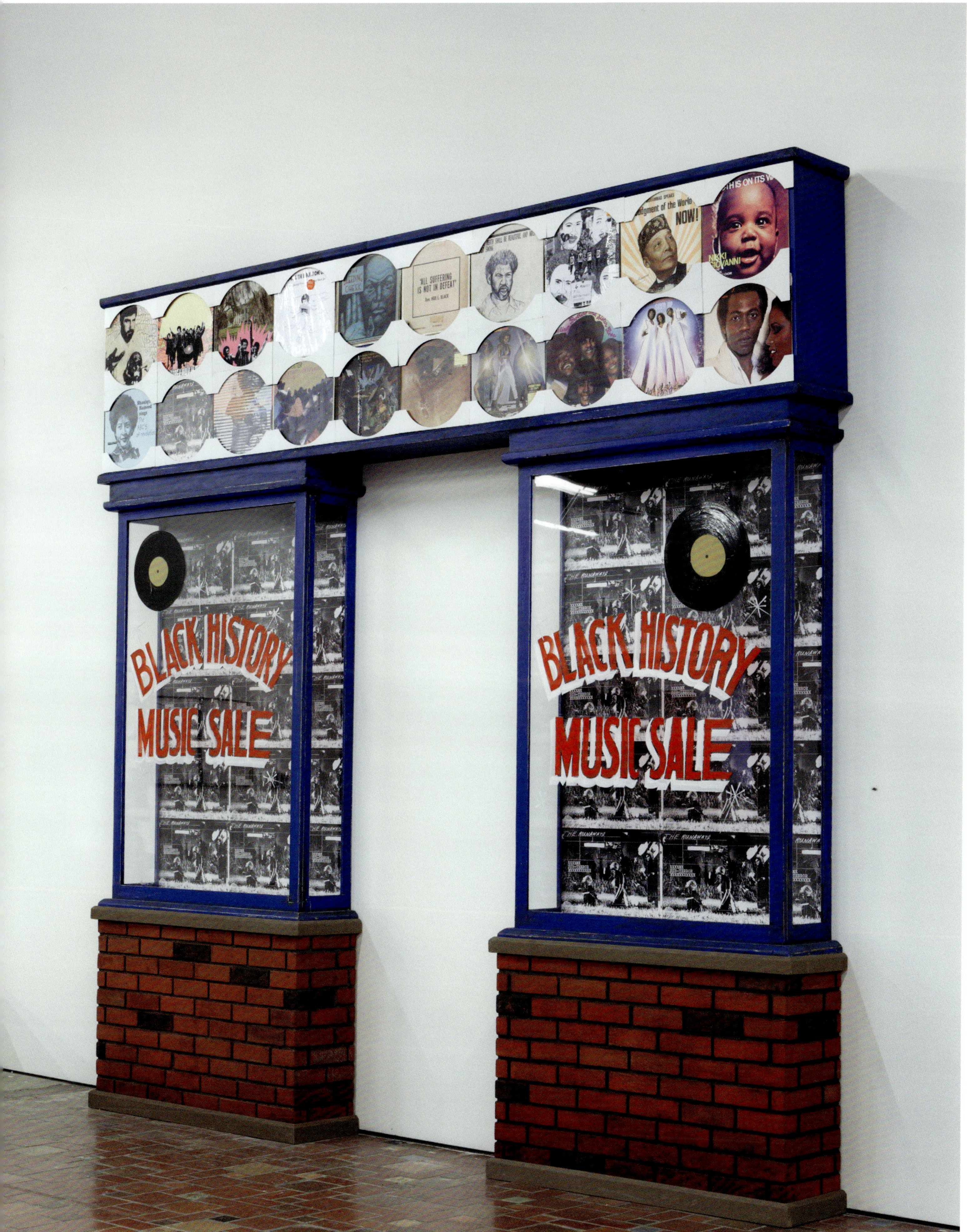
"ALL SUFFERING IS NOT IN DEFEAT!"
NOW!
BLACK HISTORY
MUSIC SALE
BLACK HISTORY
MUSIC SALE
THE RUNAWAYS

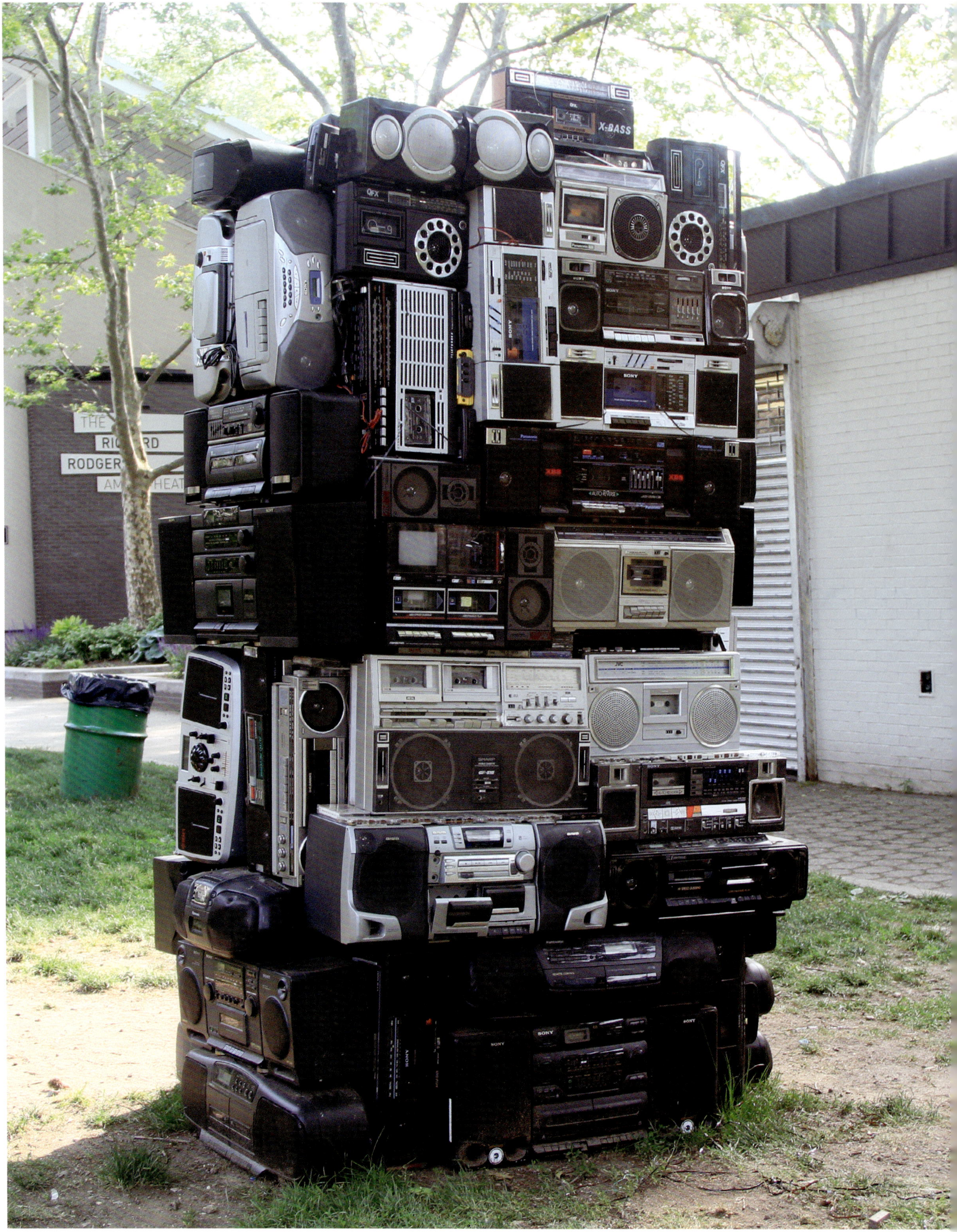
X-BASS
QFX
SONY

BAYETÉ ROSS SMITH

Got the Power: Detroit
2017
Dimensions variable
Vintage boom boxes, custom mixtape
Courtesy the artist

Bayeté Ross Smith works directly with local communities to create site-specific installations in his *Got the Power* series. Comprising a tower of boom boxes and a custom mixtape, the work offers an audio portrait of the city's residents. In this iteration, Smith conducted oral history interviews with an array of Detroiters, asking participants open-ended questions about their lives in the city and how music has been important to them. He then made a unique mixtape, approximately three hours long, that includes excerpts from the interviews and music people had mentioned as part of their stories. The mixtape plays through the boom box speakers in the installation, creating an audio archive of everyday life in the city and a contemporary monument to the urban landscape.

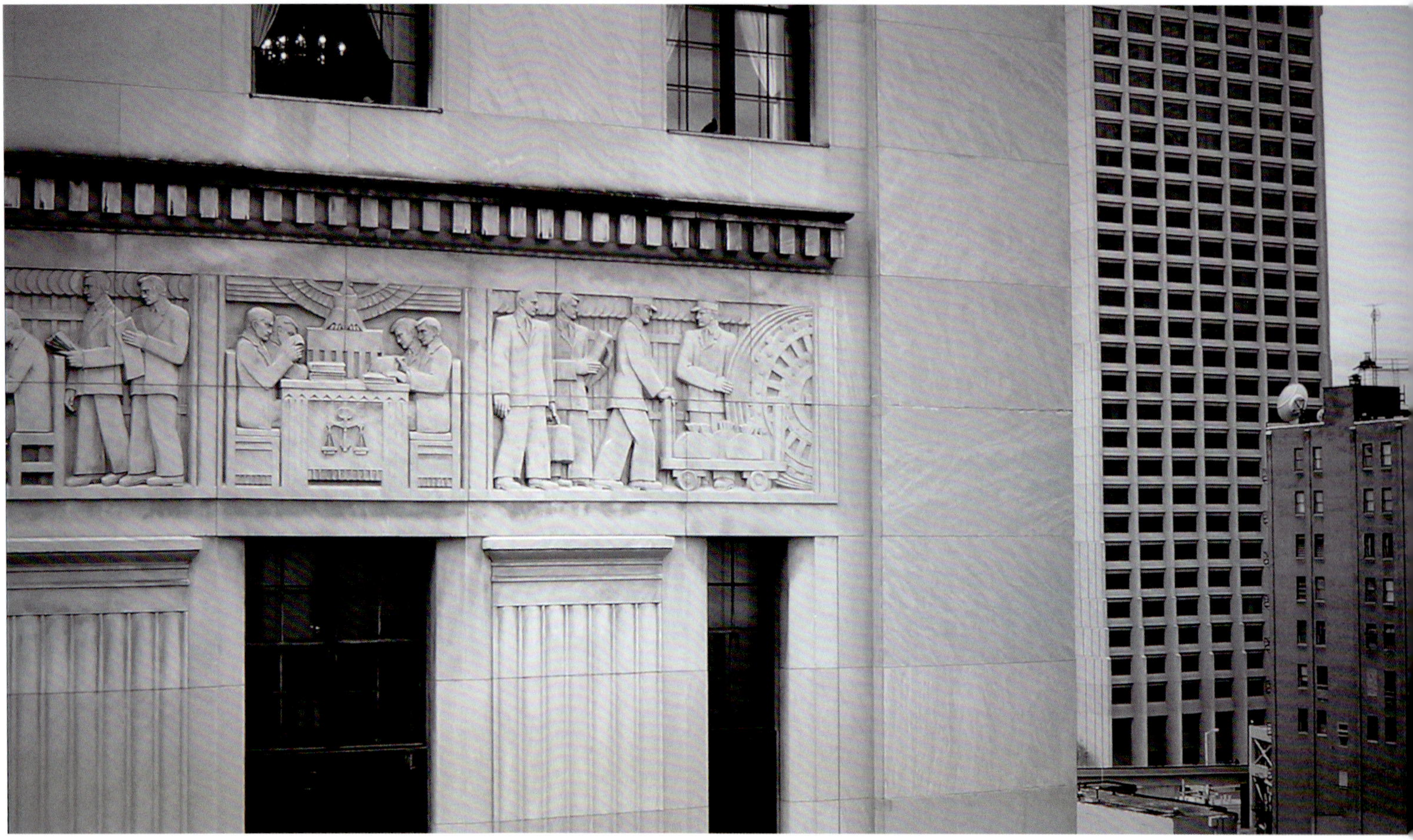

DAVID HARTT

The Republic
2014
HD video, 16:08 minutes with score by Sam Prekop
Courtesy the artist and David Nolan Gallery, New York

David Hartt's *The Republic* explores the interconnected histories of Detroit and Athens, Greece. In the 1960s, both cities commissioned Greek urban planner Constantinos Doxiadis to design and implement an urban redevelopment plan to create the future city. His efforts were interrupted, however, by the 1967 urban rebellion in Detroit and by the fall of the Greek junta in 1974, and none of his plans for either city came to be. Hartt's film intersperses shots of Athens and Detroit, creating a hybrid of the urban landscapes and drawing historical connections between their respective fates. Paired with a soundtrack by Chicago musician Sam Prekop, *The Republic* looks at the life of the city through the lens of social unrest.

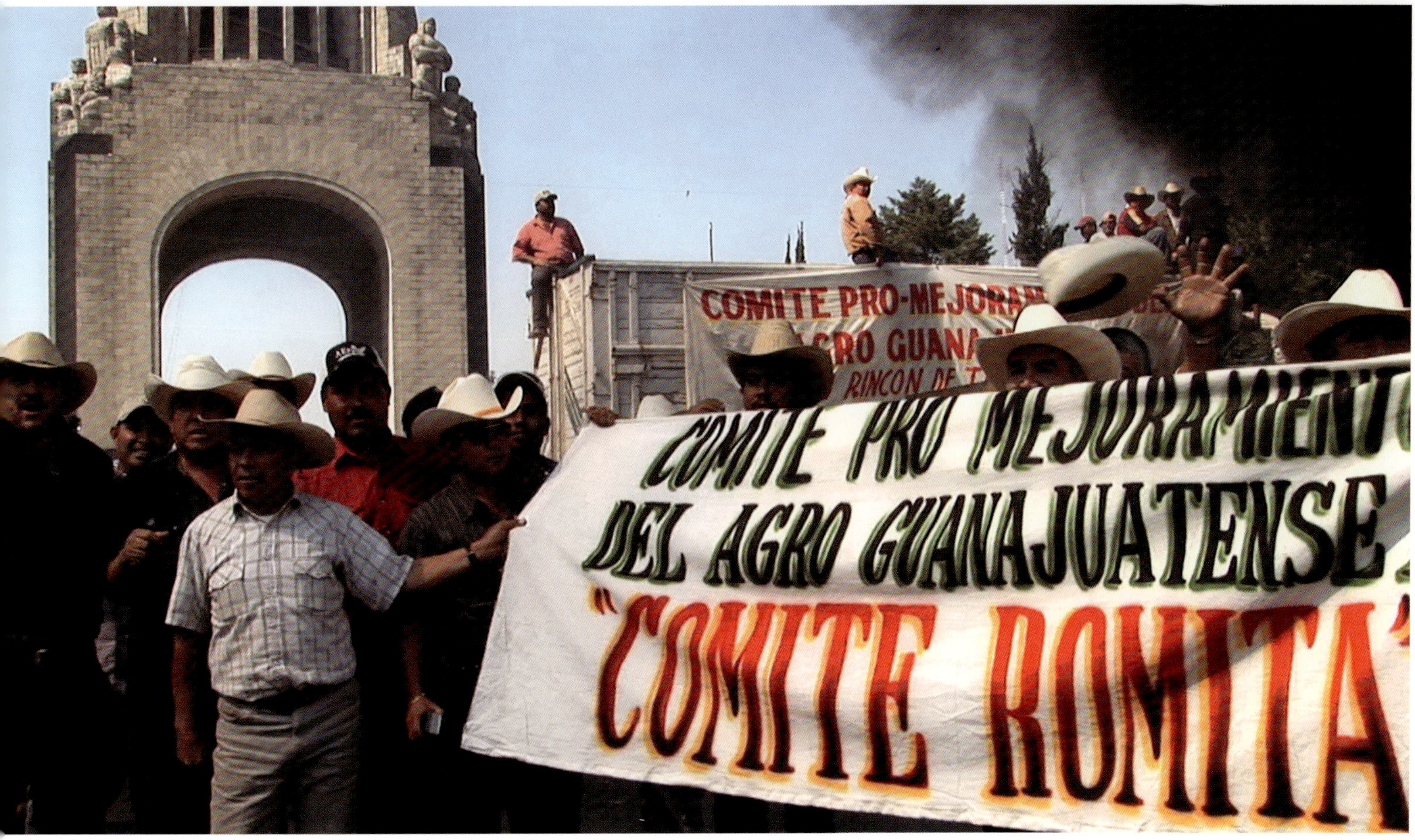

MINERVA CUEVAS

Disidencia v. 2.0
2008–10
HD video, 25:43 minutes, sound
Courtesy the artist and Kurimazutto, Mexico City

Minerva Cuevas investigates the political, social, and economic realities of individuals living under contemporary capitalist conditions. In *Disidencia v. 2.0*, Cuevas records moments of protest and resistance in Mexico City, consolidating them into a dense collage of powerful images. Turning our attention toward both overt and more clandestine forms of resistance, Cuevas creates a filmic archive of political and social activism. Accompanied by a soundtrack by the Mexican composer Pablo Salazar, the film provides a stirring record of citizen protest and defiance against an unjust social regime.

KEVIN JEROME EVERSON

It Seems to Hang On
2015
HD video, 19:50 minutes, sound, color and B&W
Courtesy the artist and Picture Palace Pictures, New York

It Seems to Hang On is based on the true story of the serial killers Alton Coleman and Debra Brown, a young black couple who cut a violent path through the American Midwest in the summer of 1984. The dialogue is based on the American soul duo (and couple) Ashford and Simpson's 1979 hit song *It Seems to Hang On*, whose lyrics refer to a couple struggling to hang on and stay together through adversity. Kevin Jerome Everson's film depicts a desperate, violent, but loving couple on the run from the law.

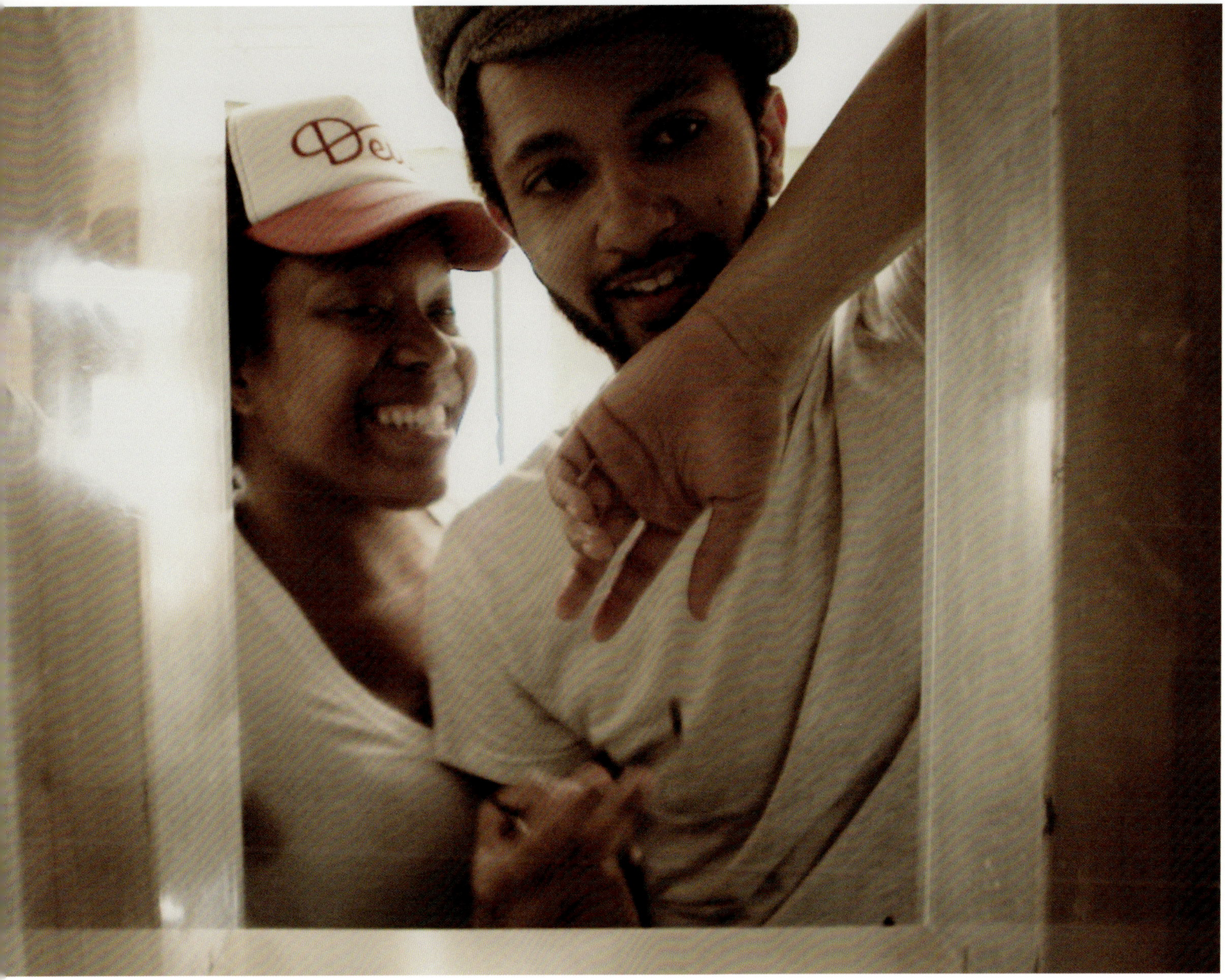

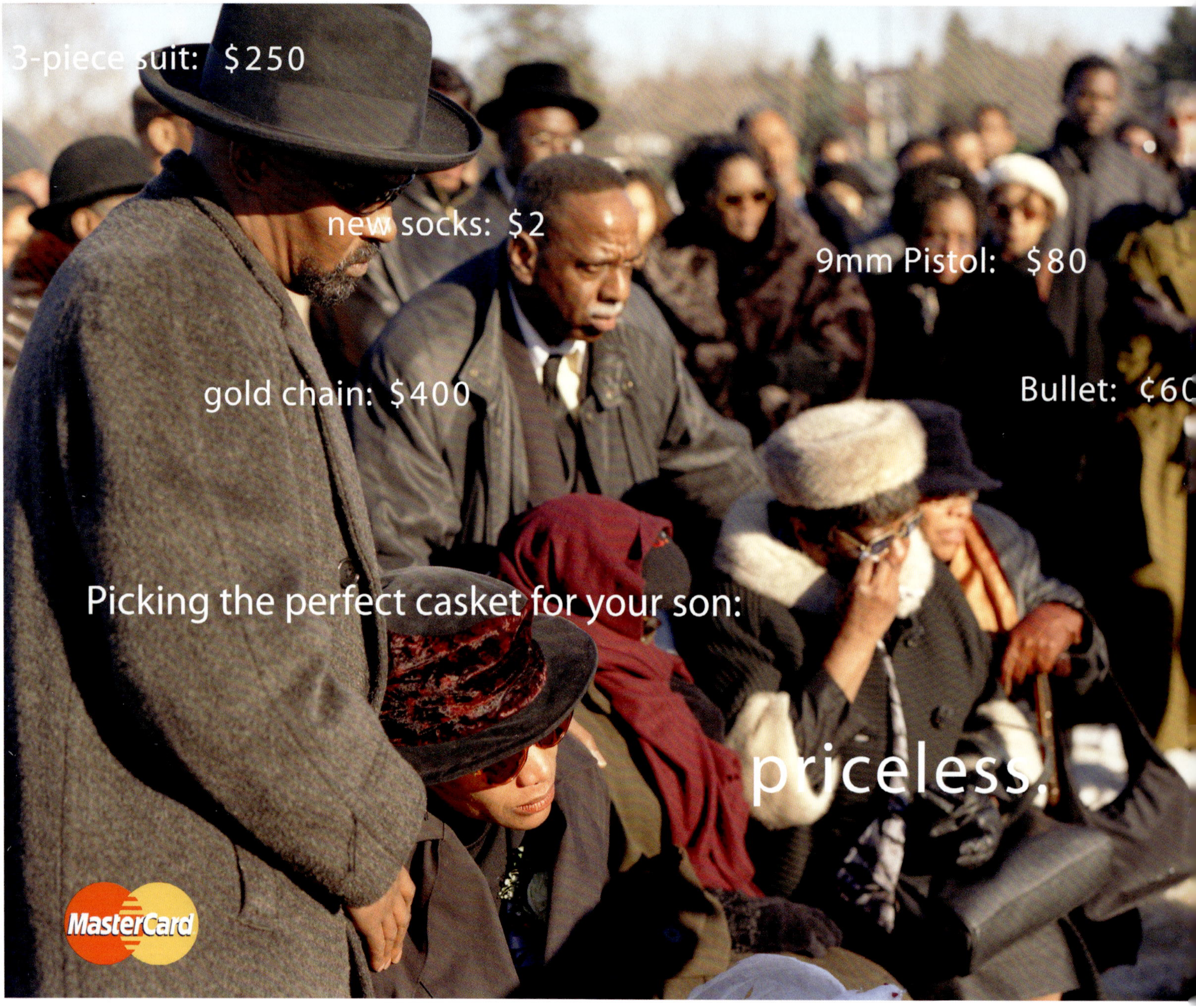

HANK WILLIS THOMAS

Priceless
2004
Lambda print
70 x 96 inches
Courtesy the artist and Jack Shainman Gallery, New York

What Goes Without Saying
2012
Wooden pillory and microphone
64 x 66 x 36 inches installed
Courtesy the artist and Jack Shainman Gallery, New York

Interdisciplinary artist Hank Willis Thomas makes works about black American identity, politics, and history. In *Priceless*, he appropriates the look, logo, and language of Mastercard commercials and print ads that ran in the early 2000s. Following the ad campaign's familiar formula, this photograph of a black family (the artist's own, in fact) is overlaid with objects and prices: "3-piece suit: $250; new socks: $2; gold chain: $400," and so on. Yet, Thomas's work culminates in a line that subverts the expected up-beat message: "Picking the perfect casket for your son: Priceless." The work responds to the murder of the artist's cousin, Songha Willis Thomas, in particular, while also speaking more broadly to the violence disproportionately enacted against black men in America.

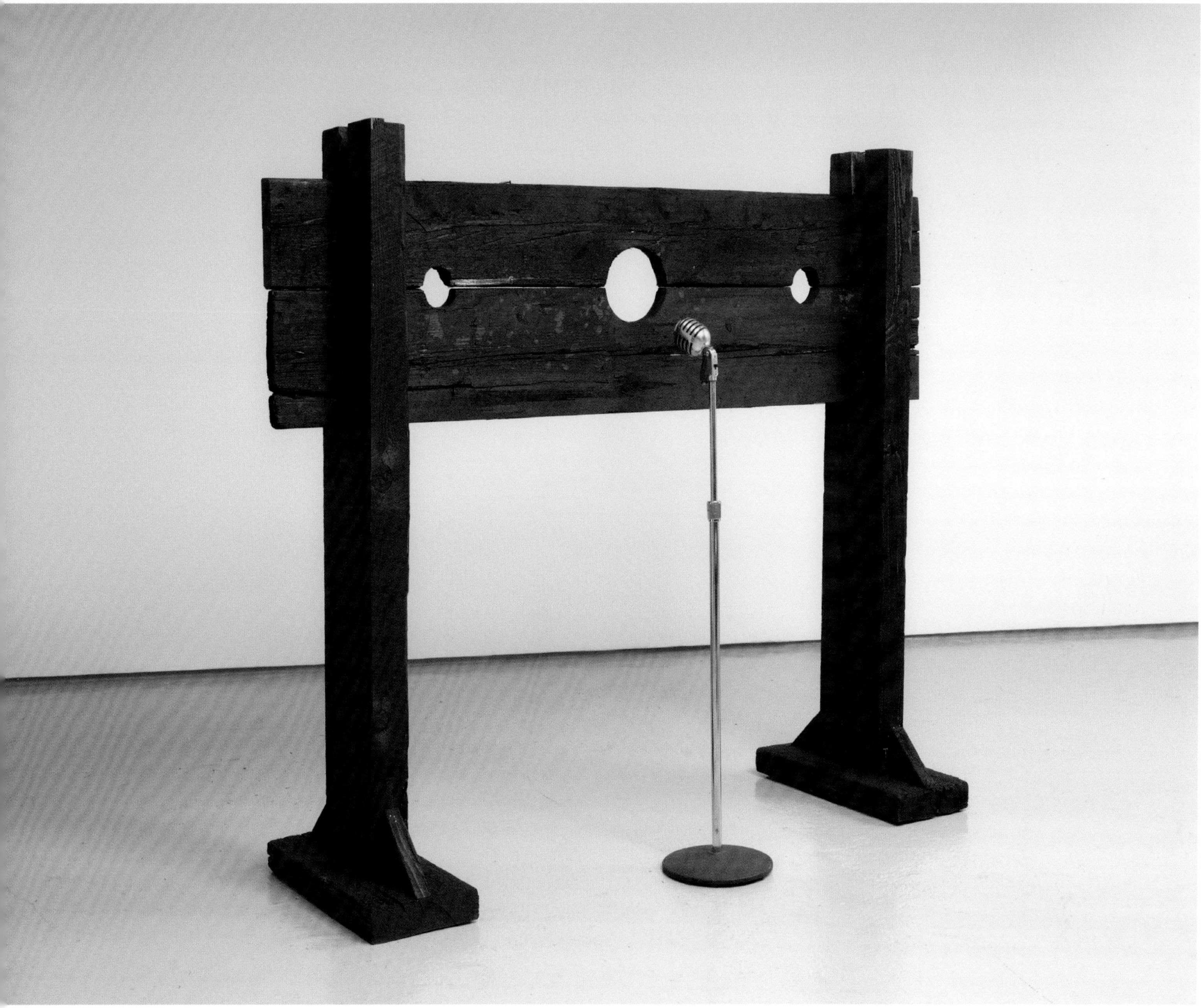

In Hank Willis Thomas's *What Goes Without Saying*, the artist presents a wooden pillory—the type formerly used to punish American slaves for even small infractions—with a microphone. The title comes from a passage in Roland Barthes' *Mythologies* (1957): "I resented seeing Nature and History confused at every turn, and I wanted to track down, in the decorative display of *what-goes-without-saying*, the ideological abuse which, in my view, is hidden there." Pointing to the ingrained but nonetheless contrived belief in European superiority that enabled American slavery and persists today, Thomas reminds us that it is History, not Nature. Placed in front of the pillory where the victim's head would be, the microphone symbolically listens for the unheard voices of the enslaved.

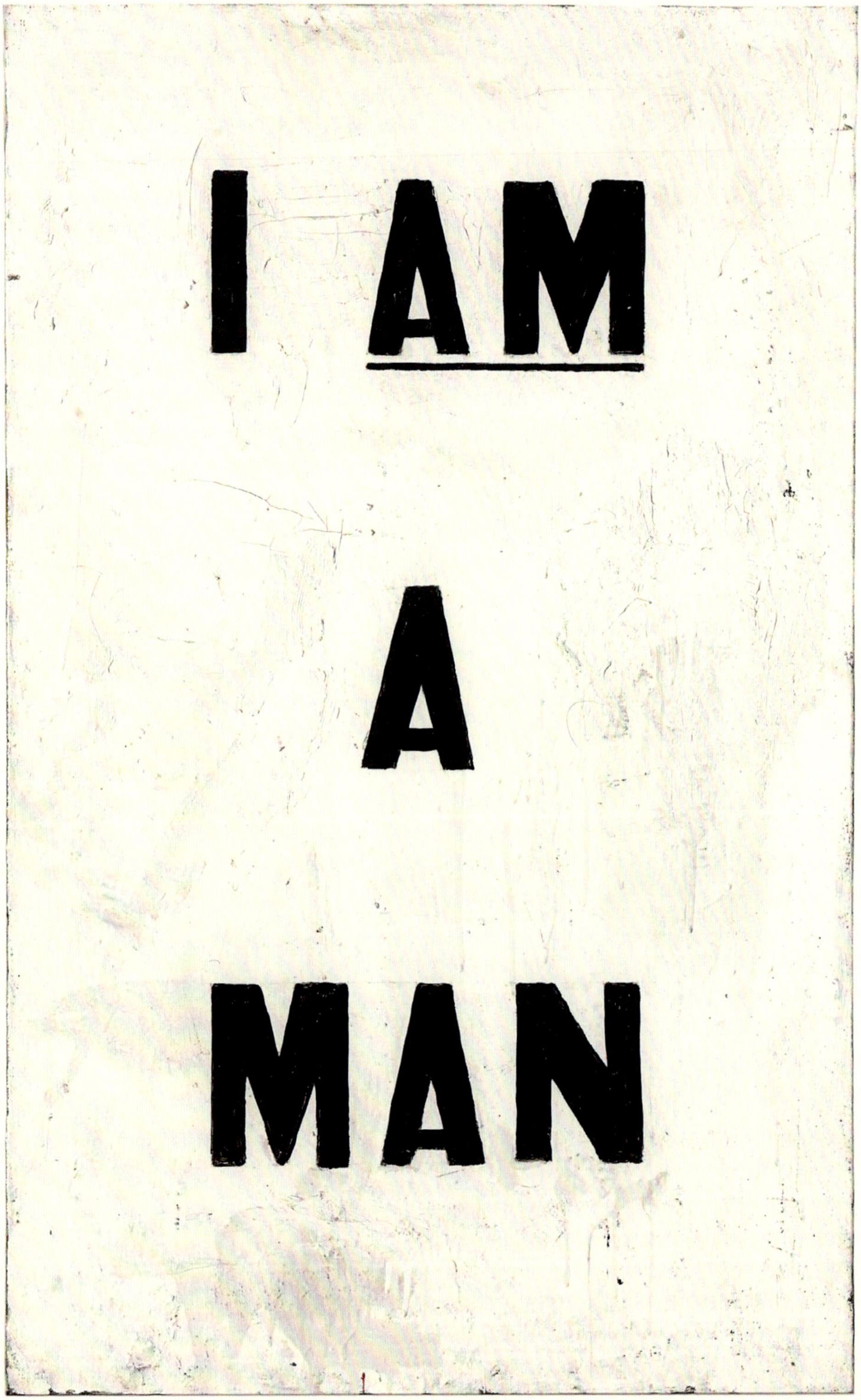
I AM
A
MAN

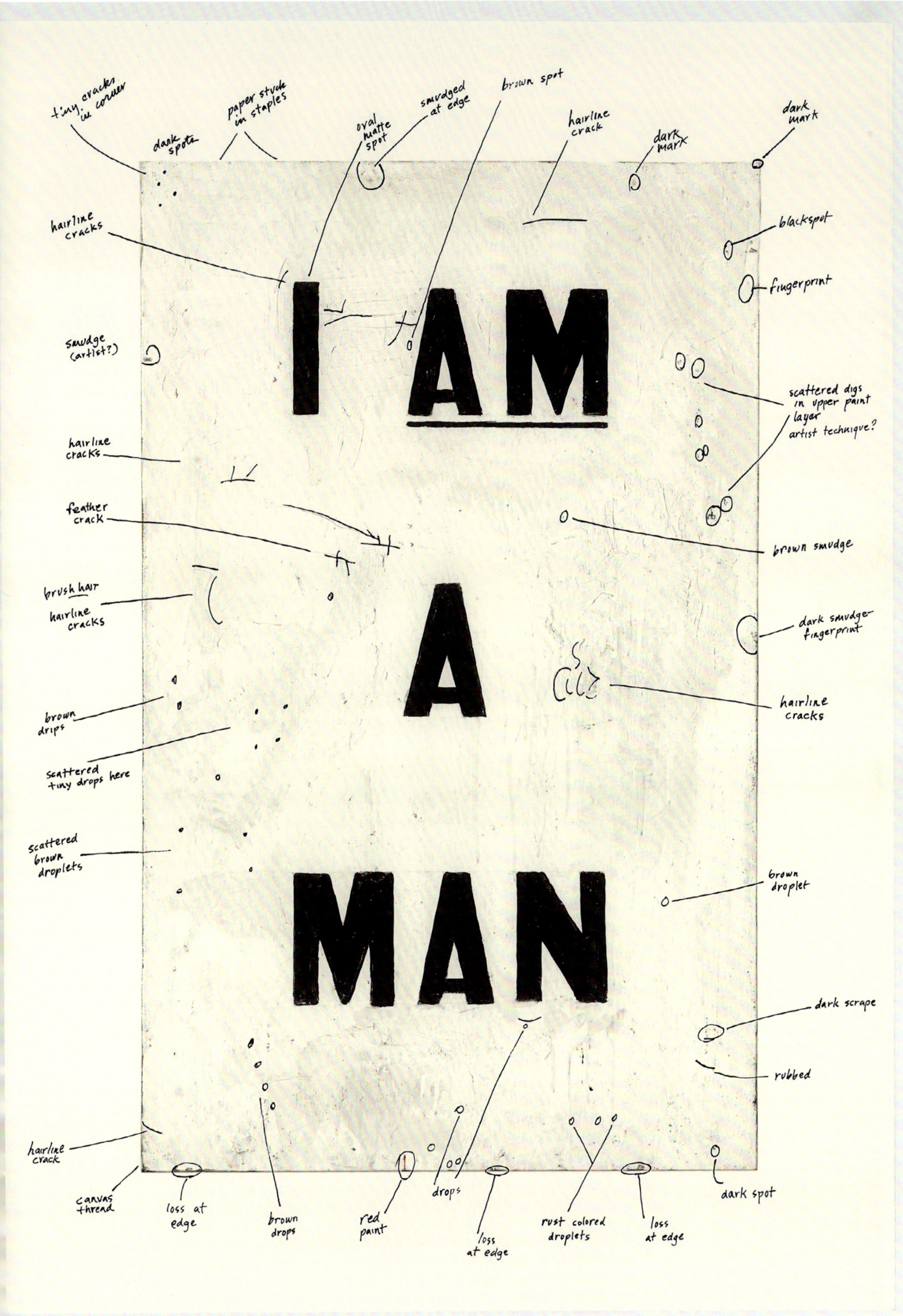
tiny cracks in corner
paper stuck in staples
dark spots
oval matte spot
smudged at edge
brown spot
hairline crack
dark mark
dark mark
hairline cracks
blackspot
fingerprint
I AM A MAN
smudge (artist?)
scattered digs in upper paint layer
artist technique?
hairline cracks
feather crack
brown smudge
brush hair
hairline cracks
dark smudge-fingerprint
hairline cracks
brown drips
scattered tiny drops here
scattered brown droplets
brown droplet
dark scrape
rubbed
hairline crack
canvas thread
loss at edge
brown drops
red paint
drops
loss at edge
rust colored droplets
loss at edge
dark spot

Previous page:

GLENN LIGON

Condition Report
2000
Iris print and Iris print with serigraph, 2 parts
Edition of 20, 7 Aps and 2 PPs
Published by Jean Noblet Studio
32 x 22 3/4 inches each
Collection of KADIST, San Francisco and Paris

Glenn Ligon's diptych *Condition Report* contains a nested set of historical and self-referential quotations. Both prints depict a version of the artist's 1988 painting, *Untitled (I Am A Man)*, which in turn quotes the iconic protest signs carried in the Memphis Sanitation Workers Strike at the height of the Civil Rights Movement. The left-hand print is a simple reproduction of Ligon's 1988 painting, whereas the right-hand print reproduces this painting along with the conservator's annotations cataloging the minor impurities such as hairline cracks, smudges, and fingerprints that accrued on the work's surface—the "condition report" of the title. Tracing a simple phrase—I AM A MAN—through these iterations as declaration, symbol, object, and surface, Ligon levies questions of representation and race, commodification and history, and the value and preciousness of one's identity.

JIBADE-KAHLIL HUFFMAN

Yesterday (Our Love Went into a Coma)
2011–ongoing
Video, monitor, microphone, love poem
Color, 3:51 minutes, silent
Courtesy the artist and Anat Ebgi Gallery, Los Angeles

Born in Detroit and based in Los Angeles, Jibade-Khalil Huffman uses video, installation, photography, and text to create narratives that are both readable and intangible. He started out as a poet and began incorporating projections into his readings when he found words alone incapable of expressing what he wanted. In *Yesterday (Our Love Went into a Coma)*, Huffman employs the signature blue screen and white lettering of a karaoke machine to create an disenchanted love song with no sound. The timing of the karaoke's slow scroll elongates our experiences of anticipation and confusion as this strange ode unravels, punctuated by (silent) instrumental breaks and drawn out syllables.

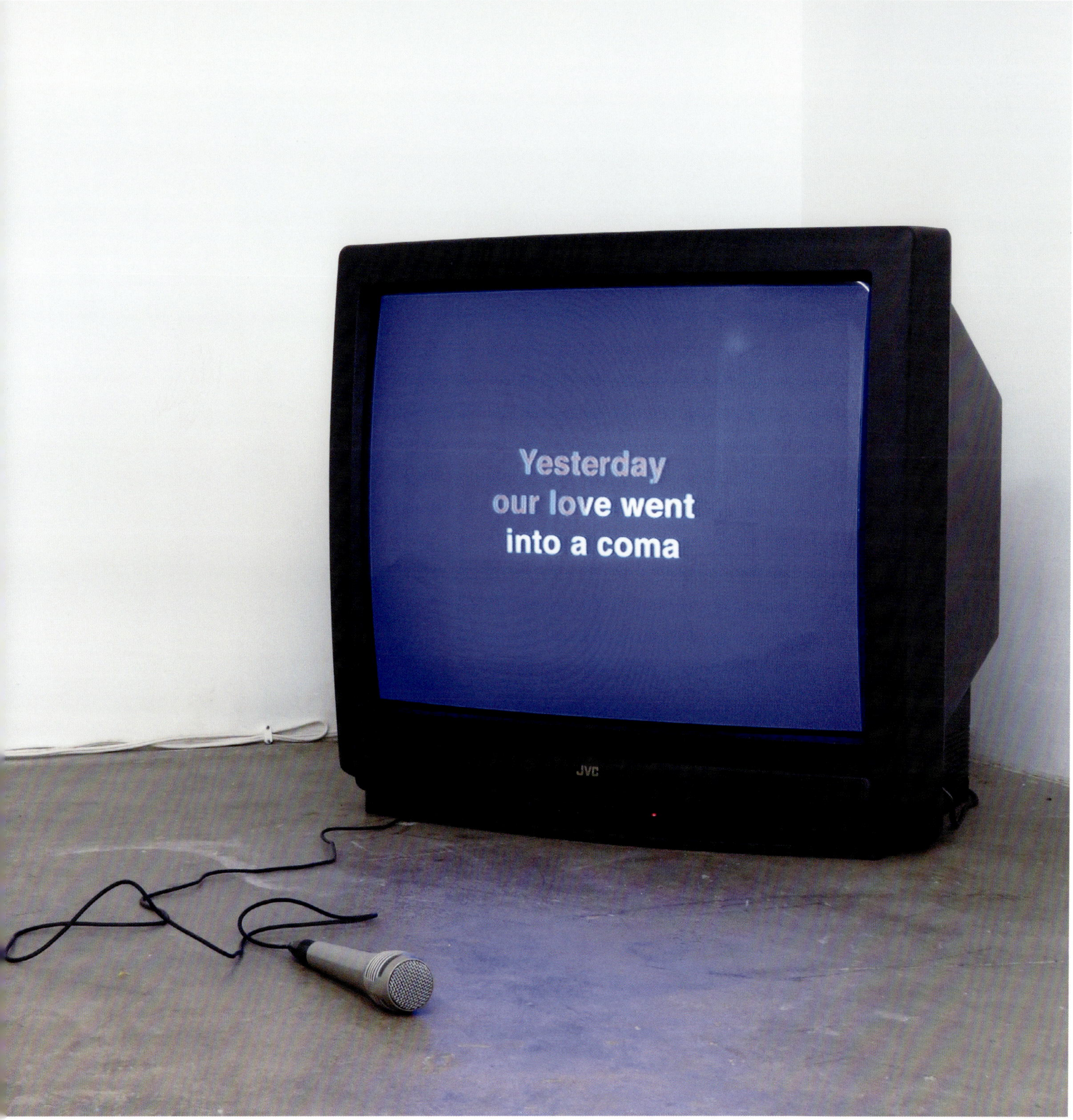
Yesterday
our love went
into a coma
JVC

ANTHONY WARNICK

You May Choose
2017
Prisoner-produced offset prints
12 x 18 inches each
Courtesy the artist

The posters comprising Anthony Warnick's *You May Choose* were printed by prisoners at the Pickaway Correctional Institution in Orient, Ohio. Although the artist has worked directly with prisoners in print-making workshops in the past, for this work he went through the established bureaucracy enabling the public to order products produced within the Ohio prison system. This work forms part of a larger series in which Warnick confronts the exploitation of those incarcerated by the state—the legal history of which originates in the 13th amendment to the U.S. Constitution, which abolished slavery and involuntary servitude except as punishment for a crime. The sentence Warnick selected for this set of prisoner-produced prints is a quotation from a well-known speech by British abolitionist William Wilberforce: "You may choose to look the other way but you can never again say that you did not know." Museum visitors are invited to take a print as a lasting reminder of the injustices the work calls to attention.

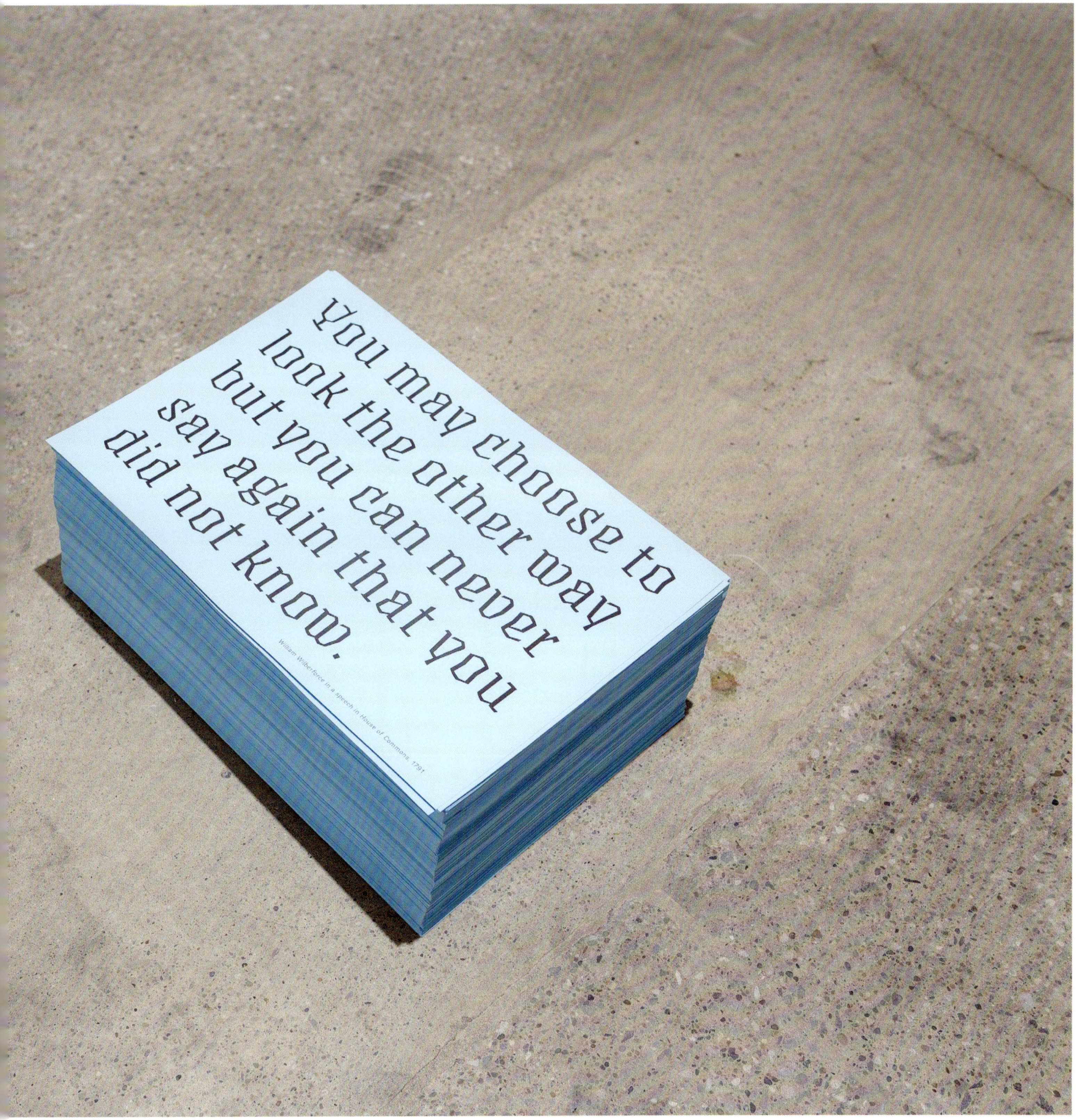
You may choose to
look the other way
but you can never
say again that you
did not know.
William Wilberforce in a speech in House of Commons, 1791

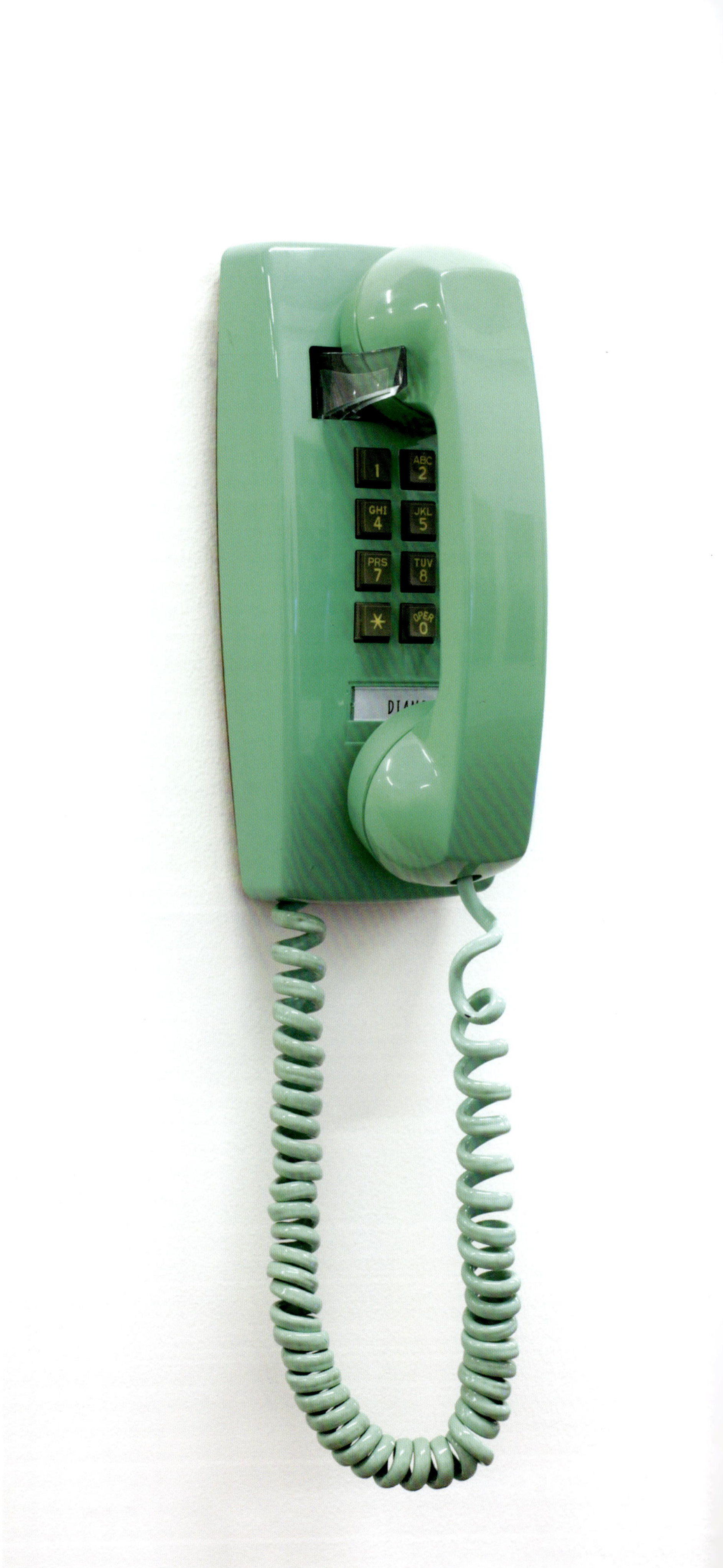
1
ABC 2
GHI 4
JKL 5
PRS 7
TUV 8
*
OPER 0

DIAMOND STINGILY

Dad is Byron
2017
Audio, vintage telephone
42:32 minutes
Courtesy the artist

Born in Chicago and based in New York, Diamond Stingily works in a variety of media—from spoken word, video, and audio to sculpture and installation. *Dad is Byron* is a new audio work in which the artist recorded a telephone conversation with her father, the house musician Byron Stingily. The artist initially planned for the conversation to focus on the violence her father witnessed growing up on Chicago's West Side and how music helped him to cope. *Dad is Byron* begins there, but the casual, familial conversation roves among a range of topics, including Byron's relationships to certain musicians and how becoming a father had changed him. He even sings a little—a special touch for this father-daughter portrait.

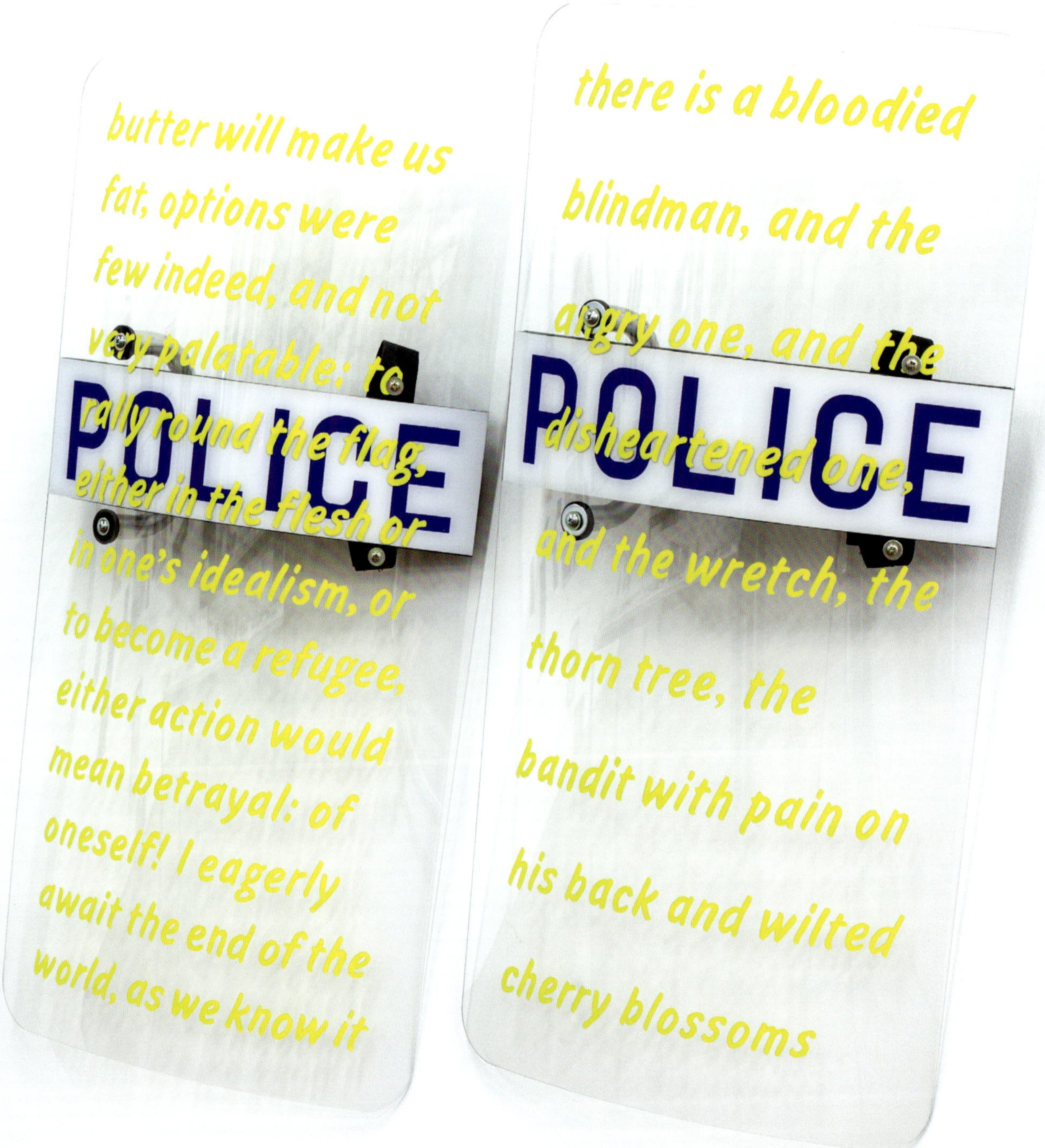
butter will make us fat, options were few indeed, and not very palatable: to rally round the flag, either in the flesh or in one's idealism, or to become a refugee, either action would mean betrayal: of oneself! I eagerly await the end of the world, as we know it
POLICE
there is a bloodied blindman, and the angry one, and the disheartened one, and the wretch, the thorn tree, the bandit with pain on his back and wilted cherry blossoms
POLICE

DANIEL JOSEPH MARTINEZ

Riot Shield (Butter), 2012
Riot Shield (Cherry Blossom), 2012
Riot shields with paint
39 3/8 x 19 1/8 x 5 3/4 inches each
Courtesy the artist and Roberts and Tilton, Los Angeles

Never hesitant to take on controversial issues in direct and provocative ways, Daniel Joseph Martinez creates works that confront American social, economic, and political systems. In *Riot Shield (Butter)* and *Riot Shield (Cherry Blossom)* the artist emblazoned unfathomable poems onto standard police riot shields. The titles of the works reference the video game *Call of Duty: Black Ops II* (2012), which at the time of its launch became the highest-grossing video game in history with over $500 million in sales within the first 24 hours of its release. The gamer has to collect various weapons and riots shields to attack and defend her- or himself. Martinez's work takes on complex issues of American history, democracy, racial politics, and the downsides of capitalist societies.

DANIEL JOSEPH MARTINEZ

A Meditation on the Possibility of Romantic Love; or, Where You Goin' with That Gun in Your Hand: Bobby Seale and Huey Newton Discuss the Relationships between Expressionism and Social Reality Present in Hitler's Paintings
2005
White Carrara marble
11 x 4 1/2 x 1 inches each
Courtesy the artist and Roberts and Tilton, Los Angeles

Martinez's sculpture renders Black Panther Party co-founders Bobby Seale and Huey P. Newton in pristine white marble. The artist sourced the marble from Carrara, Italy, the Tuscan quarry that has supplied marble for monumental architecture and sculpture since Roman antiquity, including the Pantheon and Michelangelo's *David*. Martinez subverts the majestic presumptions encoded in this Western heritage by applying the same material, in miniature form, to honoring persecuted leaders of the Black freedom struggle.

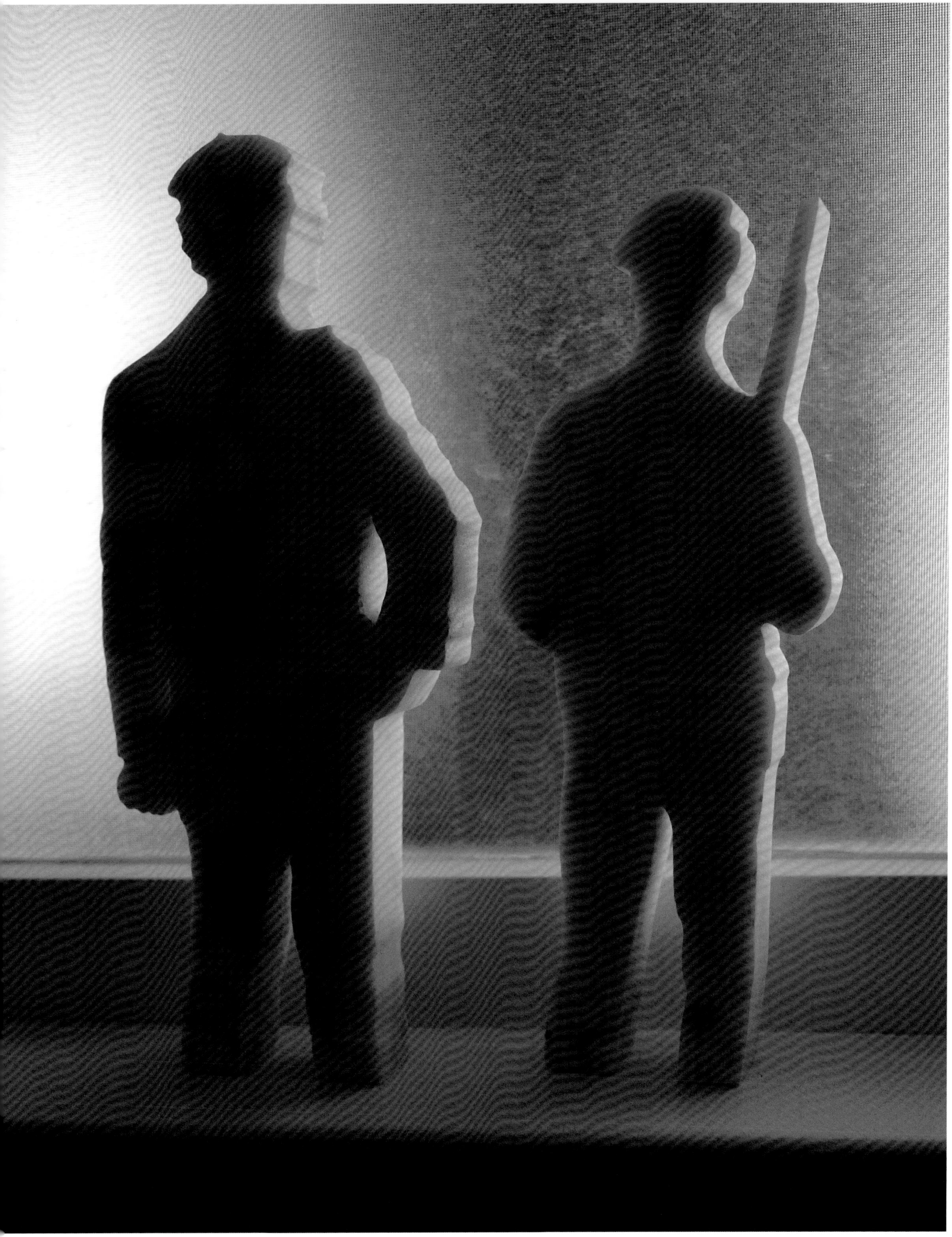

BEN HALL

Orwell in Burma
2017
Stretched Fleece
90 x 90 inches
Courtesy the artist and Young World Gallery, Detroit

George Orwell's time as a British imperial policeman in Burma during the 1920s ended in his becoming resolutely anti-state and anti-colonial—and to his becoming one of the twentieth-century's best-known anti-authoritarian writers. Combining a reference to Orwell with an image of popular British band The Police, Ben Hall implies the interdependence of political and cultural imperialism.

The Police's version of reggae music constitutes a form of colonial theft—an appropriation of a colonized people's folkways for foreign profit. Reggae emerged in the 1960s as a protest music against institutionalized racism and oppression in Jamaica, where the vast majority of people descend from Africans once enslaved by the English. Its absorption within mainstream British music depoliticizes it, diminishing its revolutionary potential.

Having also emerged from the British Empire, The United States participates in this colonial legacy, though many of its citizens prefer to ignore this. Evoking Orwell's call for disarmament of the police state, Hall provokes viewers to acknowledge the country's colonial foundations and its current ramifications, including ongoing police violence against African Americans. Hall says, "we forget because of the long-term occupation of this land that America is a colonial project, and the framework for oppression has been laid and relaid, repaired, reified, and reinforced over 500 years—all for profit with the police acting as the front line for occupation." Viewers may also consider how oppositional African American cultural forms become absorbed and diluted within the commodified mainstream.

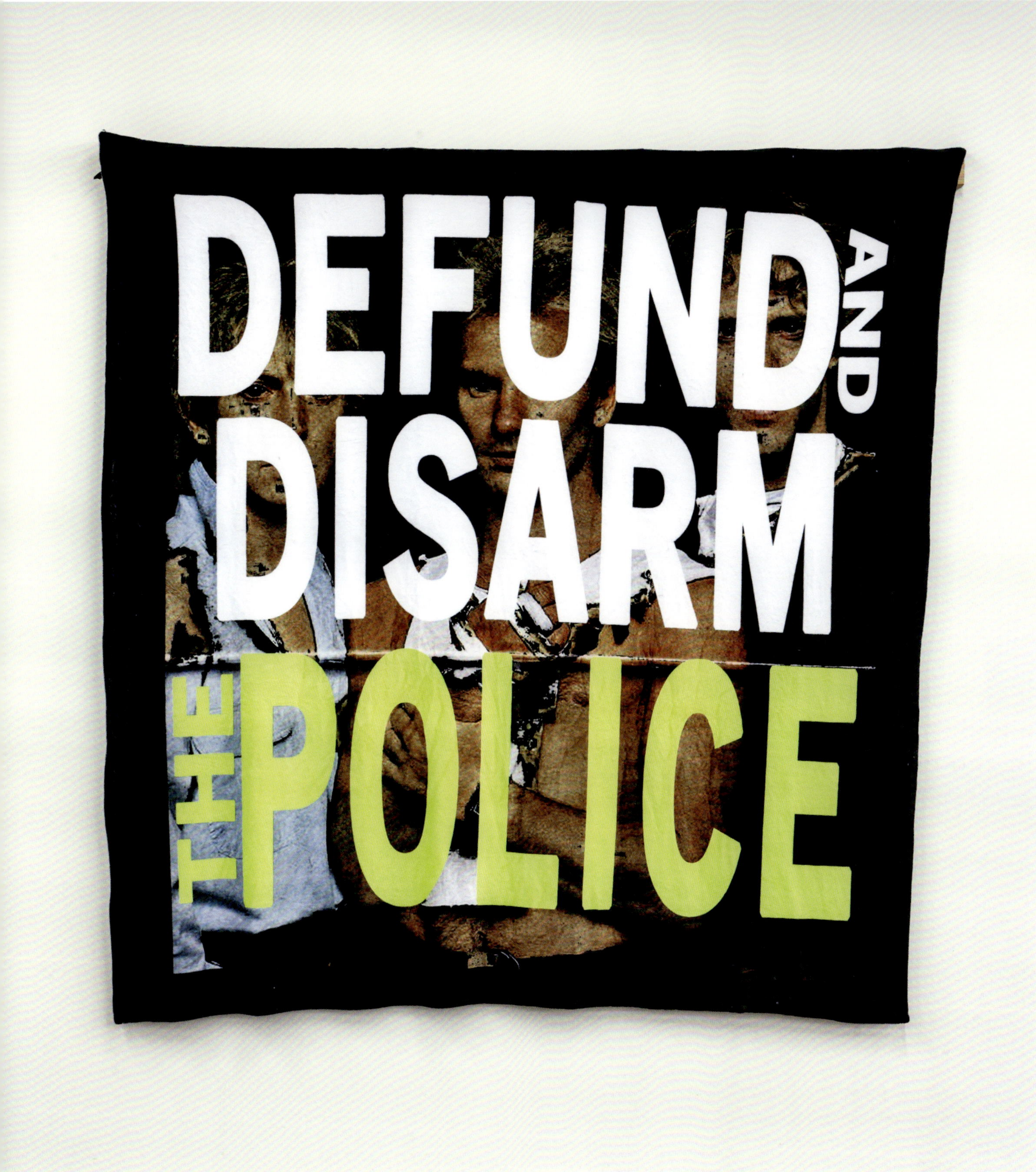
DEFUND
AND
DISARM
THE
POLICE

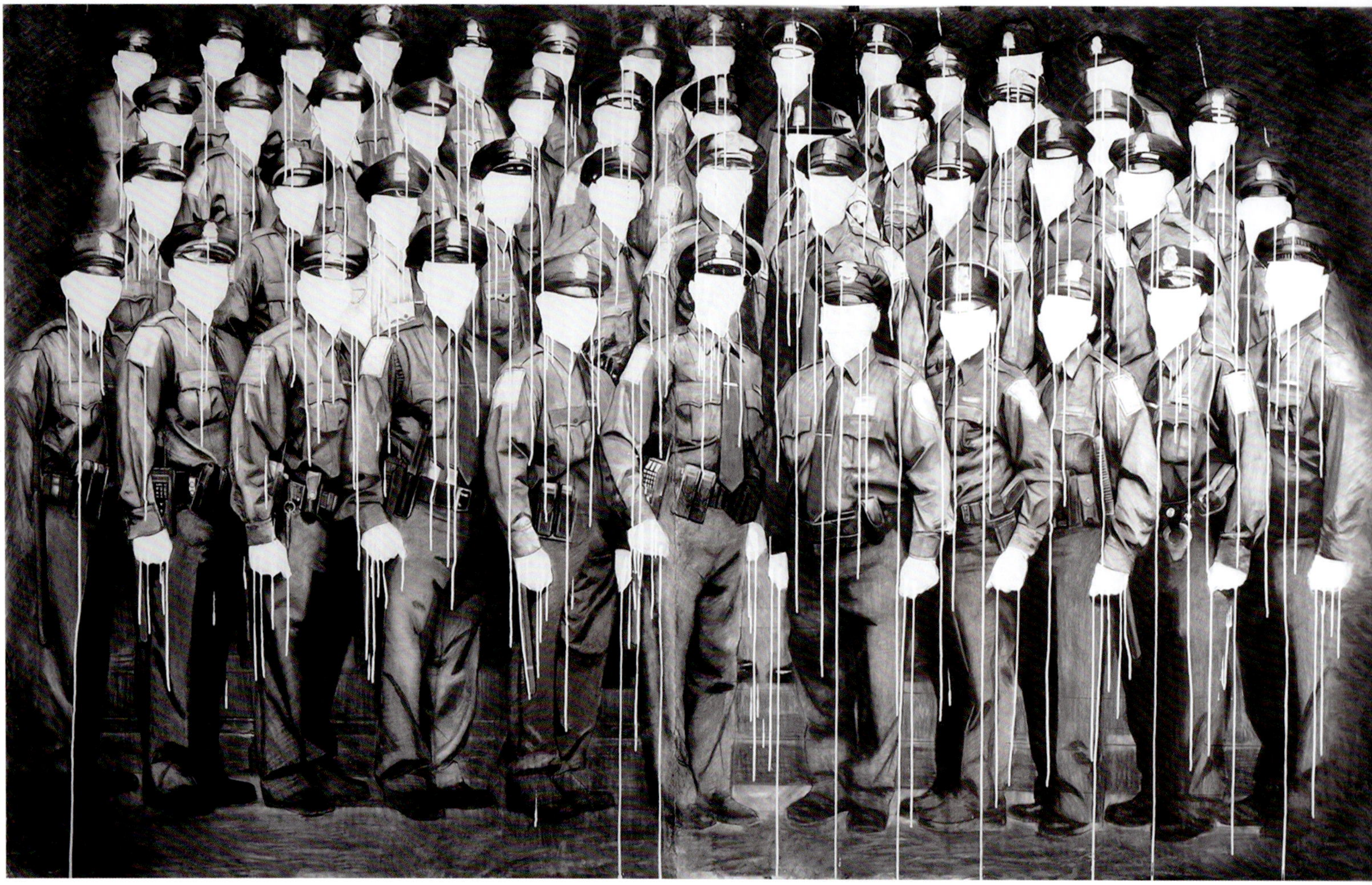

TYLONN SAWYER

Cabal: Class of 2016
2016
Charcoal drawing and mixed media on canvas
60 x 96 inches
Courtesy the DeAndre and Desiré Levy Collection

Tylonn Sawyer's large-scale drawing *Cabal: Class of 2016* presents rows of uniformed men posing for a group portrait. The black-and-white image conceals the figures' flesh and features, their faces and hands covered in thick glosses of white paint that drip down the canvas. Evidently a class of police officers, although the details of their uniforms are not too crisp, the figures appear homogeneous and white, any differences among them—including race and gender—neutralized and subsumed under the signifier of the uniform. Anonymous but unified and powerful, the group projects a disturbing image mirroring the fear, intimidation, and distrust that many people, particularly in black communities, feel toward law enforcement in an era of rampant police brutality.

Class Photo #3: Black Convening
Class Photo #4: Black Convening
2017
Oil, collage, and glitter on canvas
70 x 46 inches each
Courtesy the artist

The paintings in Sawyer's ongoing series *Black Masquerade* depict anonymous contemporary figures donning masks of cultural leaders who have historically given voice to black resistance. In *Class Photo #3: Black Convening*, five identically-dressed female figures wear Nina Simone masks, seeming to adopt through their physical postures the singer's defiance and strength. Similarly, in *Class Photo #4: Black Convening*, Sawyer depicts five male figures wearing matching red ties, black suspenders, white shirts, and masks of the iconic writer and social critic James Baldwin. The works raise questions about how twenty-first century Americans can connect with and further the work of such groundbreaking figures from the past.

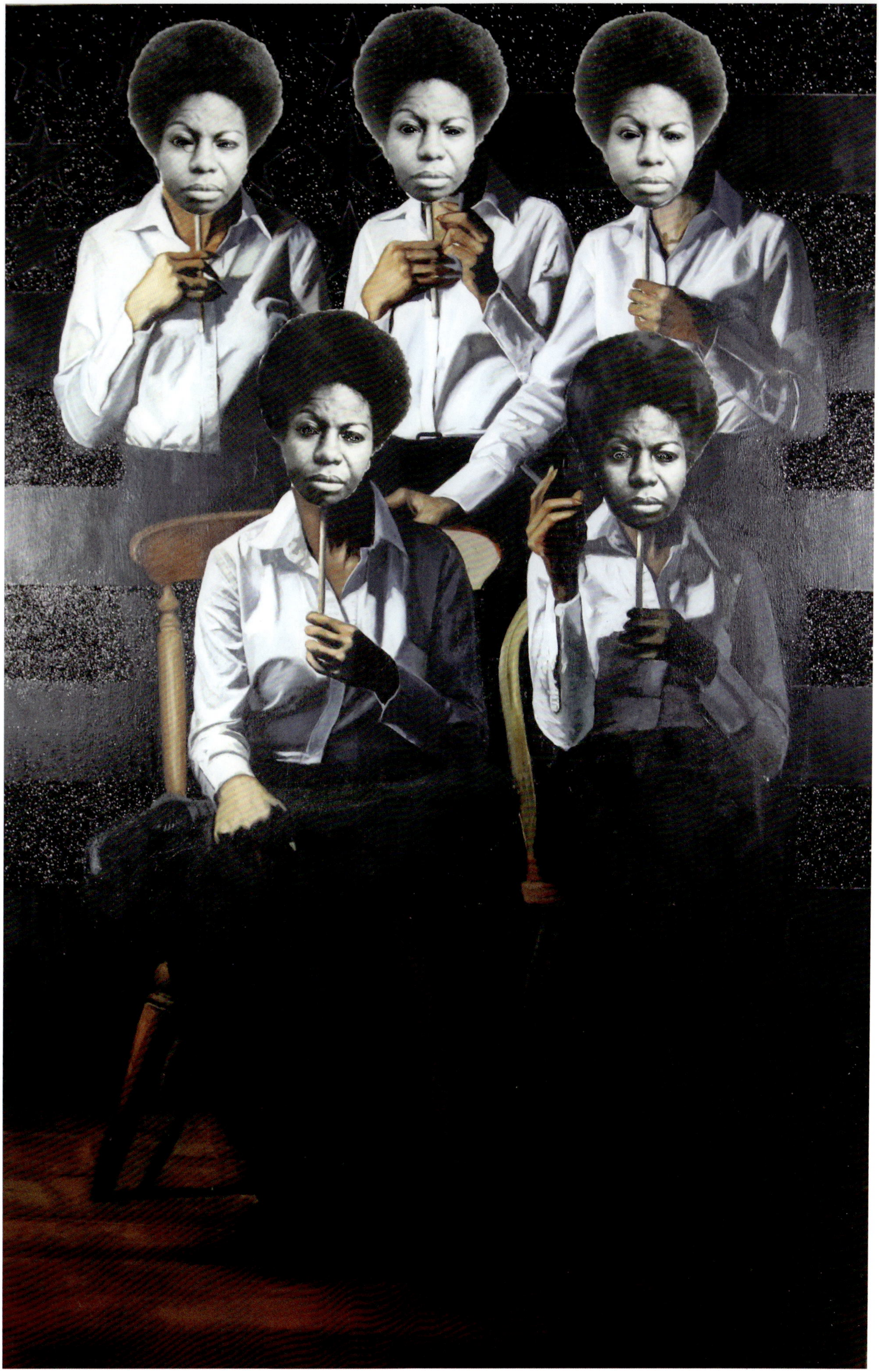

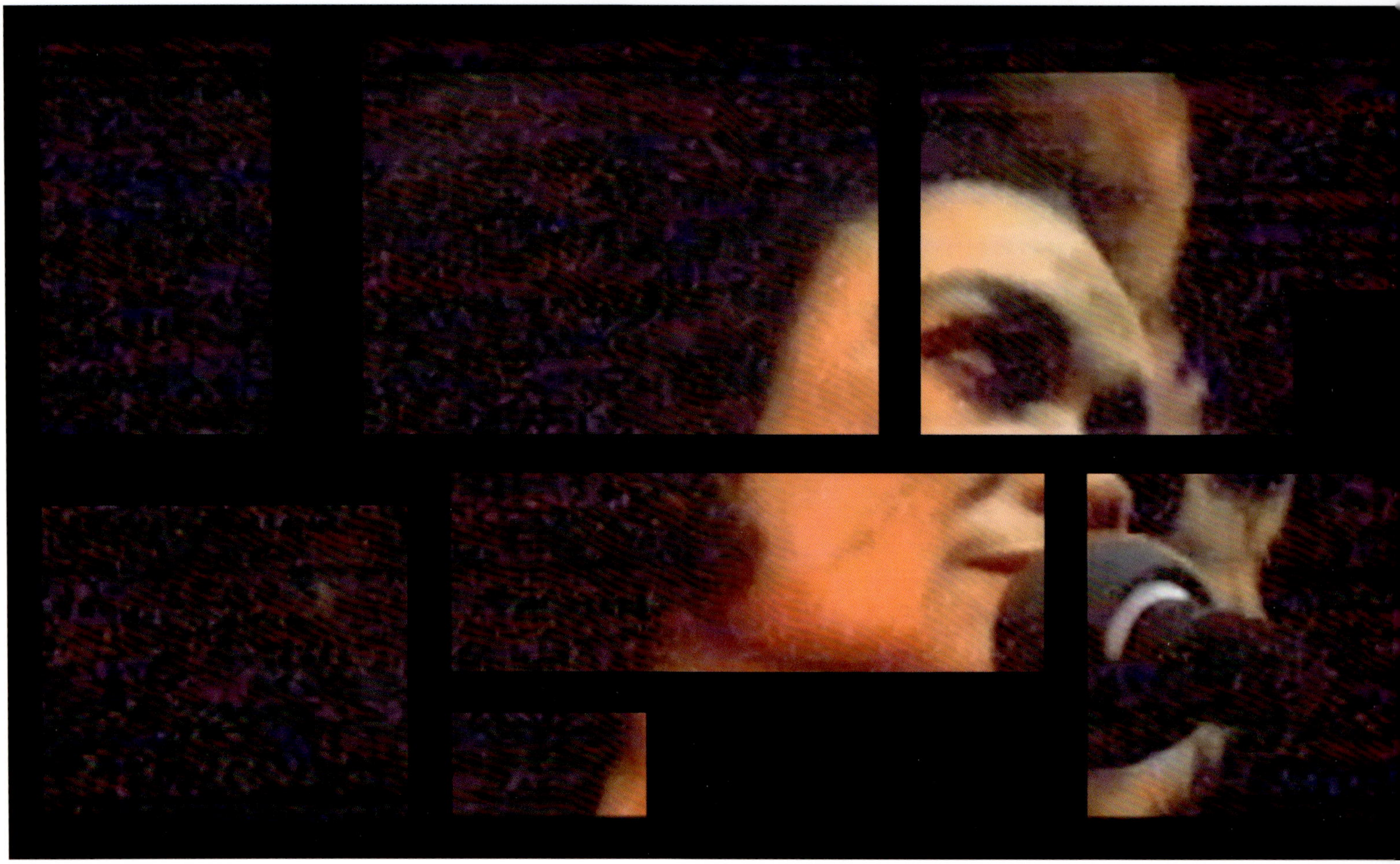

MICKALENE THOMAS

Do I Look Like a Lady?
2016
Mixed media installation
Installation views, LA MOCA

Courtesy the artist and Lehmann Maupin, New York and Hong Kong.

Mickalane Thomas's elaborate, rhinestone-studded paintings, installations, and photographs deal with conceptions of femininity, beauty, and black identity. For her two-channel video installation, *Do I Look Like a Lady? (Comedians and Singers)*, Thomas joined together video clips featuring iconic performers speaking and singing about their experiences as black women. Whitney Houston, Josephine Baker, Jackie "Moms" Mabley, Eartha Kitt, Nina Simone, Wanda Sykes, and others, form a rich collage of black female voices. Punctuated by the static of analog TV and partitioned into grids of images and sound, Thomas's installation confronts issues of representation, conceptions of beauty, and the powerful legacies of black female entertainers.

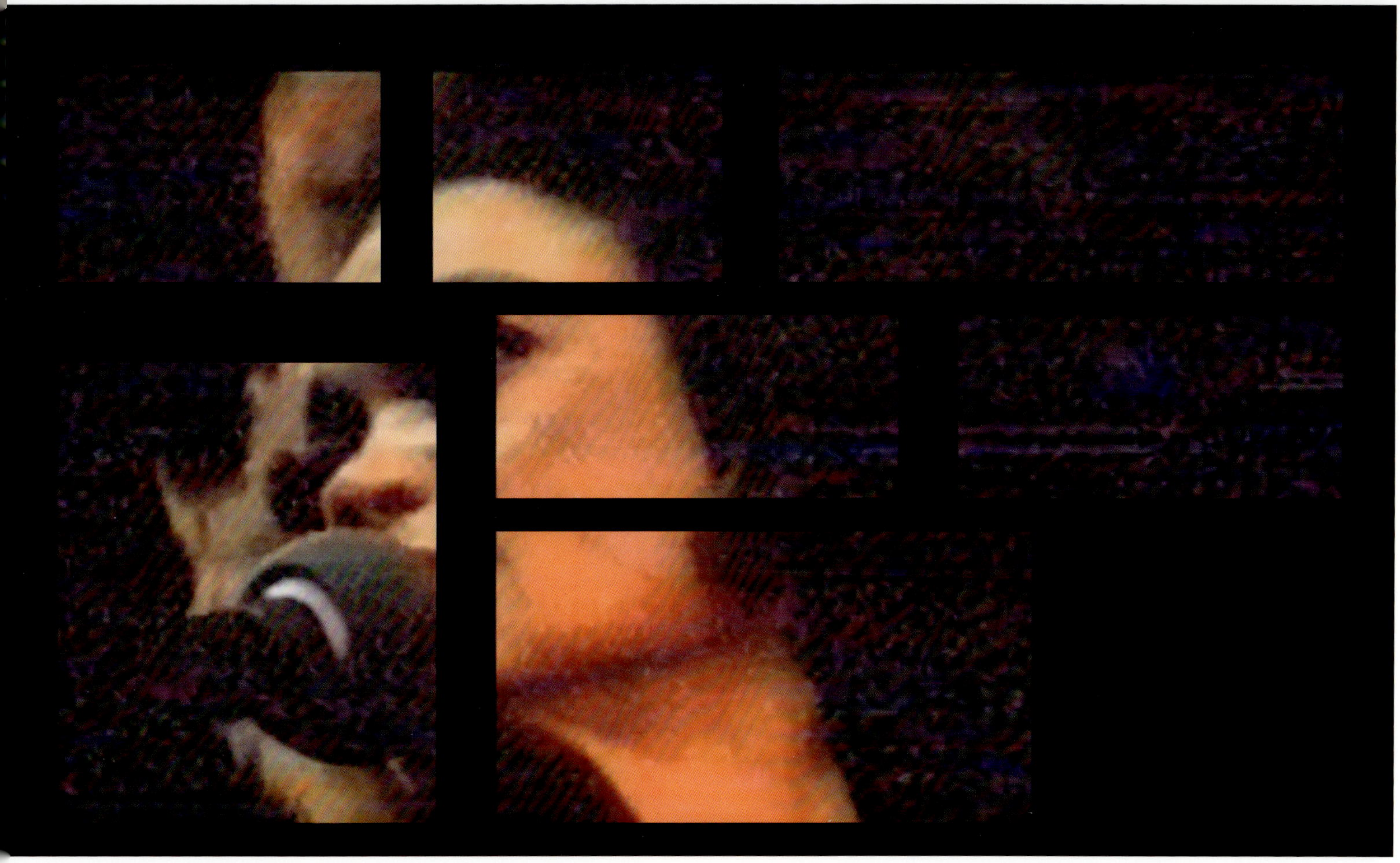

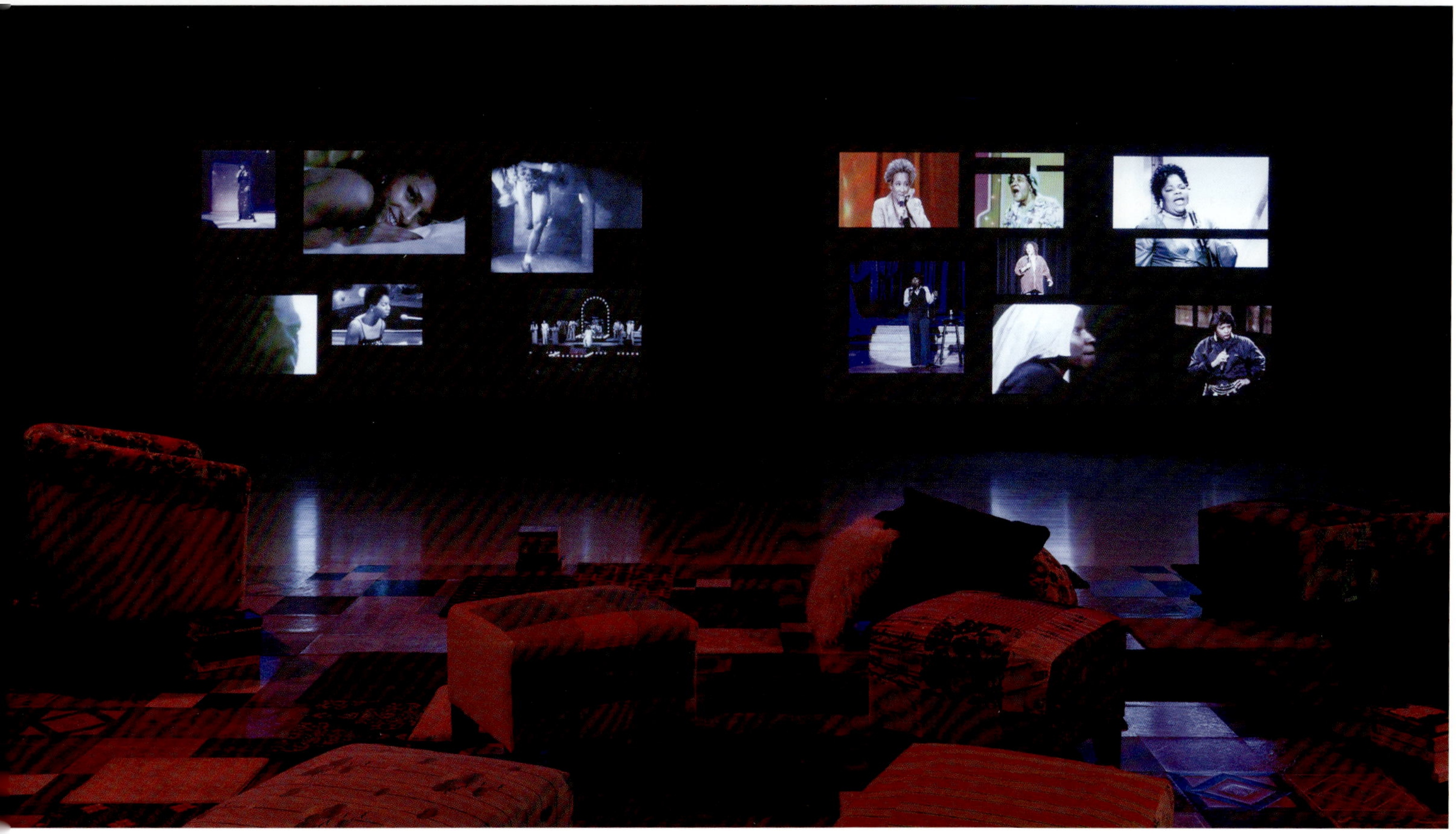

IMANI ROACH

Good to Me as I Am to You (After Aretha)
2017
Paraffin wax
18 sculptures
5 x 4 x 3 inches each
Courtesy the artist

Good to Me as I Am to You (After Aretha) is inspired by Imani Roach's long-standing fascination with Aretha Franklin's song of the same name, released on her 1968 album *Lady Soul.* In addition, Roach recalls Franklin's performance of "Natural Woman" at the 2015 Kennedy Center Honors, when the singer casually, yet triumphantly, removed her fur coat and let it drop to the floor during the song's dramatic crescendo. For *Sonic Rebellion*, Roach created eighteen miniature casts of Franklin's fur coat for display in a grid recalling helicopter views of Detroit's street grid, comprising burned and badly damaged buildings, after the 1967 uprising.

Aretha Franklin was raised in Detroit, and her father C.L. Franklin's church was located near the geographic epicenter of the rioting. 1967 was also the year Aretha catapulted to international stardom with songs like "Respect" and "Chain of Fools." Roach is interested in the emergence of Soul music, circa 1967, as what she calls a "sonic warning" or "a lifting of the mask to reveal the righteous rage at the heart of the political moment for many black people in America." She regards Franklin's black, female body and voice as a vessel for rage. Viewing Franklin's Kennedy Center performance nearly fifty years later, Roach sees the Queen of Soul's discarding of her coat not only as a declaration of her diva status but also as a cathartic shedding of her vessel—and her sculpture maps that catharsis back onto the landscape from which the singer and her music emerged.

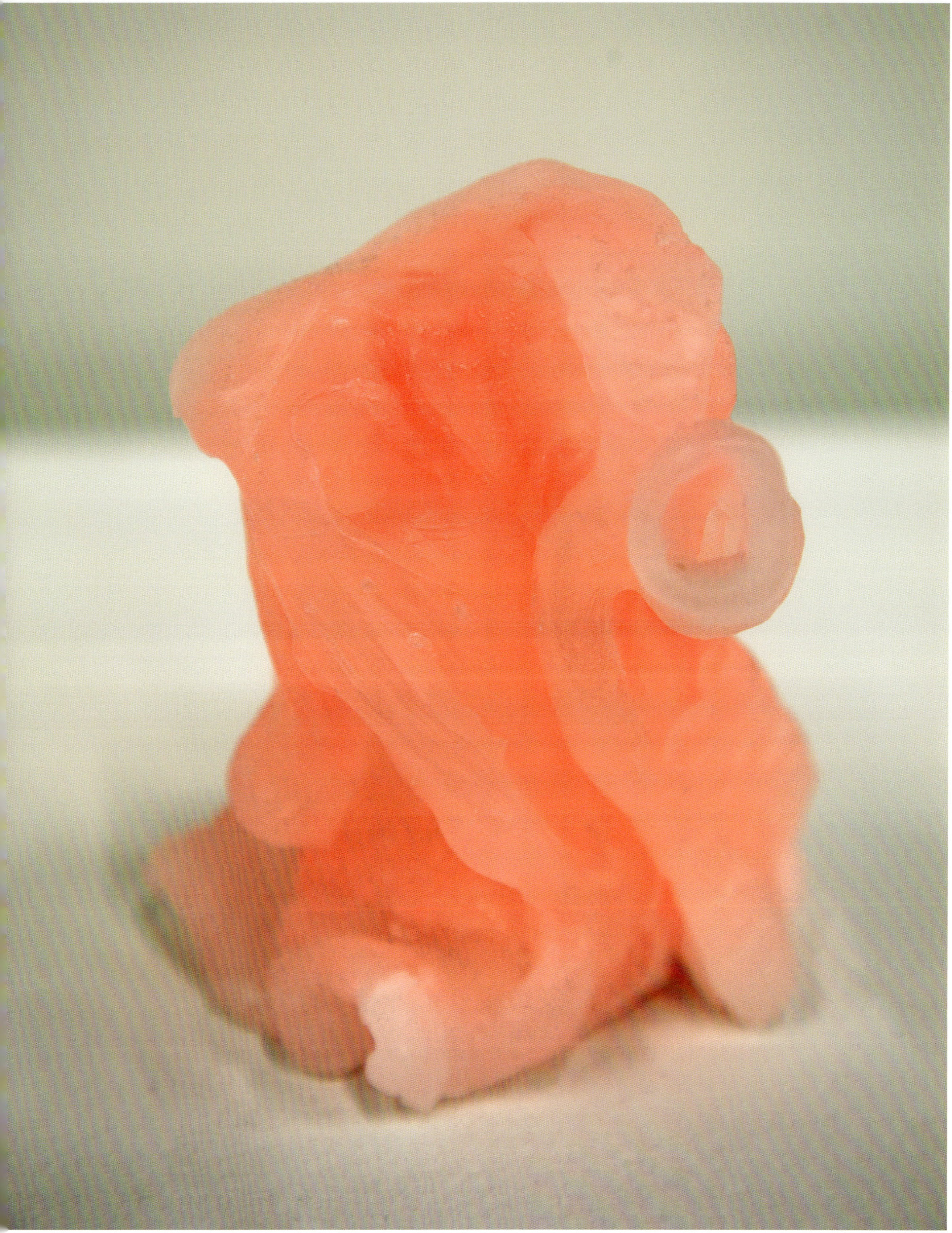

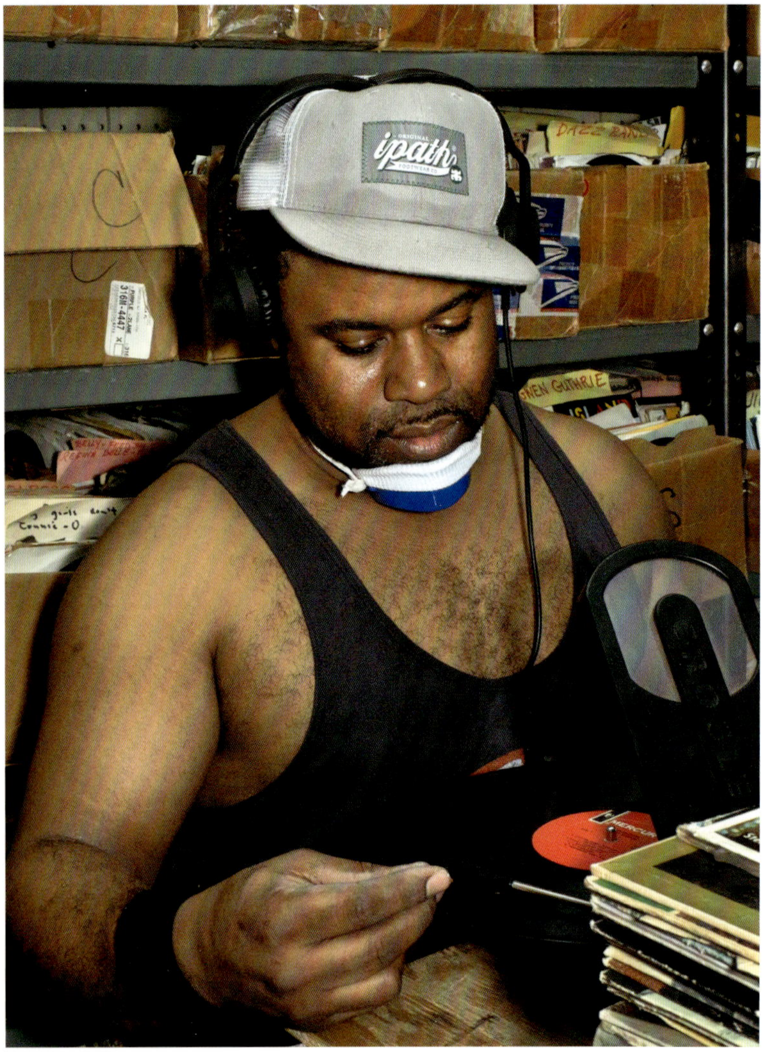

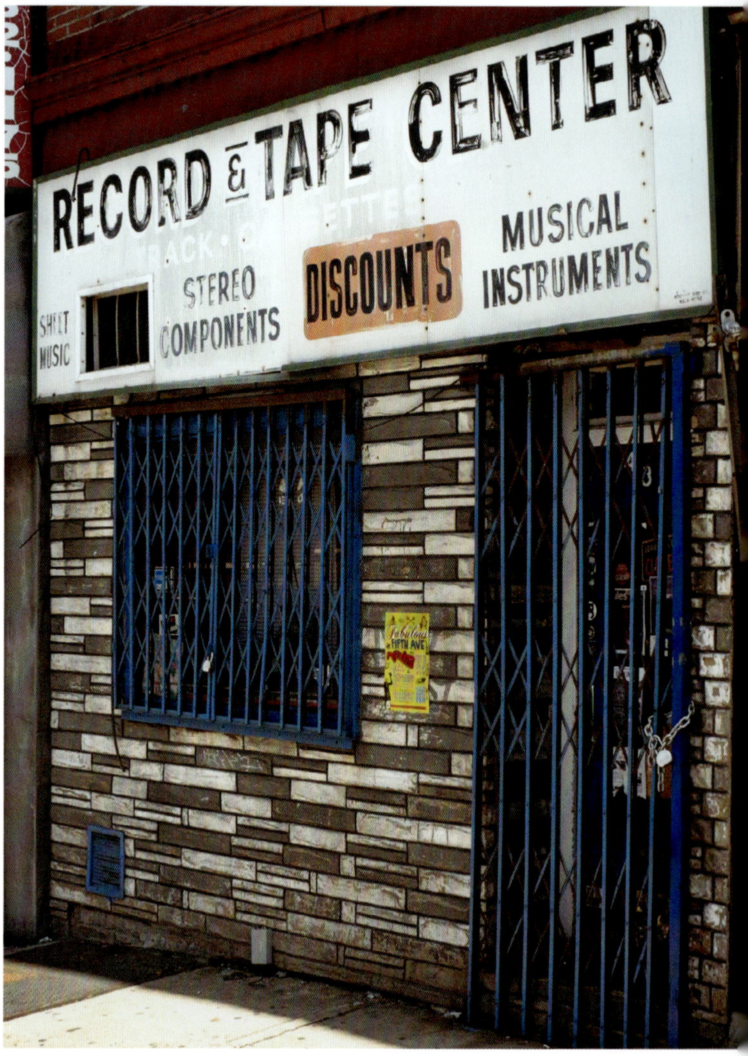

DARIN MICKEY

Death Takes a Holiday
2014–15
Archival pigment prints
Dimensions variable
Courtesy the artist

Left to right:
"Dusty Fingers," Platter World, Garfield, NJ 2015
"5th Ave Facade," Fifth Avenue Records and Tapes, Brooklyn, NY 2014
"Mosaic," Attic Records, Millvale, PA 2015
"Milk Bone," Platter World, Garfield, NJ 2015

This selection of photographs comes from a project titled *Death Takes a Holiday*, in which over three years Darin Mickey documented a handful of record shops in New York, New Jersey, and Pennsylvania. An important aspect of photography, from its inception, has been its capacity to enumerate typologies of objects, as laid out in Henry Fox Talbot's book *The Pencil of Nature* (1844–46). Here Mickey applies this photographic archival impulse to the dusty accumulations of records apparently rotting away inside America's used record stores. The collection of photographs comprises an archive of an archive, as the stores themselves constitute storehouses of rare records, cultural documents of moments and music from the past.

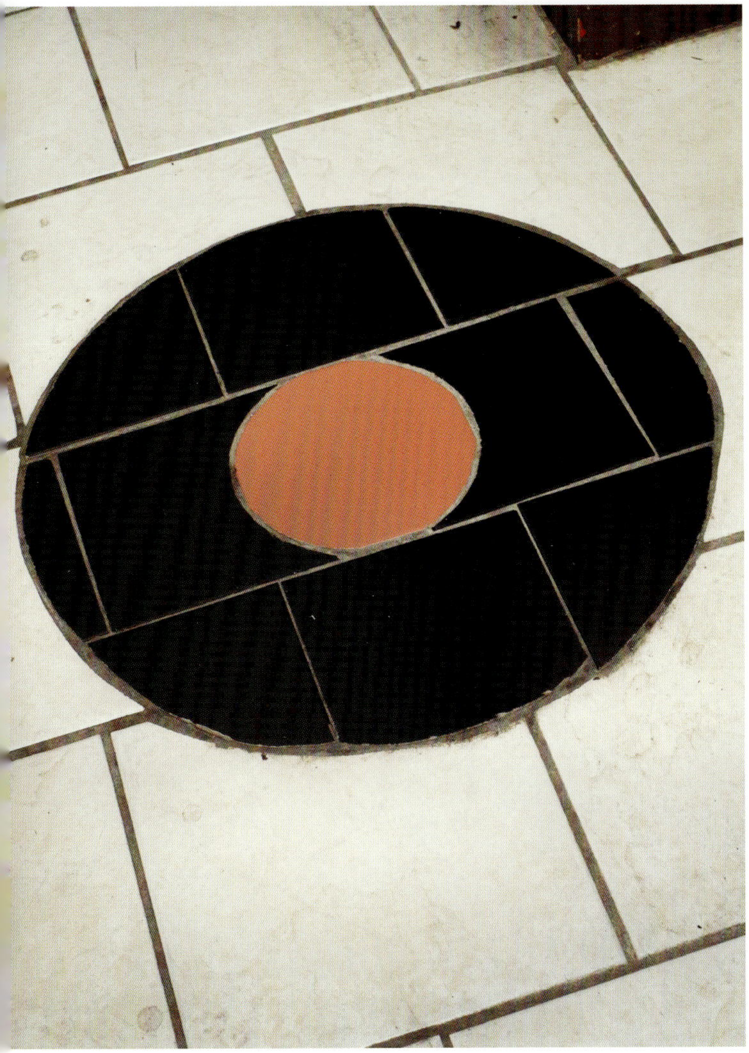

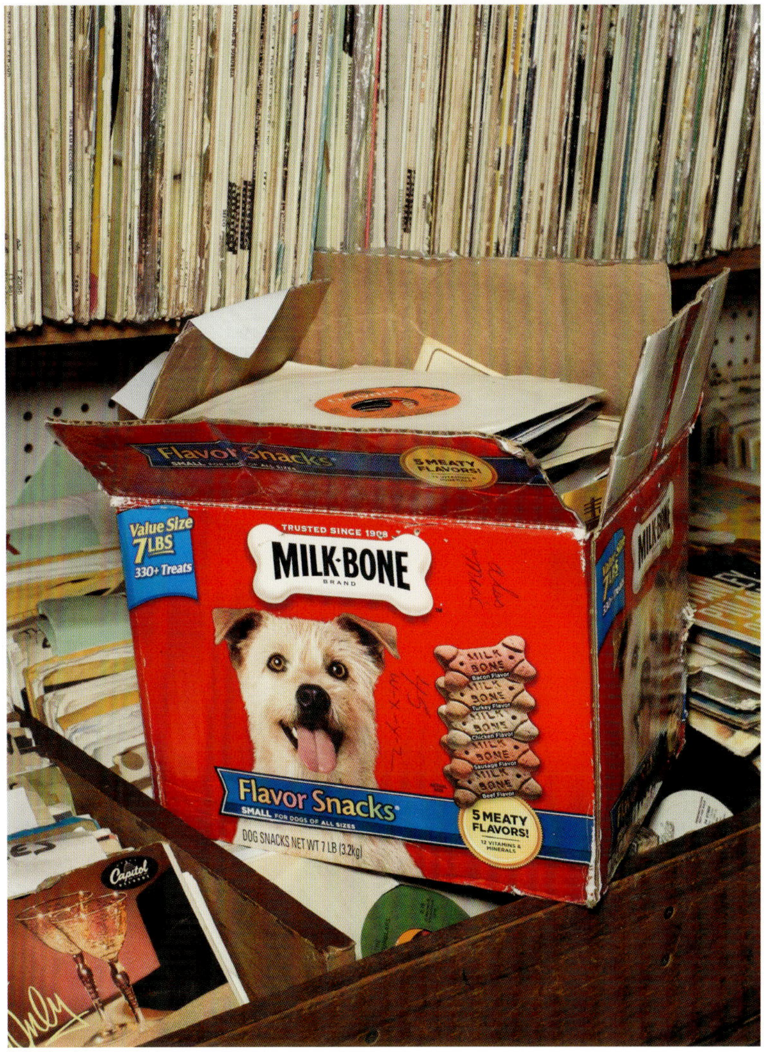
Flavor Snacks
5 MEATY FLAVORS!
Value Size
7LBS
330+ Treats
TRUSTED SINCE 1908
MILK-BONE
Flavor Snacks
SMALL FOR DOGS OF ALL SIZES
DOG SNACKS NET WT 7 LB (3.2kg)
5 MEATY FLAVORS!
Capitol

RASHID JOHNSON

Birth of Cool
2014
Black soap, wax
48 ½ x 72 ½ x 2 ½ inches
Courtesy the artist and David Kordansky Gallery

Rashid Johnson's *Birth of Cool* is a kind of drawing in relief. Created from some of the artist's signature materials—black soap and wax—the energetic and frenetic lines incised across the dark, expansive surface create a dynamic field, while the work's materials and title draw in other cultural references. Black soap, a material used often by Johnson, is thought to have healing powers in its originating nation of Ghana. And the title, *Birth of Cool*, refers to Miles Davis' iconic 1957 jazz compilation album, *Birth of the Cool*, the lines and curves perhaps mimicking Davis' mind-bending trumpet arrangements. Davis' album also inspired the title of a 2008 retrospective of famed black portrait artist Barkley Hendricks, who has also directly influenced Johnson's practice. *Birth of Cool* forms part of a series of works Johnson calls *Cosmic Slop*, in reference to the 1973 Funkadelic album of the same name. "It refers to a fictional dance," the artist explains, "and I like the idea that this dance has something to do with the performance of making a painting."

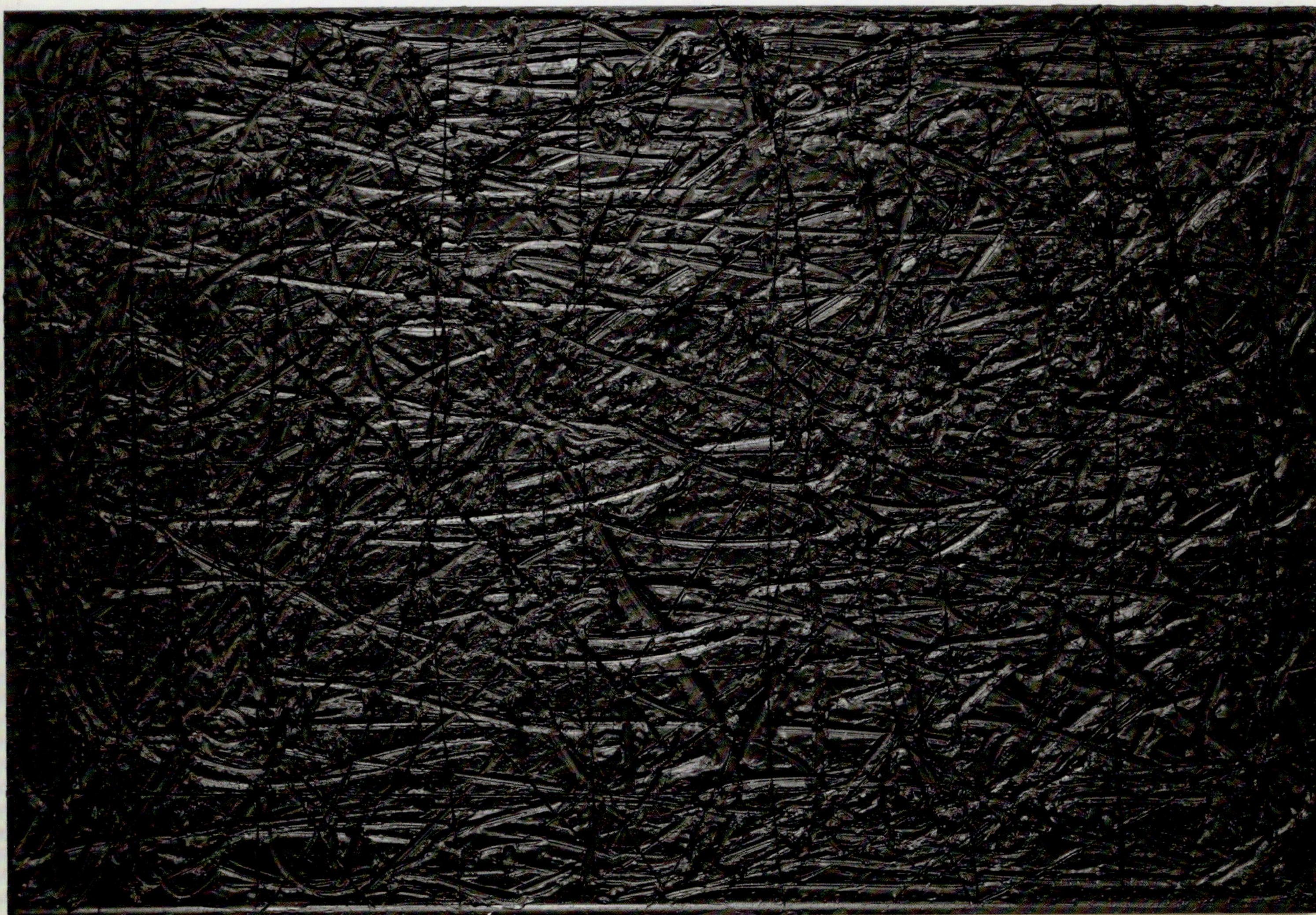

MARCELO CIDADE

Monumento ao Monumento
2010
Galvanized iron containment gates
236 7/32 x 78 ¾ x 78 ¾ inches
Courtesy the artist and Galeria Vermelho, São Paulo

Drawing from graffiti and skateboard culture, among other things, Brazillian artist Marcelo Cidade explores forms of resistance deployed on the streets of São Paulo. Using a variety of materials, he often references and recreates forms of obstruction—objects of presumed authority functioning to protect property, exclude certain people from certain spaces, and project a sense of "security." Thinking about the ways in which authoritative implementations of these objects typically value property over people, enable and reconstitute social barriers, and act to symbolize and enact structures of power, Cidade reconfigures them as towering and yet precarious monuments to stymied marginalization.

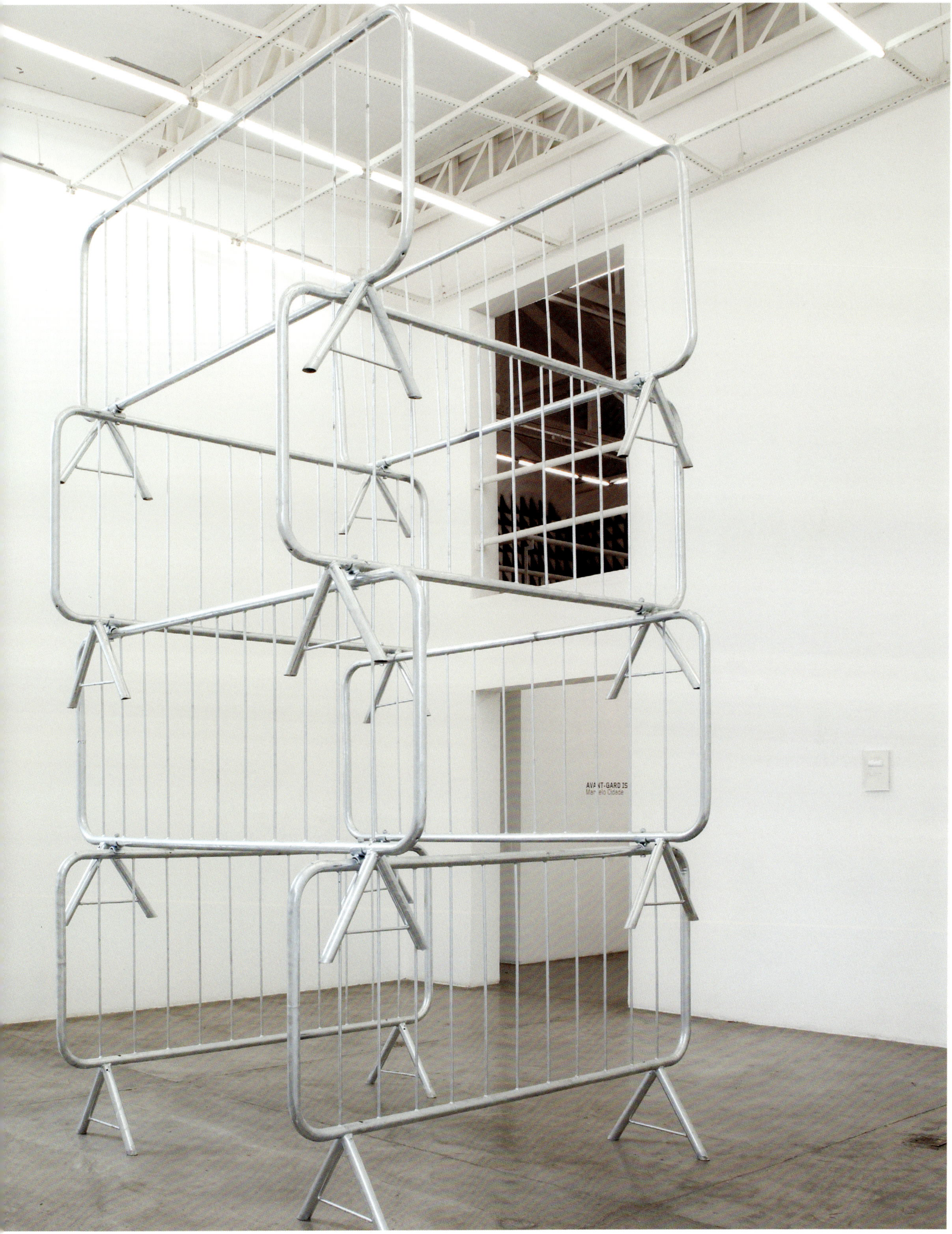

HERE IS A SONG WITH NO FACE ... A BEAT AND MELODY MADE BY AND FOR THE FACELESS

FACELESS PEOPLE FILL FACELESS BUILDINGS THAT OCCASIONALLY EXPRESS THEMSELVES ... A BEAT
BUMPS, DROPS A BRICK HERE, A CINDERBLOCK SMILE
AN ELBOW FROM ONE OF THE FACELESS RESTS ON A WINDOW STOOL CRUMBLES THE HOLLOW GRIDS
HOLDING TARNISHED GLASS IN PLACE THERE, EDIFICE EYES

A SMILE, NO ....
AN ABDOMEN PULLED IN MID CIRCLE, MAYBE ...
A GREEN LIGHT SHIMMERING ON SHOULDERS RAPIDLY SWERVING AN ANALEMA

ITS LIKE THIS WITH US
WE COULD HAVE SOMETHING LIKE A FACE
WITH THE RECOGNITION IT ENTAILS
BUT WHAT HAS THAT EVER GOTTEN ANY OF US

A FACE
LIKE A HANDS INFLUENCE
LIKE PROMISES IN CONTRACTS WITH PRECONDITIONS AND QUALIFIERS
LIKE HARDWARE OUTMODED BY SOFTWARE
IS TOO OFTEN THE FORCED STEWARD OF ITS OWN OBSOLESCENCE

WE WERE ALL FIGHTING FOR A FACE ONCE, EVEN HAD THEM AT ONE POINT
THE SONGS THEN WERE MARVELOUS ... GLAMOROUS SOLOS AND MONOLOGUES ABOUT LOVING
THOSE WITH FACES, LOVING
ADONIS CITIES, BRIGHT AND WIDE-EYED
BELIEVING IN THEIR REFLECTIONS
JUST UNTIL THEY RUSTED,
SUDDENLY LOST THEIR SHIMMERING POLISHED STEEL FACES
HEADLIGHTS FELL OUT
TRANSMITTERS ABANDONED

THE FACELESS COULD ONLY MISRECOGNIZE AND SUBSEQUENTLY MISUSE ... FACELESS SPACES ...
FACELESS LEFT BEHINDS,

NOT YET DUST BUT LONG SINCE IN HANDS OF, RE-DEPLOYED

IN THIS GRAND MISRECOGNITION A BEAT AND A MELODY WERE BORN ... AND CERTAIN FACELESS
PEOPLE REBORN IN THE BRIGHT SHADOWS OF

A FACELESS REVIVAL

HERE IS A SONG WITH NO FACE ... A BEAT AND MELODY MADE BY AND FOR THE FACELESS ... AND
FOR ABSOLUTELY NO ONE ELSE

JULIANA HUXTABLE

Untitled (Faceless)
2017
Vinyl text
Dimensions variable
Courtesy the artist and Reena Spaulding Fine Arts, New York

Juliana Huxtable's text piece for *Sonic Rebellion* offers a theme of "facelessness" as a meditation on identity formation in connection with the city of Detroit. She offers the work in homage to Detroit techno, especially the collective, label, and production hub Underground Resistance (UR). For Huxtable, the music and ethos of UR derives from the context of Detroit as the quintessential American "dream deferred," especially for the many African Americans who moved to the city in search of stable jobs during the Great Migration. As the auto industry abandoned the city, it left a landscape of deteriorating factories and urban life in tatters. Yet, the city's fascination with the industrial landscape birthed a unique relationship to technology as the basis for music production. With UR, this production occurs in resolved anonymity, as the collective rejects the cult of personality of the DJ/producer in a performed allegiance with the city's poor, black people who are already invisible in so many ways. Huxtable, a New York-based artist, poet, and DJ, sees this solidarity with the invisible, and possibility of anonymity within its embrace, as formative of the personal freedoms available in techno and rave culture.

Overleaf:

ADAM PENDLETON

Untitled (A Victim of American Democracy)
2017
Silkscreen ink and spray paint on canvas
84 x 60 inches
Courtesy the artist

Adam Pendleton's *Untitled (A Victim of Democracy)* diptych incorporates layers of black, spray-painted and silkscreened pigments in a collage-like field of letters and words. Though segmented and layered, the forms in Pendleton's paintings spell out "A victim of democracy"—a phrase taken from Malcolm X's famous 1964 speech, *The Ballot or The Bullet.* In the speech, Malcolm X separates his own identity from the nation in which he was born, saying: "No, I'm not an American. I'm one of the 22 million black people who are the victims of Americanism. One of the 22 million black people who are the victims of democracy, nothing but disguised hypocrisy. So, I'm not standing here speaking to you as an American, or a patriot, or a flag-saluter, or a flag-waver—no, not I. I'm speaking as a victim of this American system. And I see America through the eyes of the victim. I don't see any American dream; I see an American nightmare."

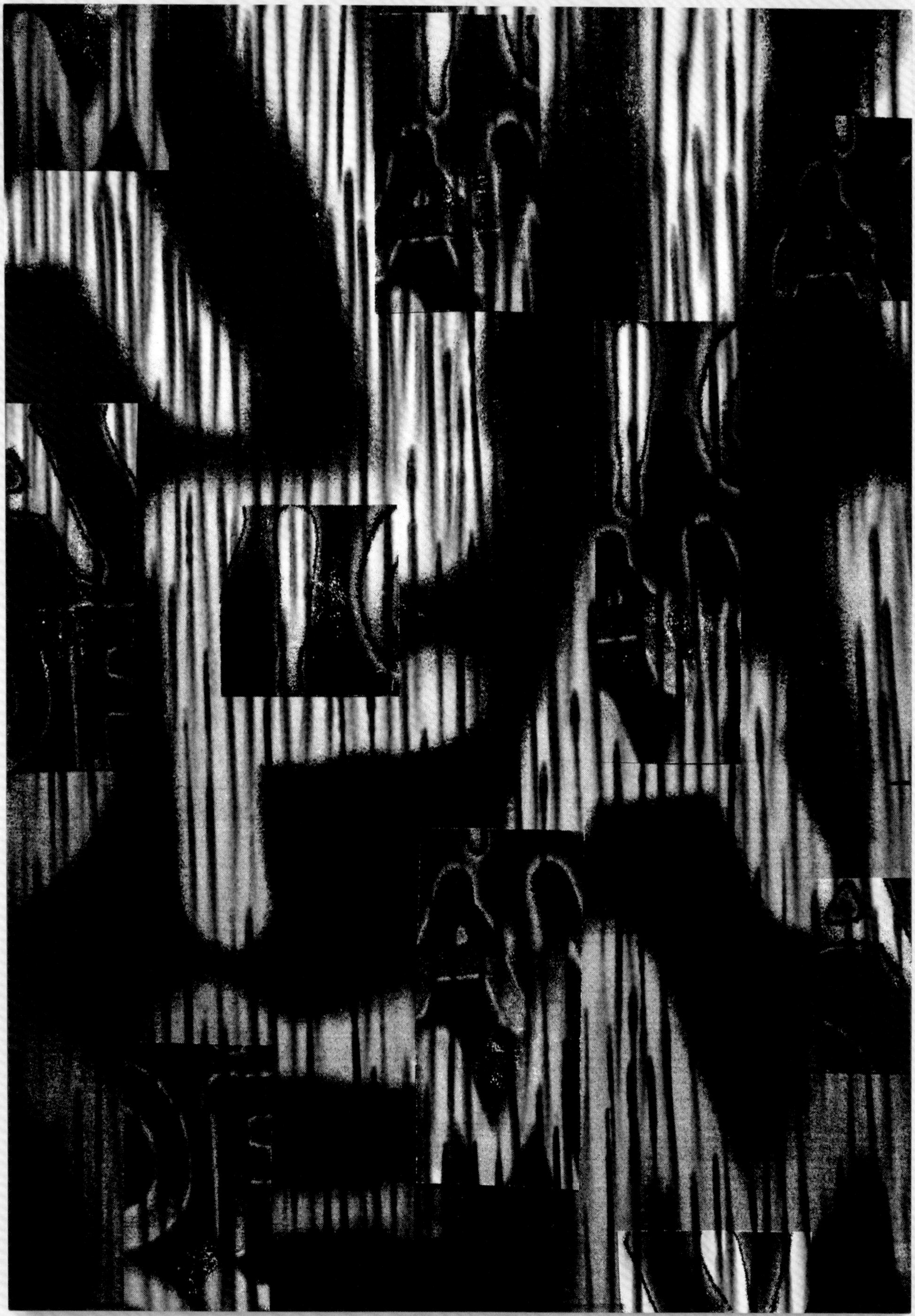

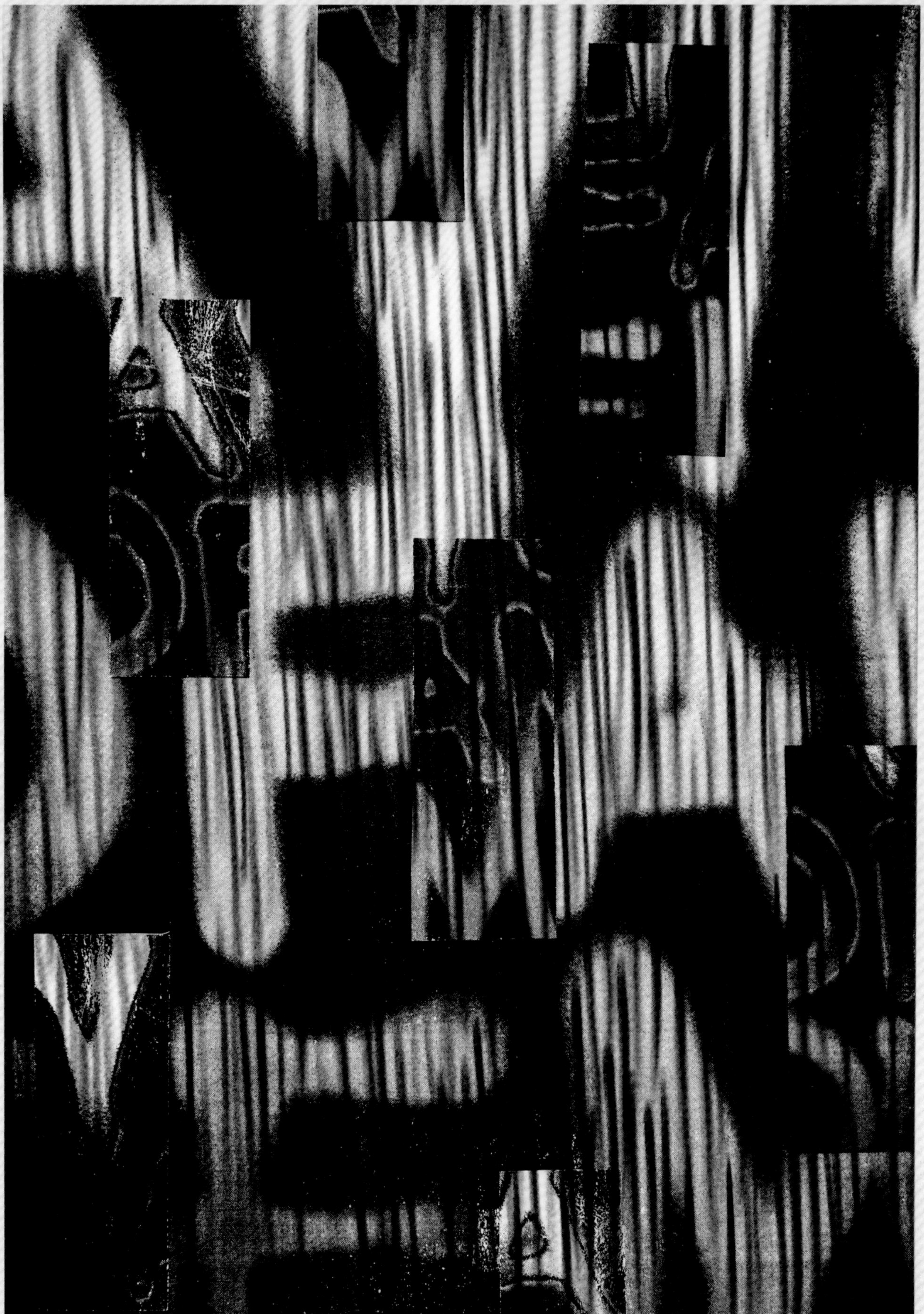

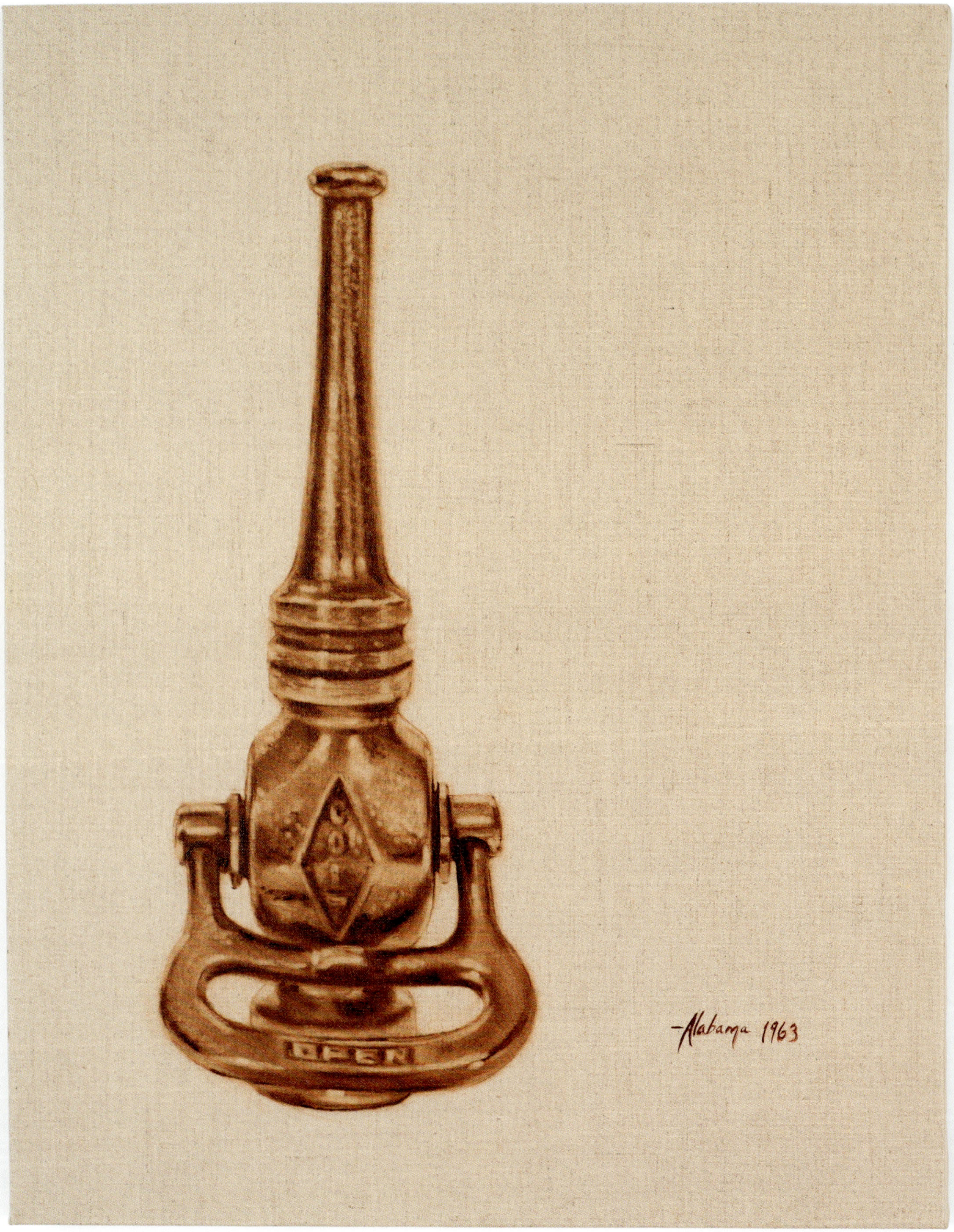
OPEN
-Alabama 1963

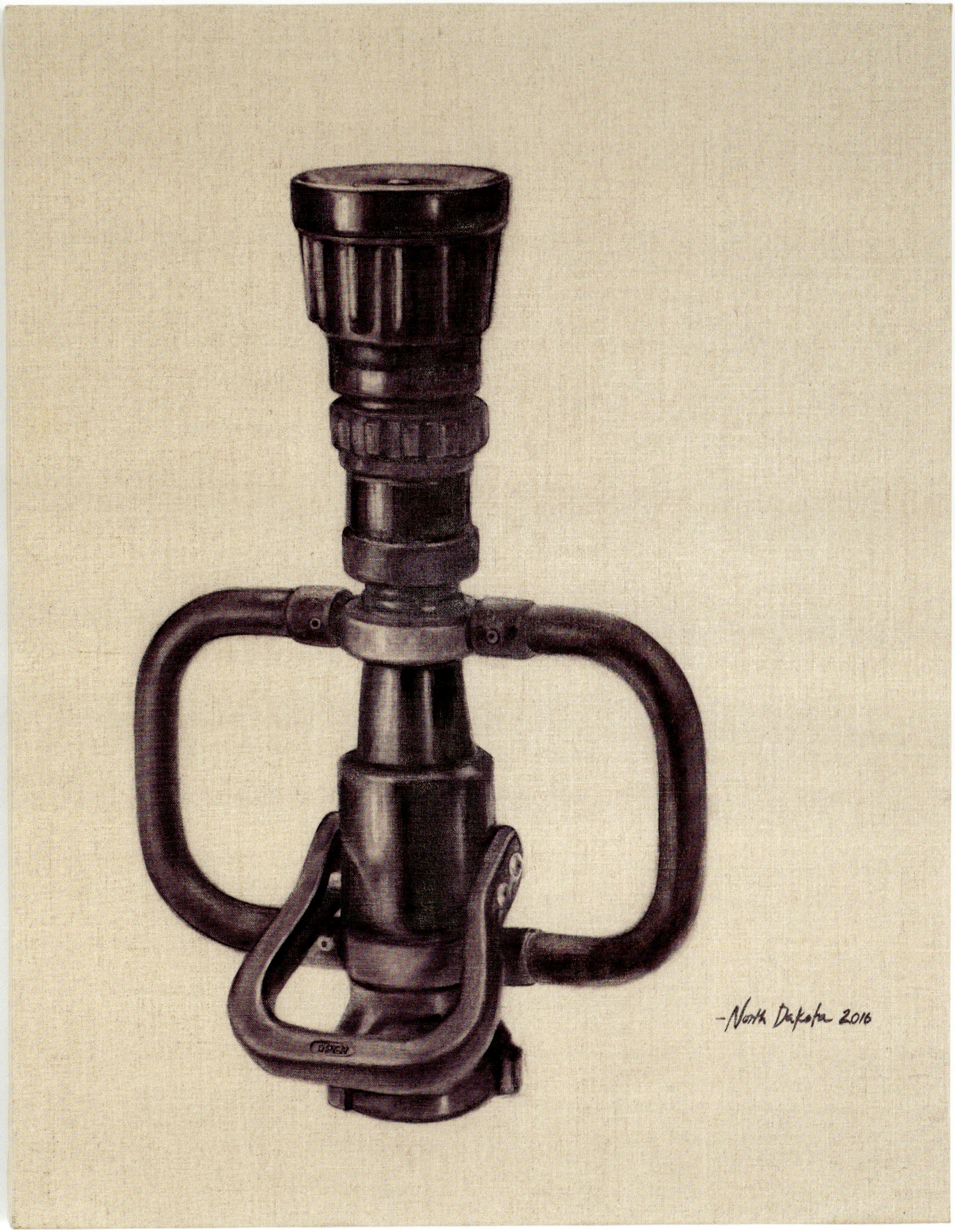
-North Dakota 2016

Previous page:

TITUS KAPHAR

2016/1963
2016
Oil on Canvas
30 x 20 inches each panel
Courtesy the artist and Jack Shainman Gallery, New York

Titus Kaphar uses classical oil painting to process everything from mug shots to historical portraiture, stills from YouTube videos, and everyday objects. The diptych *2016/1963* offers careful representations of two metallic objects—a modern-day hose nozzle and an antique one—alluding to two instances in American History when police turned fire hoses on peaceful citizen protestors. In 1963, it was Civil Rights protestors in Alabama; in 2016, it was indigenous activists protesting the Dakota Access Pipeline in North Dakota. Using simple objects to recall these historical moments, Kaphar compels us to reflect on what has changed—as well as what has not.

BRENNA YOUNGBLOOD

Revolver
2013
Mixed media
60 x 60 x 60 inches each
Courtesy Honor Fraser Gallery, Los Angeles

Los Angeles-based artist Brenna Youngblood builds textural surfaces in her assemblage works, layering paint, paper, and photographs to accumulate depth, detail, and dimension. Working with two- and three-dimensional forms, she relates her abstractions to domestic experiences, her own life and background, and the city. Youngblood's *Revolver* is a functional revolving door meant to link two spaces. The three repurposed domestic doors each show signs of wear, use, and dilapidation. Cycling through, we cannot help but think about the histories, lives, and experiences embedded in these simple objects and the idea of history's eternal return.

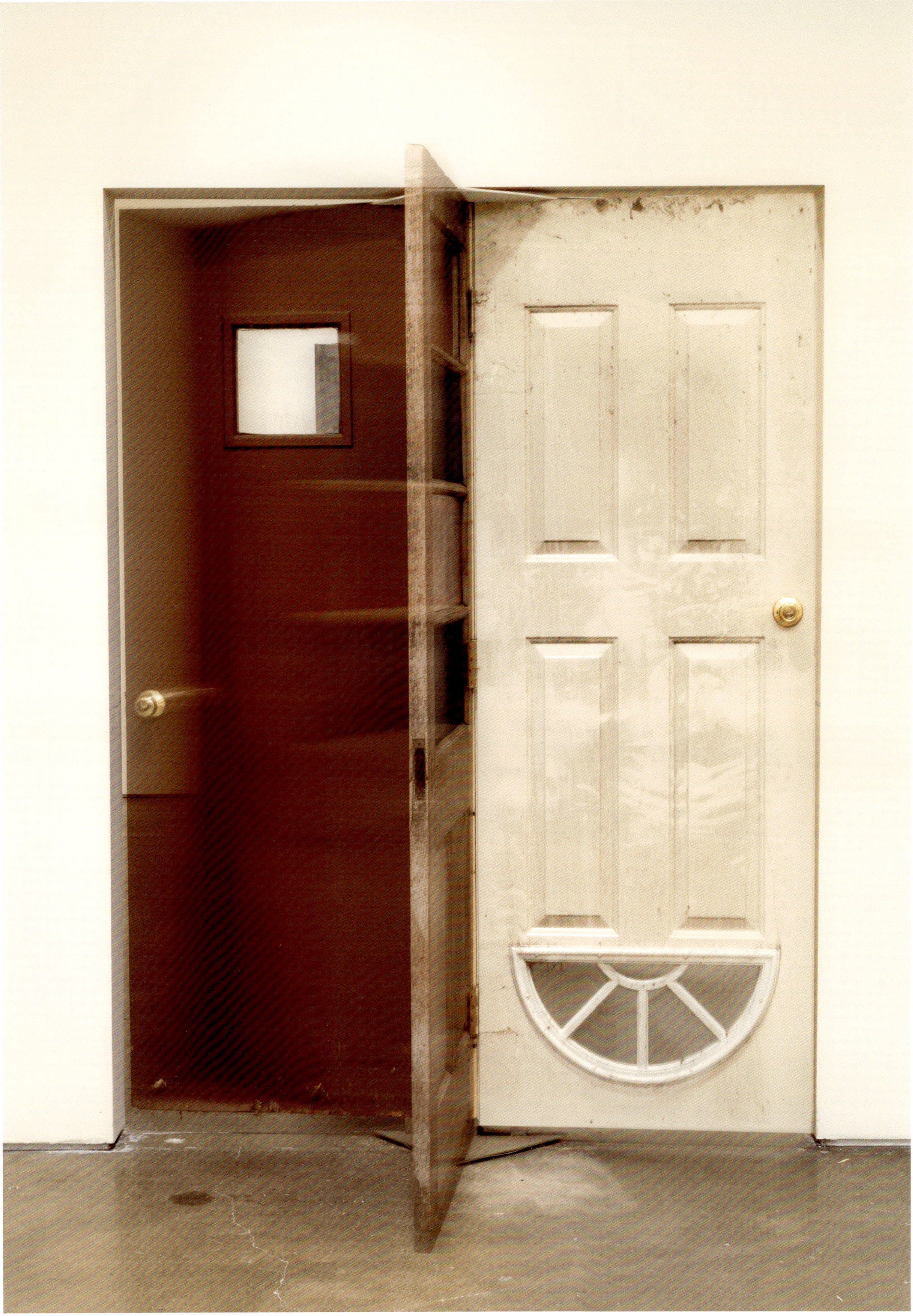

VIVIAN CACCURI

High Fidelity
2017
Vintage loudspeakers, custom soundtrack, tallow candles, framed photographs, foliage
Dimensions variable
Courtesy the artist and A Gentil Carioca, Rio de Janeiro

Brazilian artist Vivian Caccuri creates audio-visual installations with stereo equipment and unique soundtracks to tell stories with political and social significance. She created *High Fidelity* specifically in homage to Detroit's cultural and musical histories. The work comprises home stereo speakers and subwoofers sourced in Detroit, as well as archival audio and images from former Detroit radio station WDTR-FM and the former St. Margaret Mary Church on Detroit's east side.

Caccuri calls her audio composition for *High Fidelity* a spiritual radio hallucination, a fictitious radio show with only one hit: "Praying Spirit" by Detroit gospel singers the Clark Sisters. Throughout Caccuri's soundtrack audiences also hear excerpts from WDTR's programs from the 1990s and 2000s, including music by Detroit jazz artist Spencer Barefield.

High Fidelity is part of a series of works in which Caccuri stacks sound systems into altar-like formations, incorporating local foliage and lit tallow candles from Brazil. Placed in front of the subwoofers, the candles flicker with the low frequencies of the artist's custom soundtrack, creating a ritualistic atmosphere and visual metaphor for the body's internal responses to music.

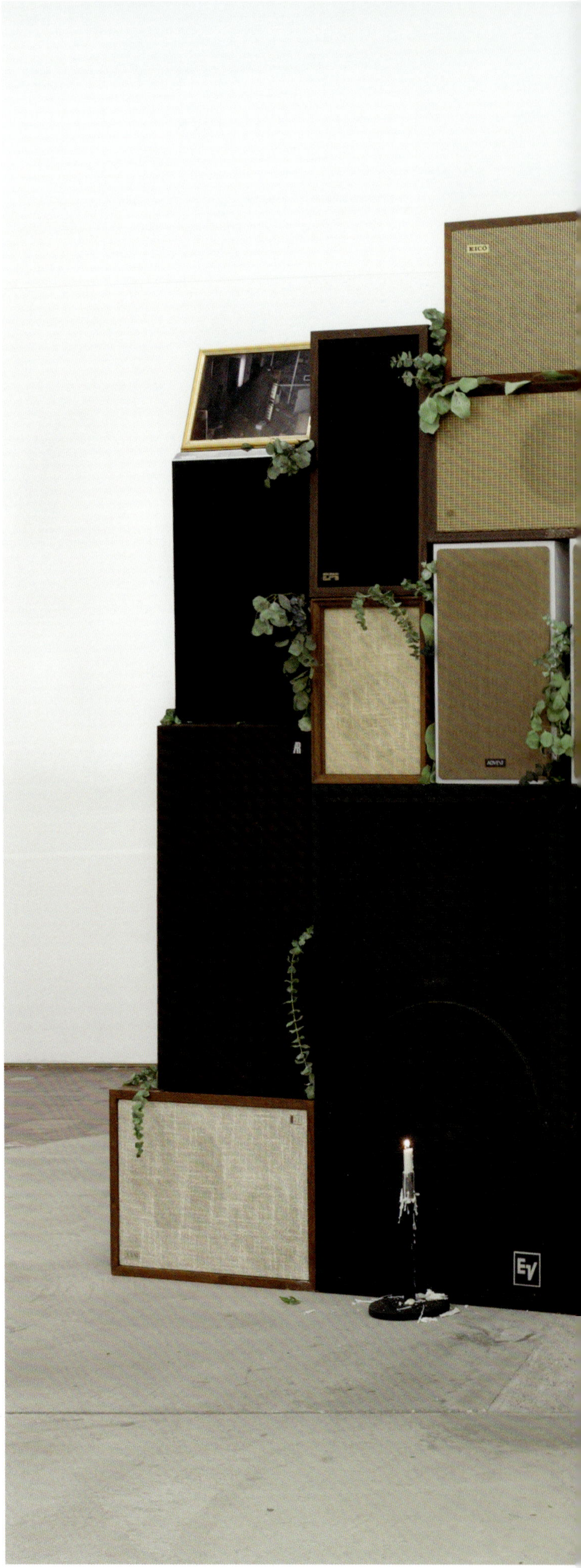

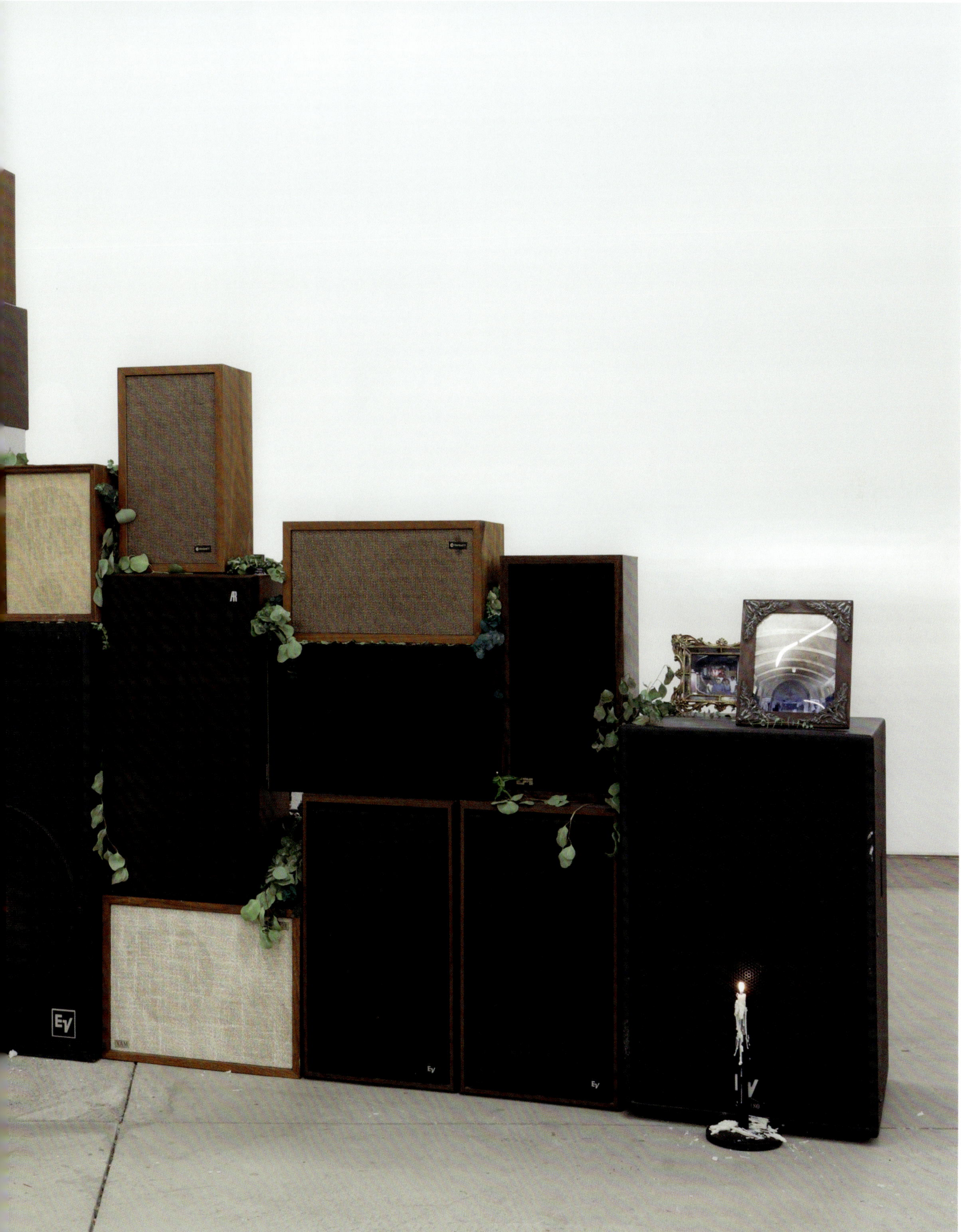

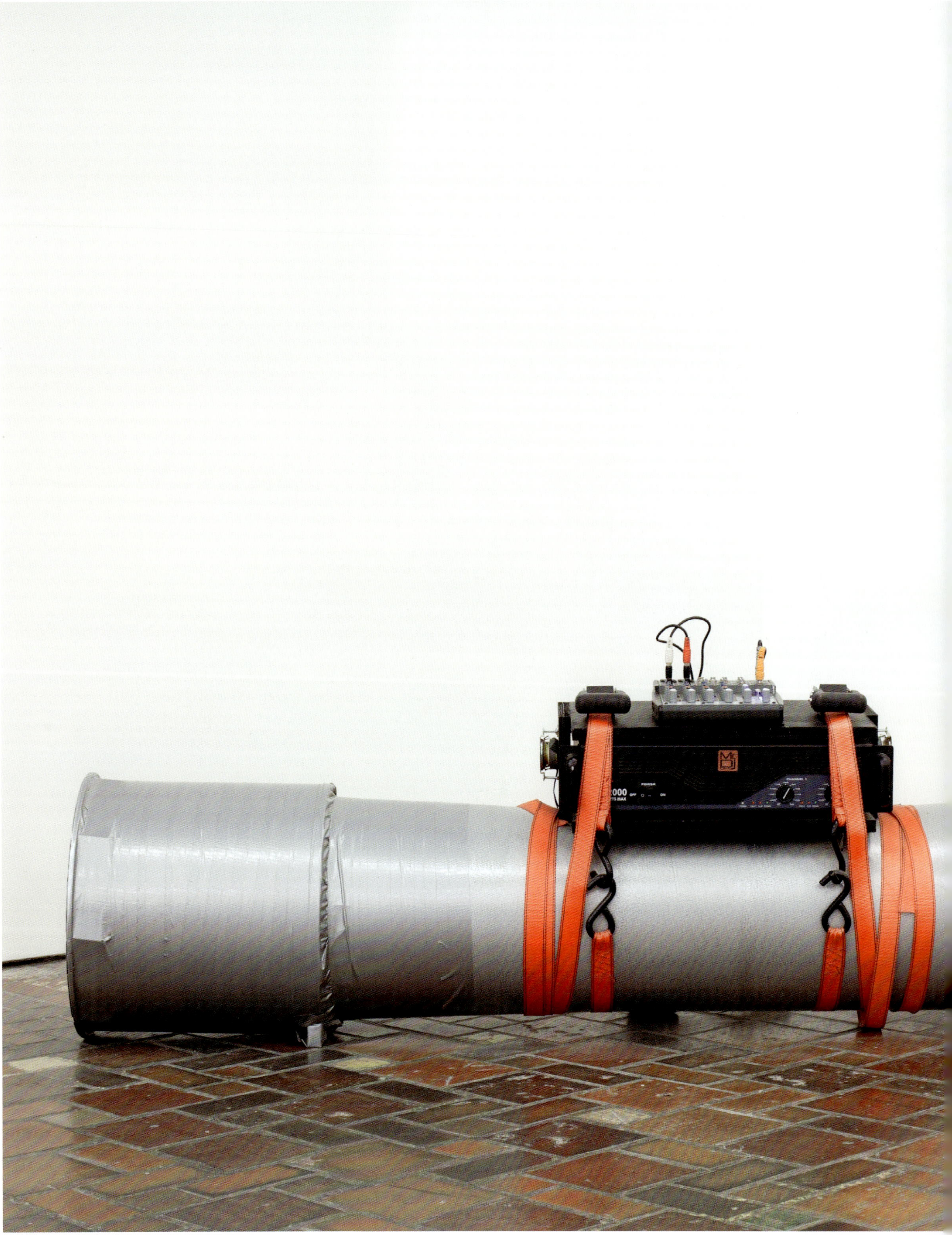

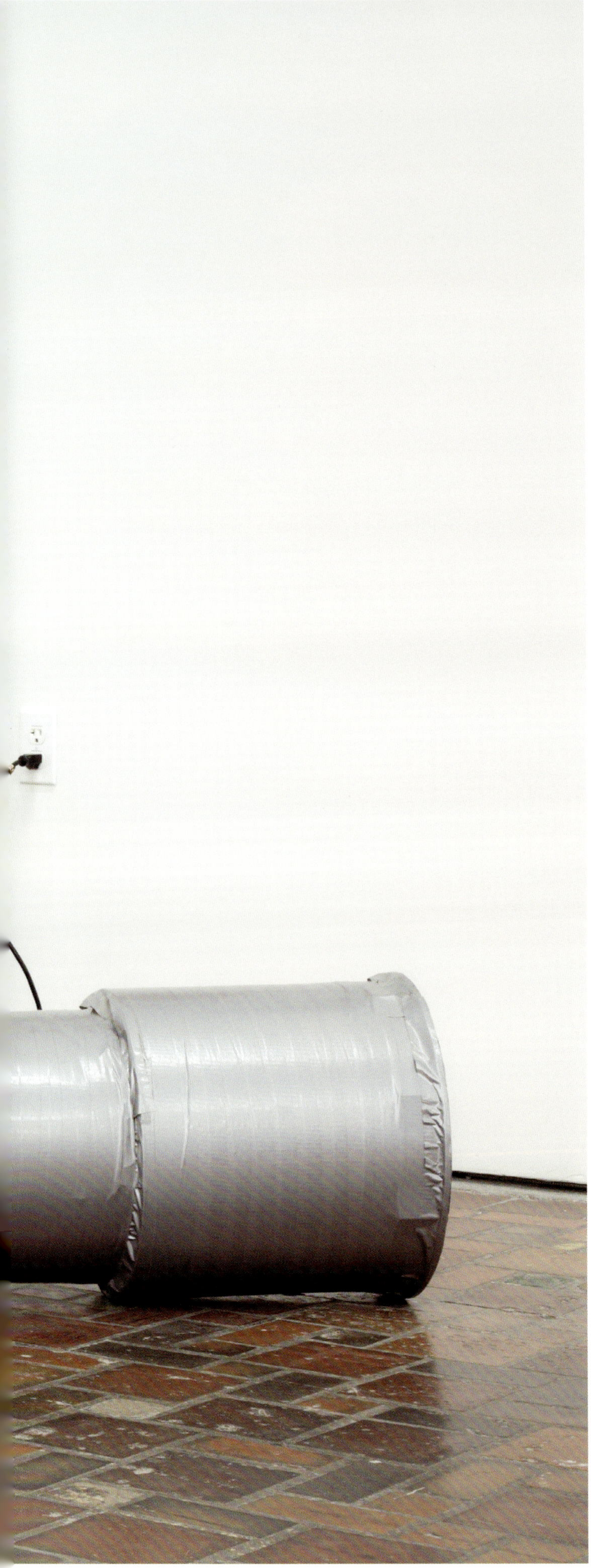

JUAN CAPISTRÁN

We Like the Cars That Go Boom…
the roar of the people could be farts
2011
Cardboard, stereo amp, speakers, sound file
14 x 24 x 84 inches
Courtesy the artist and Artists Pension Trust

The title of Juan Capistrán's sound sculpture references two 1980s tracks: L'Trimm's *We Like Cars That Go Boom* and the Minutemen's *The Roar of the Masses Could Be Farts.* L'Trimm was a female hip-hop duo from Kendall, Florida who recorded with Atlantic Records in the mid-80s and early 1990s. Their song *We Like Cars That Go Boom*, released in 1988, celebrates massive, bass-centric sound systems in cars—and the guys who drive them. Minutemen was a punk band from San Pedro, California that formed in 1980 and disbanded in 1985 when lead singer D. Boon was killed in a car accident. The humorous title of their short, energetic track from 1984 masks the poetry and sincerity of the song's lyrics. Capistrán plays with these contrasting musical cultures in this cardboard speaker creation resembling a largescale, self-made pipe bomb.

The sculpture rumbles with an audio track—Capistrán's interpretation of the Amen break programmed on a drum machine. A six-second drum solo originating in the 1969 song *Amen, Brother* by funk group The Winstons, the Amen break is famous as the most-sampled beat in electronic music and has influenced the sounds of genres like hip hop, breakbeat, hardcore techno, and jungle. Capistrán slowed the sample to 80 beats per minute and added effects. He calls the work "a meditation on the power and physicality of bass and how underground subcultures can be transgressive through the simple uses of sounds."

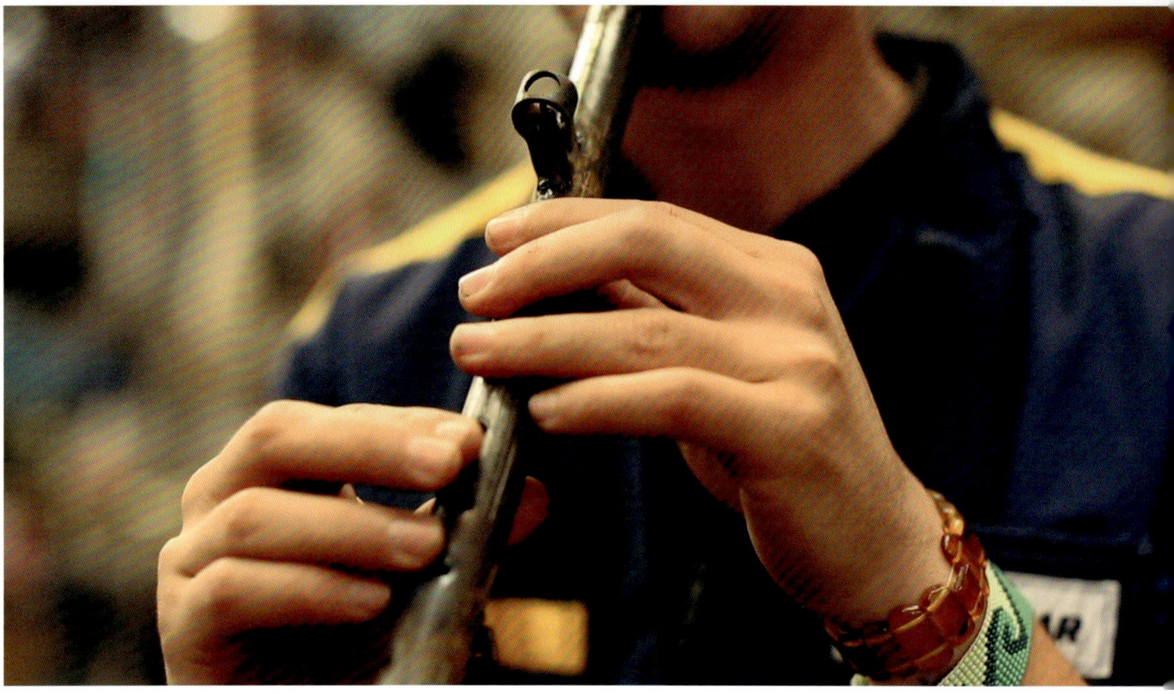

PEDRO REYES

Armas (Destruction)
2012
HD video 3:50 minutes, sound

Armas (Taller)
2012
HD video 4:25 minutes, sound

Armas (Conceierto)
2012
HD video 4:58 minutes, sound

Courtesy the artist and Lisson Gallery, London and New York

Mexican artist Pedro Reyes has long been interested in the violent history of his home country and in possibilities of breaking the cycle of brutality that has gripped it in recent decades. In works such as *Imagine* (2012) and *Disarm* (2012) Reyes collaborated with a group of musicians to turn revolvers, automatic rifles, machine guns, and shotguns confiscated by the police into musical instruments and sculptures. The three films that form the series *Armas* [Weapons] document the guns' dismantling, being remade into instruments, and finally a concert in which the former weapons are played to make music.

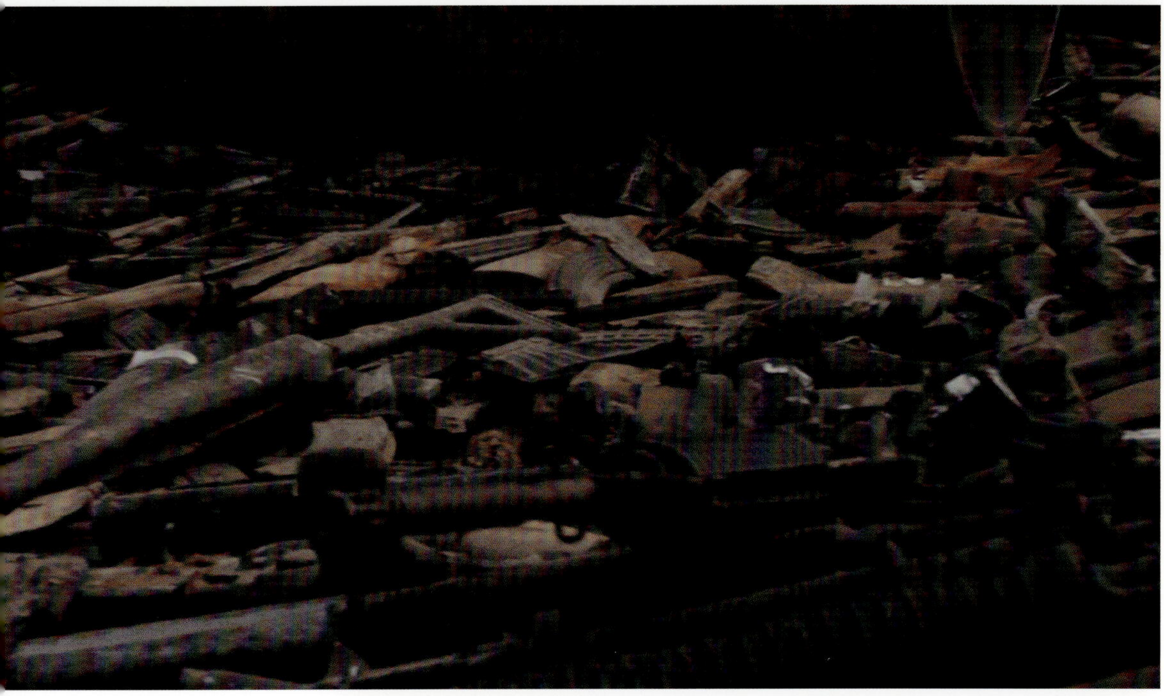

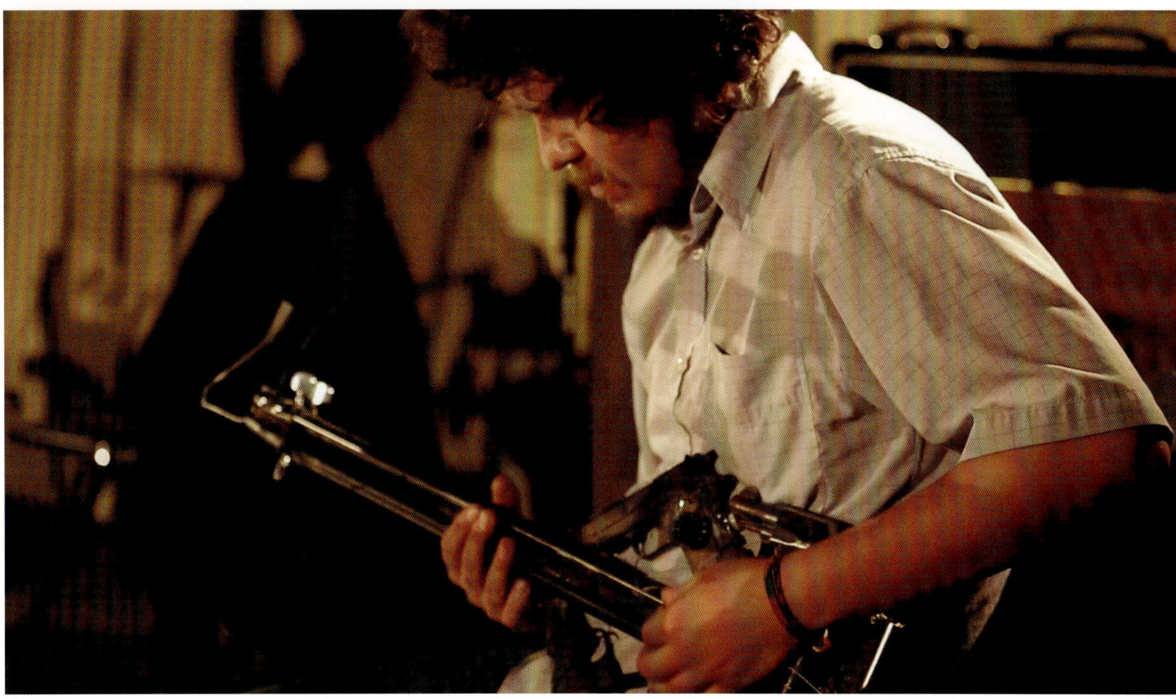

MATTHEW HARRISON AND CORINE VERMEULEN

Benign Violations
2017
HD video, 11:18 minutes, color, sound
Courtesy the artists and Jessica Silverman Gallery, San Francisco

Benign Violation is a theory of humor that examines how jokes violate social or ethical norms in benign ways to create buffers between individuals and reality. In their collaborative practice, Harrison and Vermeulen apply this notion to music and art, creating original dance music and setting it to found footage from the internet.

Like humor, music can create protective barriers between the outside world and one's mental space. For Harrison and Vermeulen, making music has emerged through an effort to stay sane in a moment when much in the world seems nuts. They seek refuge from current social and political realities in electronic music, both as a coping mechanism and as a form of personal resistance.

Track Titles:
1. c. 2013
2. c. 1976
3. Dequindre

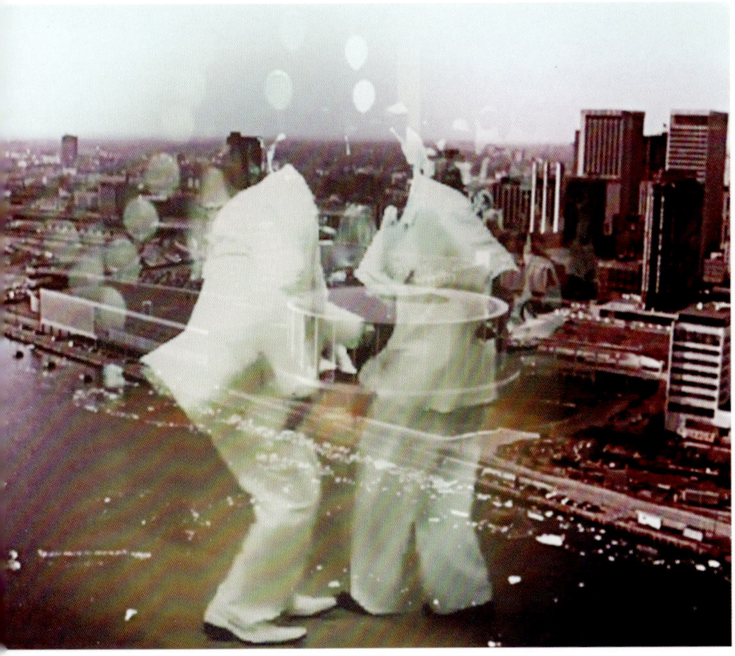

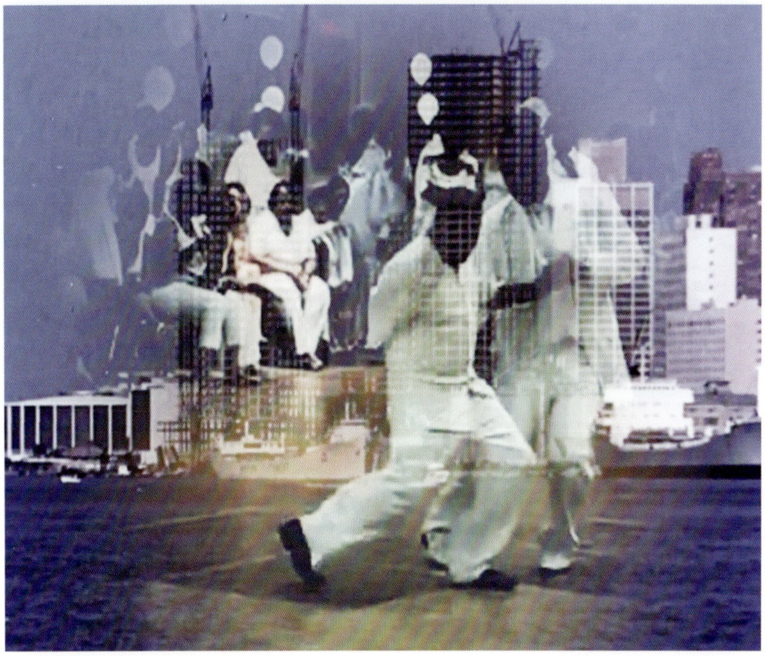

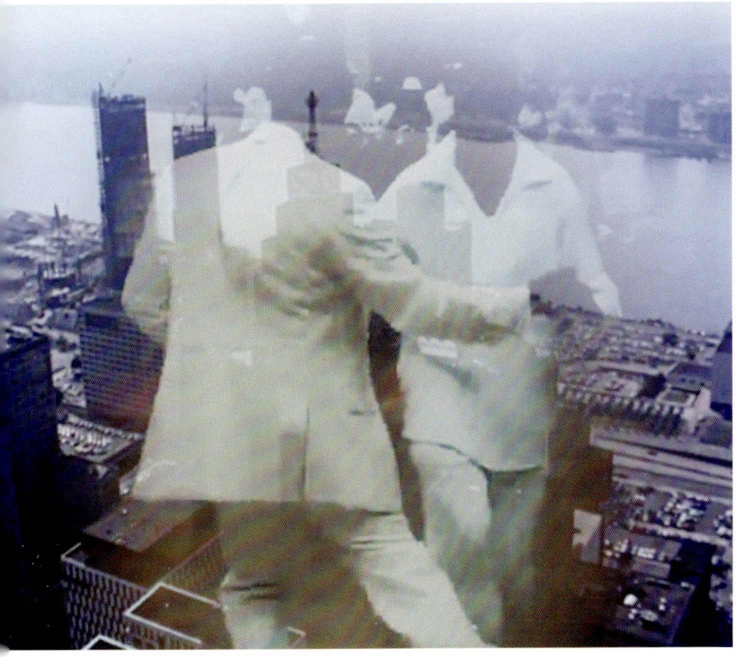

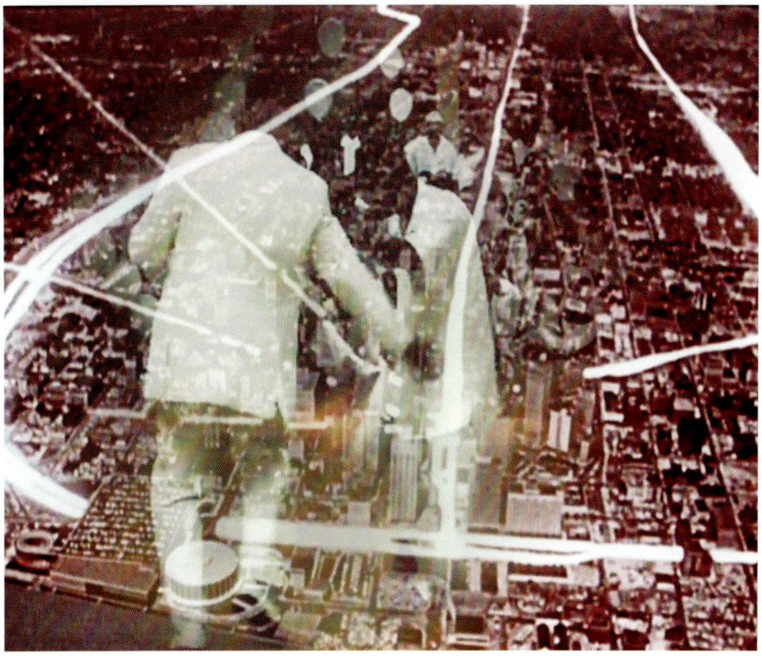

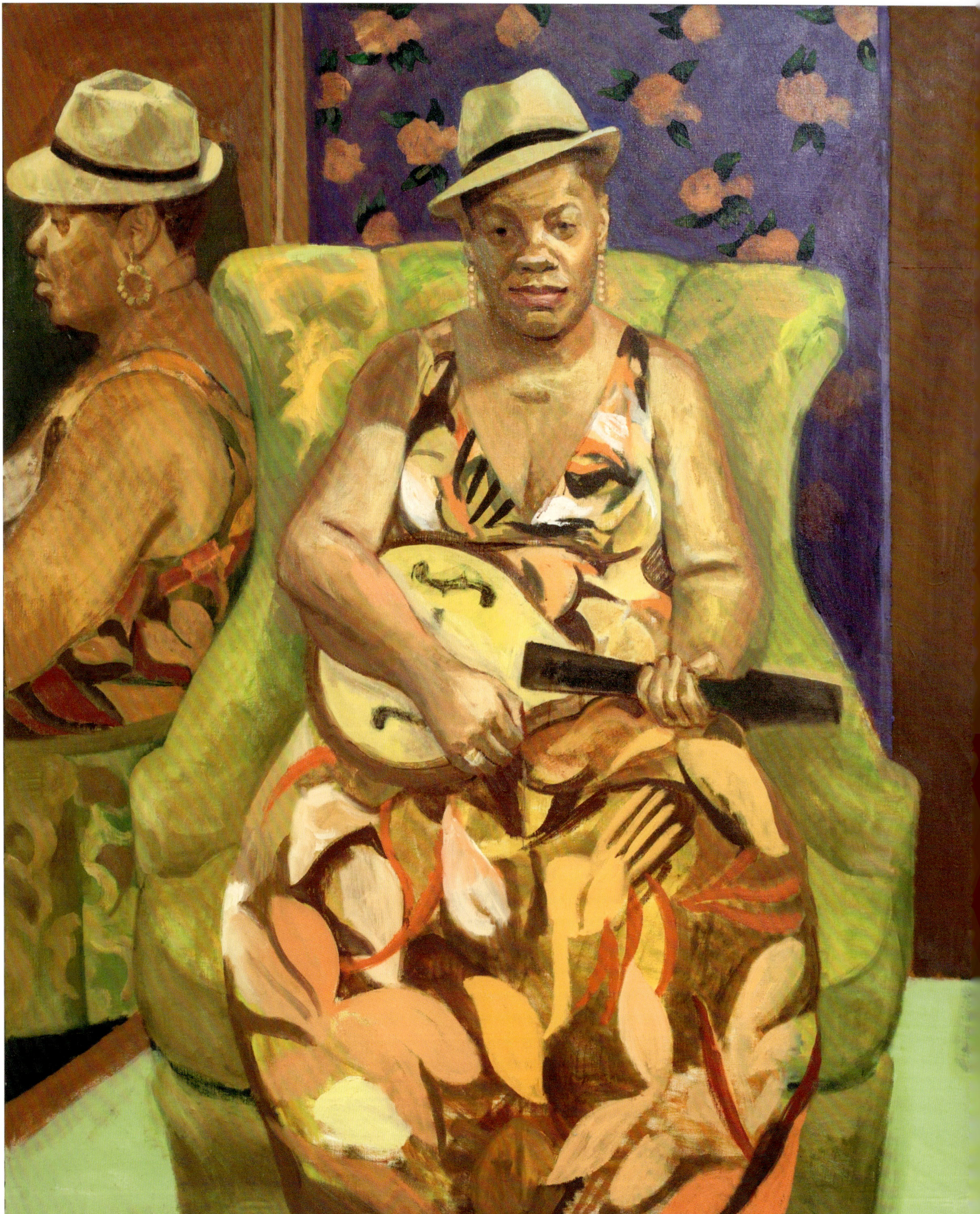

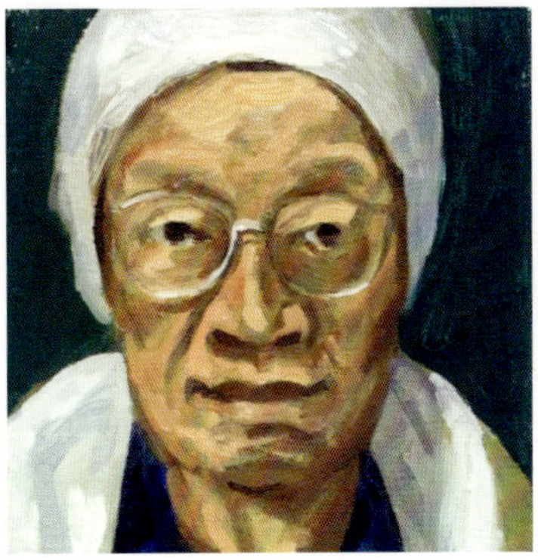

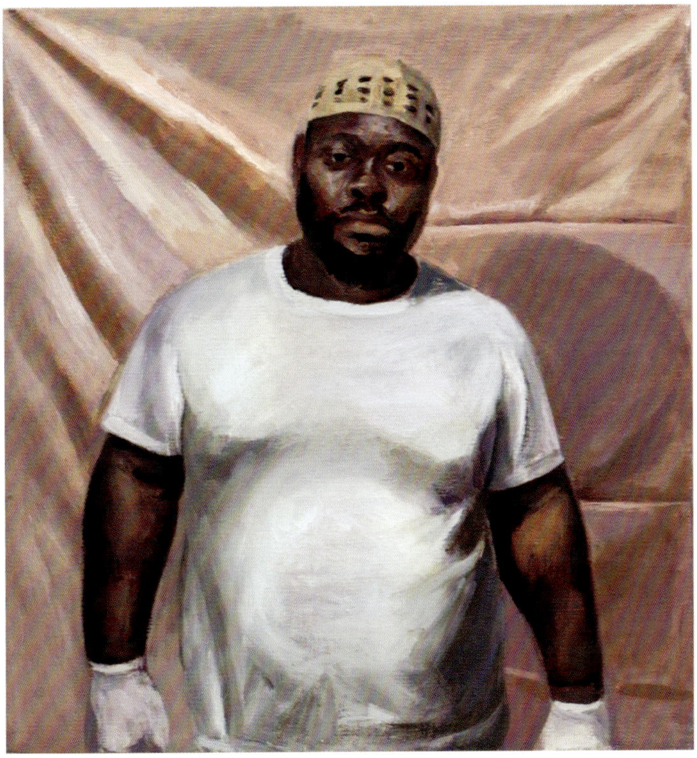

RICHARD LEWIS

Tracey With Mandolin
2013
Oil on canvas
72 x 60 inches

Self-Portrait as a Muslim
1999
Oil on canvas
24 x 24 inches

My Mother
2010
Oil on canvas
12 x 12 inches

Courtesy the artist

Richard Lewis is a Detroit-based artist who uses oil painting to represent the defiance, strength, and artistic legacies of his city. Painting people he knows—and sometimes himself—he aims to capture his community in a way that celebrates and elevates those around him. He finds points of connection between painting and music, and often casts his subjects as jazz or blues musicians.

Tracey With Mandolin is a portrait of the artist's cousin in the guise of a blues musician, simultaneously referencing and reworking a classic pose from the history of European portraiture. In the closely-cropped portrait of his mother's face, the small painting *My Mother*, Lewis presents his subject with intimacy and respect without disclosing her interiority. *Self-Portrait as a Muslim* he made while living in New York City at the dawn of the twenty-first century. Sensing a rise in Islamophobia around him, Lewis created a stoic portrayal of a Black Muslim identity.

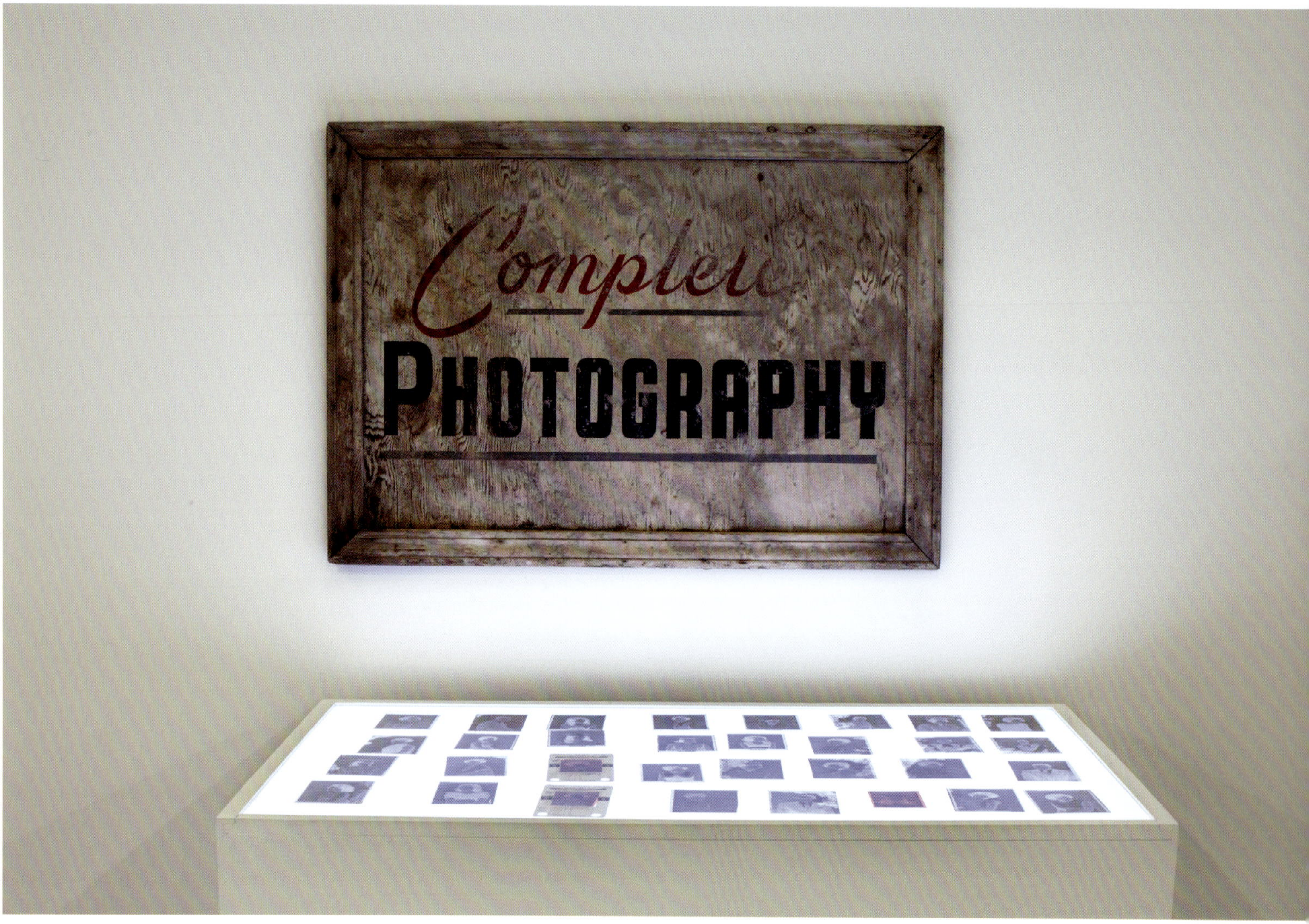
Complete
PHOTOGRAPHY

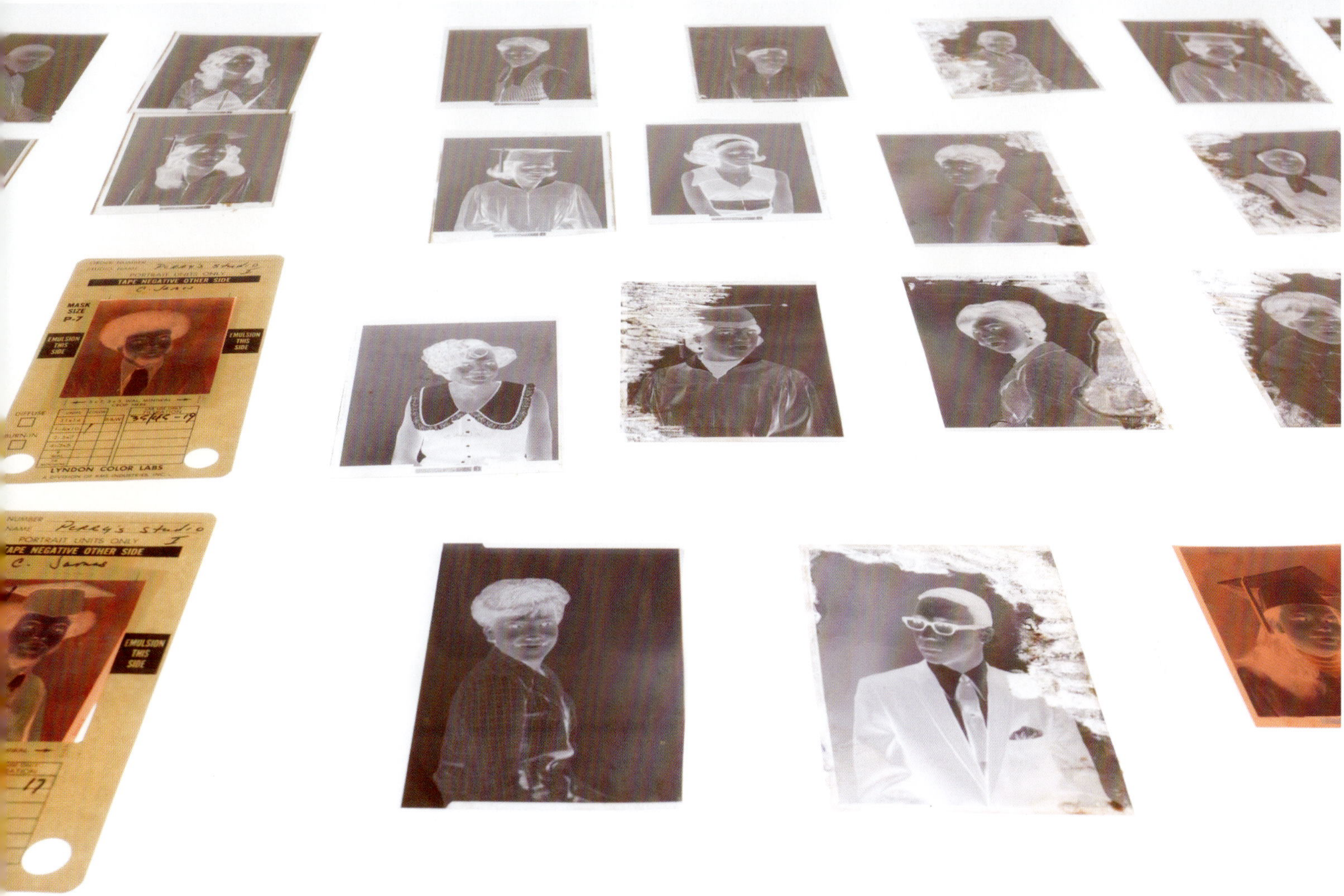

CARL PERRY

4 × 5 negatives from Perry's Photo Studio, Detroit
Courtesy T. M. Caldwell, Paul Lee, and Joseph Sopkowicz

Carl Perry's photo studio was one of the few businesses on 12th Street to survive the Detroit Rebellion and remain active in the same location into the 1990s. Perry eventually abandoned it, leaving behind boxes of 4 × 5 negatives and prints from portrait sessions individually marked with the sitters' names. Perry had also owned a drug store on 12th Street in 1967, but a fire ignited in a nearby market consumed it, despite his efforts to save it by posting "Soul Brother" signs outside. These negatives remain from photo sessions marking happy occasions in the sitters' lives, while the surface decay manifests the conditions of history.

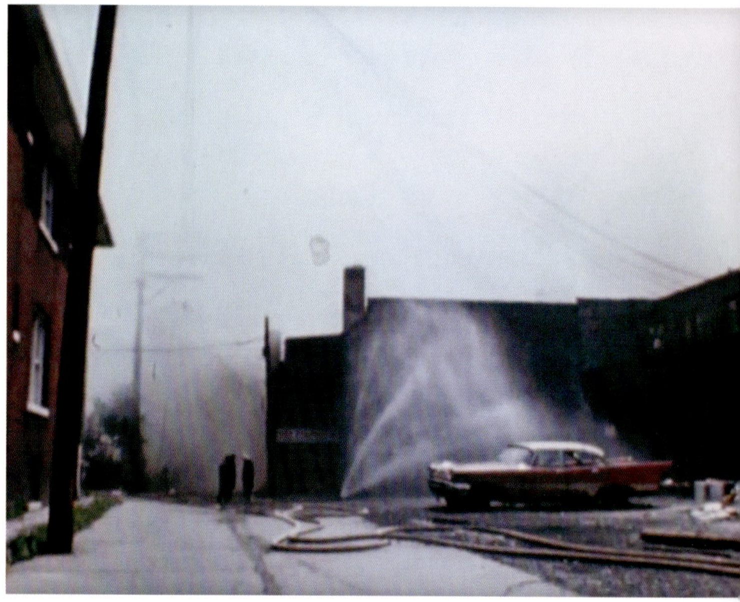

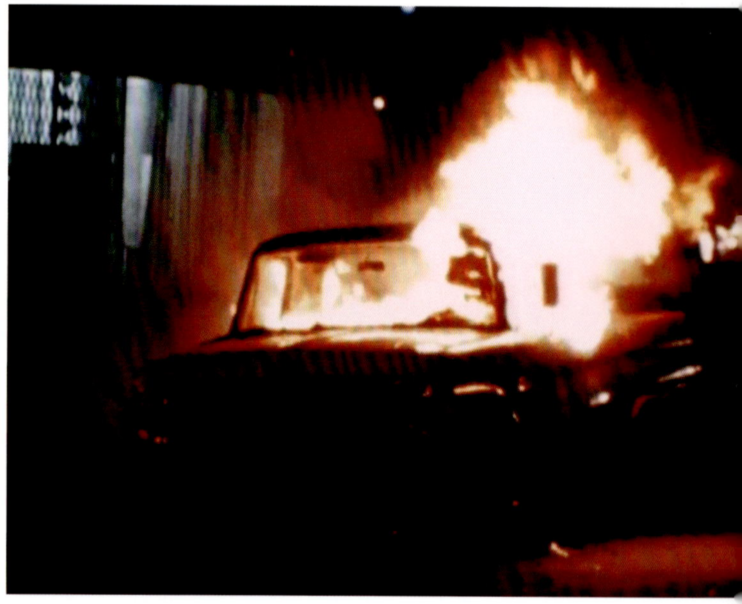

EDWARD T. BRESLIN

Riot Film, 1967
HD video transferred from 16mm film, 12:13 minutes, color, silent
Courtesy Detroit Historical Society

Edward T. Breslin was a former Detroit police beat reporter working in public relations for Chevrolet in 1967. When 12th Street erupted in July, he used his police contacts to acquire unique footage of the city inflamed. The film is hardly sensationalistic, but rather has the pacing and empathetic eye of a diary film. The unedited reel follows Breslin's path from the area around 12th and Clairmount, west to Grand River Avenue, and finally to a makeshift detention camp on Belle Isle. He recorded fire-ravaged neighborhoods, smashed storefronts, armed police and soldiers, arrests, hospitalizations, street activity, children, and relief efforts—displaying trauma as well as compassion.

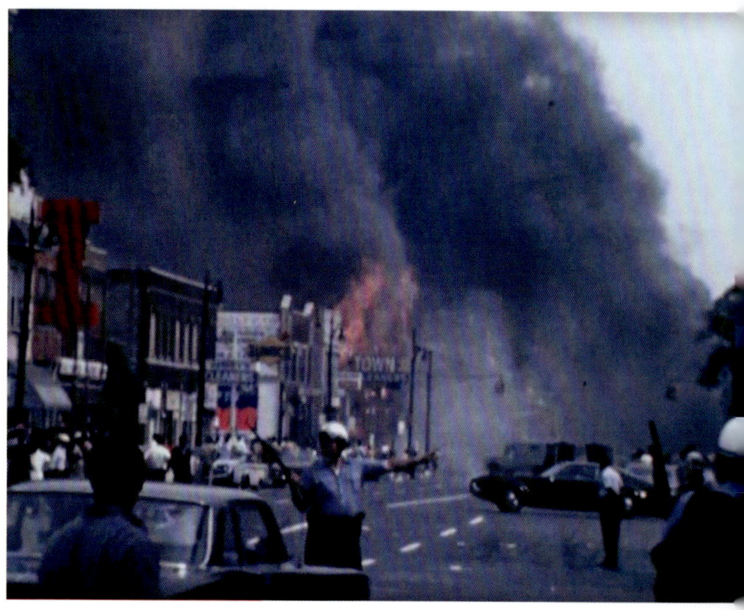

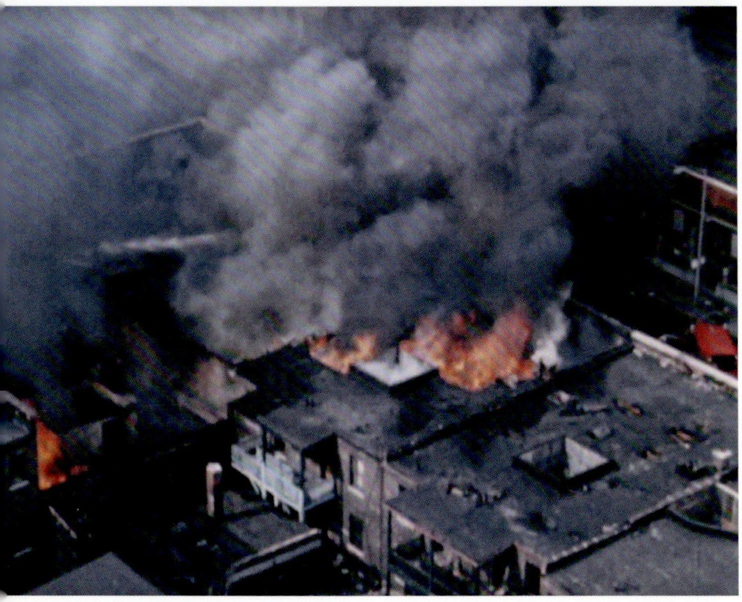
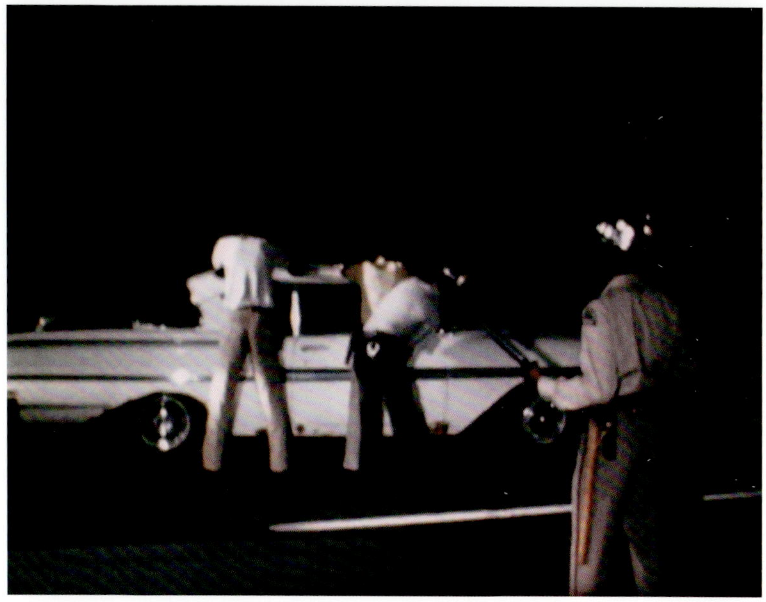
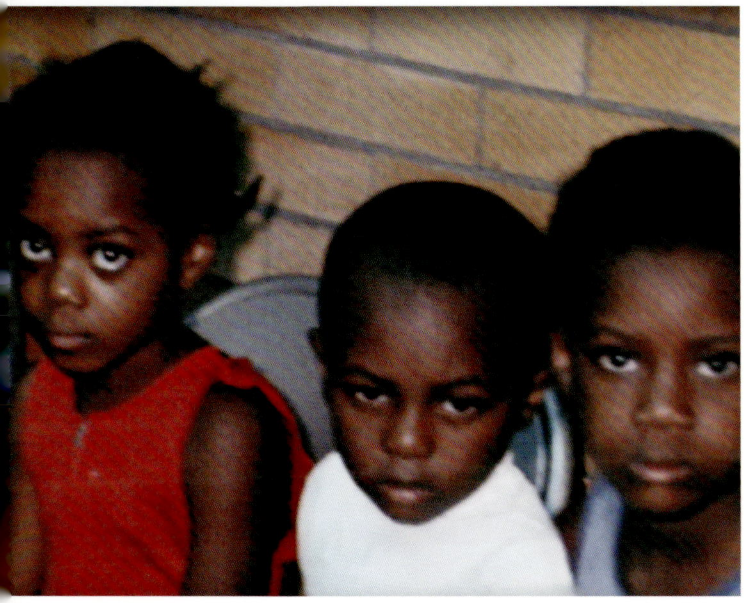
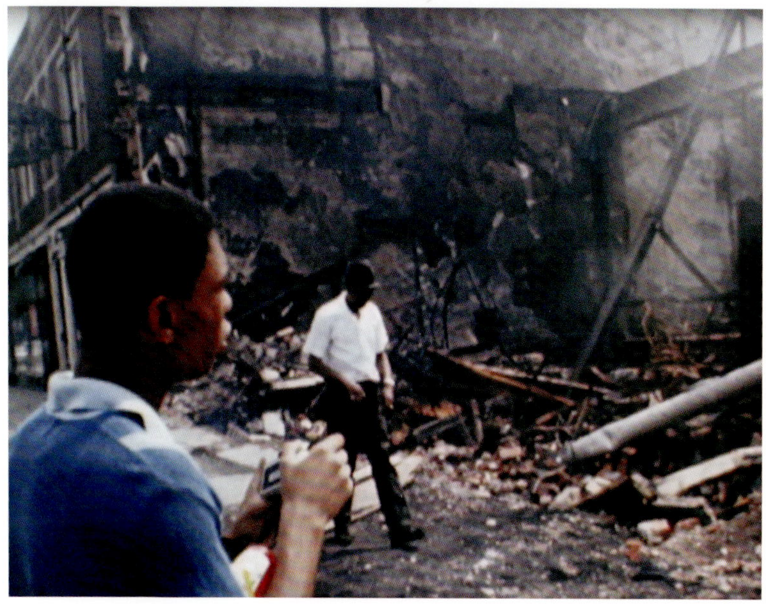
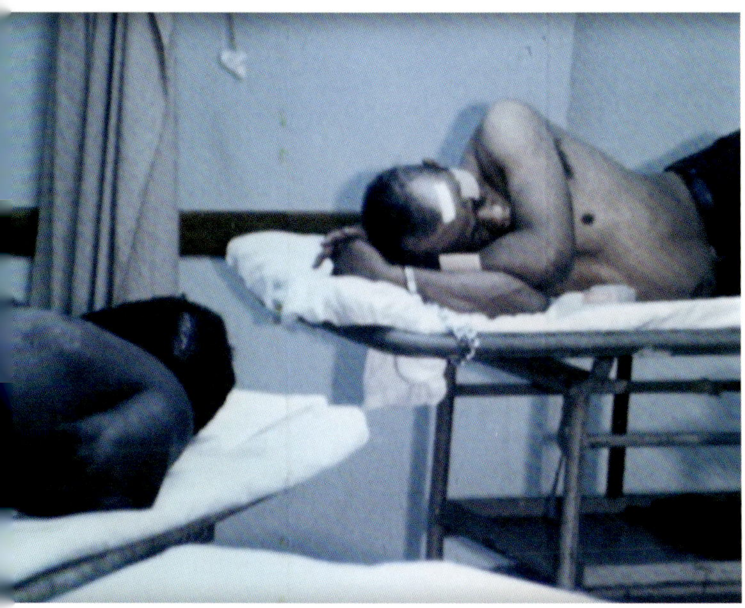
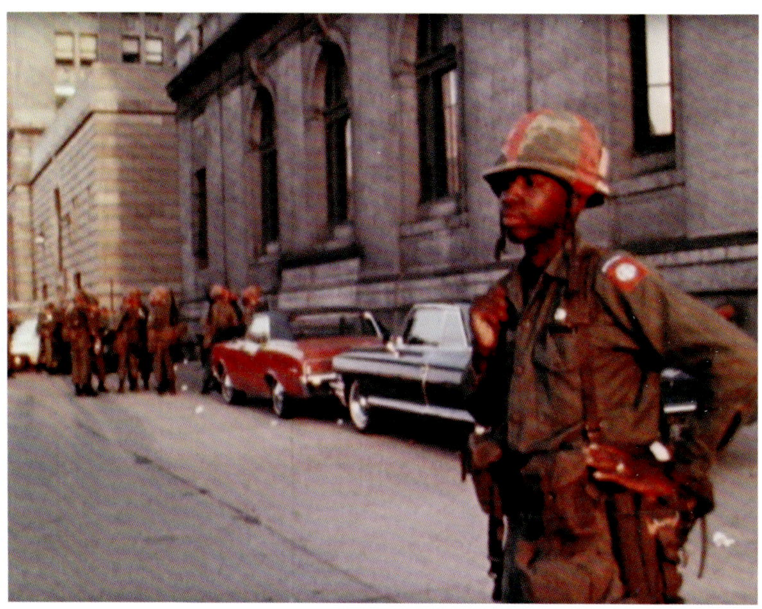

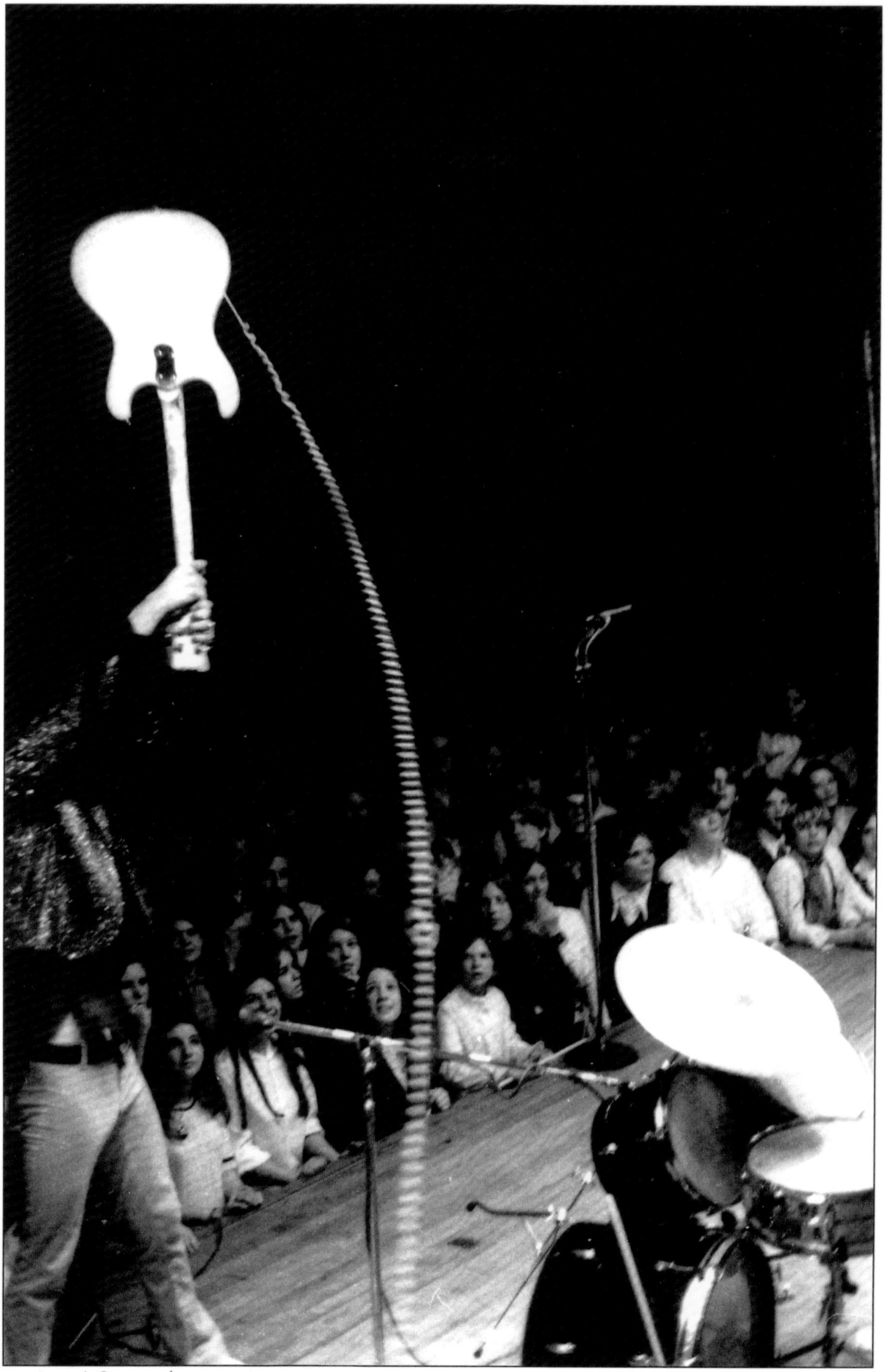

Fred "Sonic" Smith - MC5

Leni Sinclair '69

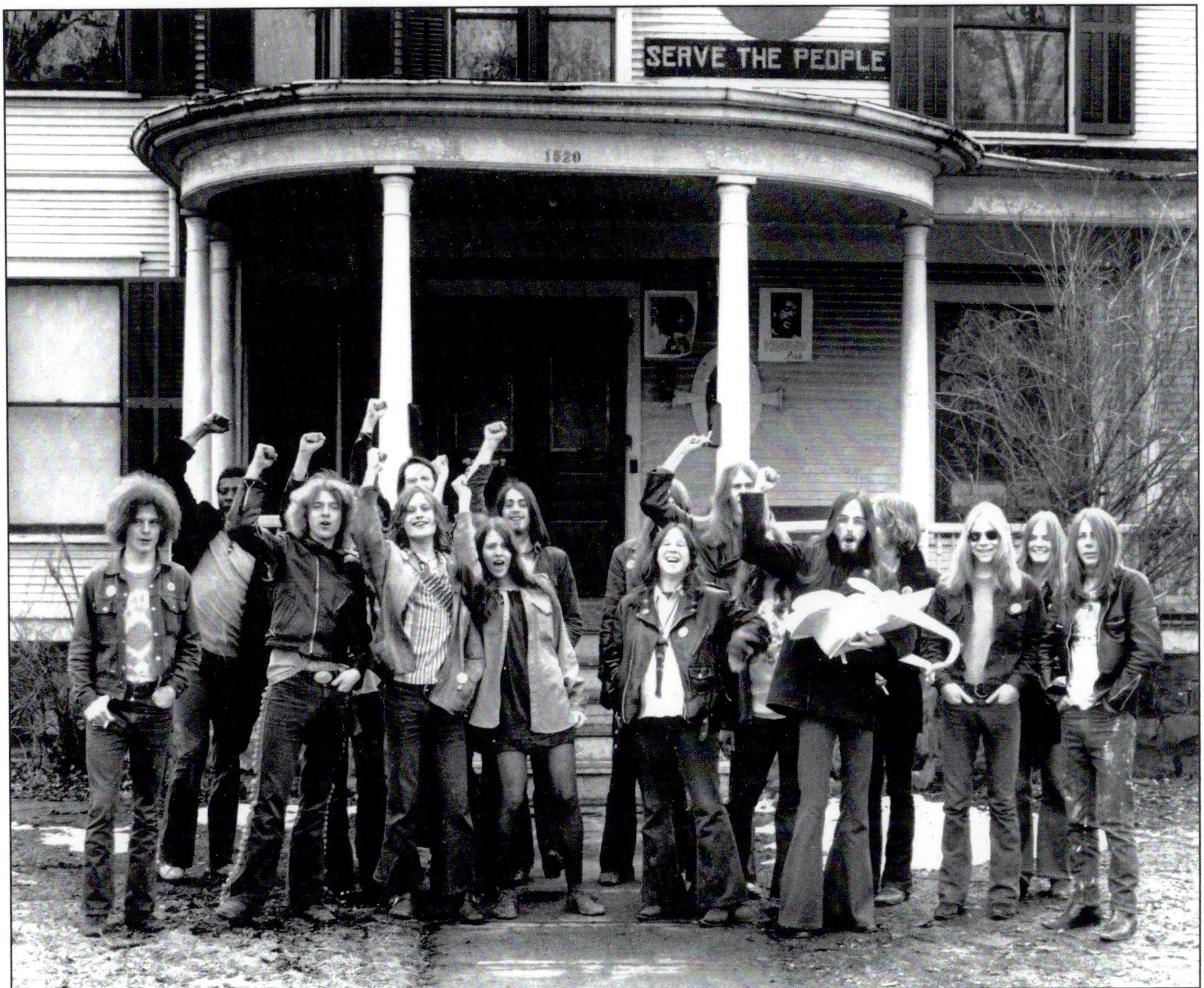

White Panthers in Ann Arbor — Leni Sinclair '70

LENI SINCLAIR

Selected photographs, 1968–92
Pigment prints, 2017
Courtesy the artist

Leni Sinclair was raised on a collective farm in East Germany. She moved to Detroit in 1959 and began photographing its people and activities, and in 1964 she cofounded the Detroit Artists Workshop in Cass Corridor with poet and activist John Sinclair and others. Leni and John married the following year, and together led numerous interconnected organizations in Detroit and Ann Arbor, including Trans-Love Energies, Rainbow Multi-Media Corporation, Ann Arbor Blues and Jazz Festival, and the Detroit Jazz Center. They also cofounded the far-left, antiracist White Panther Party in solidarity with the Black Panthers. Leni served as its Minster of Education and handled all photography for the party's incendiary band, the MC5. Her photographs beautifully document the area's artistic and cultural history, showing the vital integration of rock, jazz, art, and politics at its core.

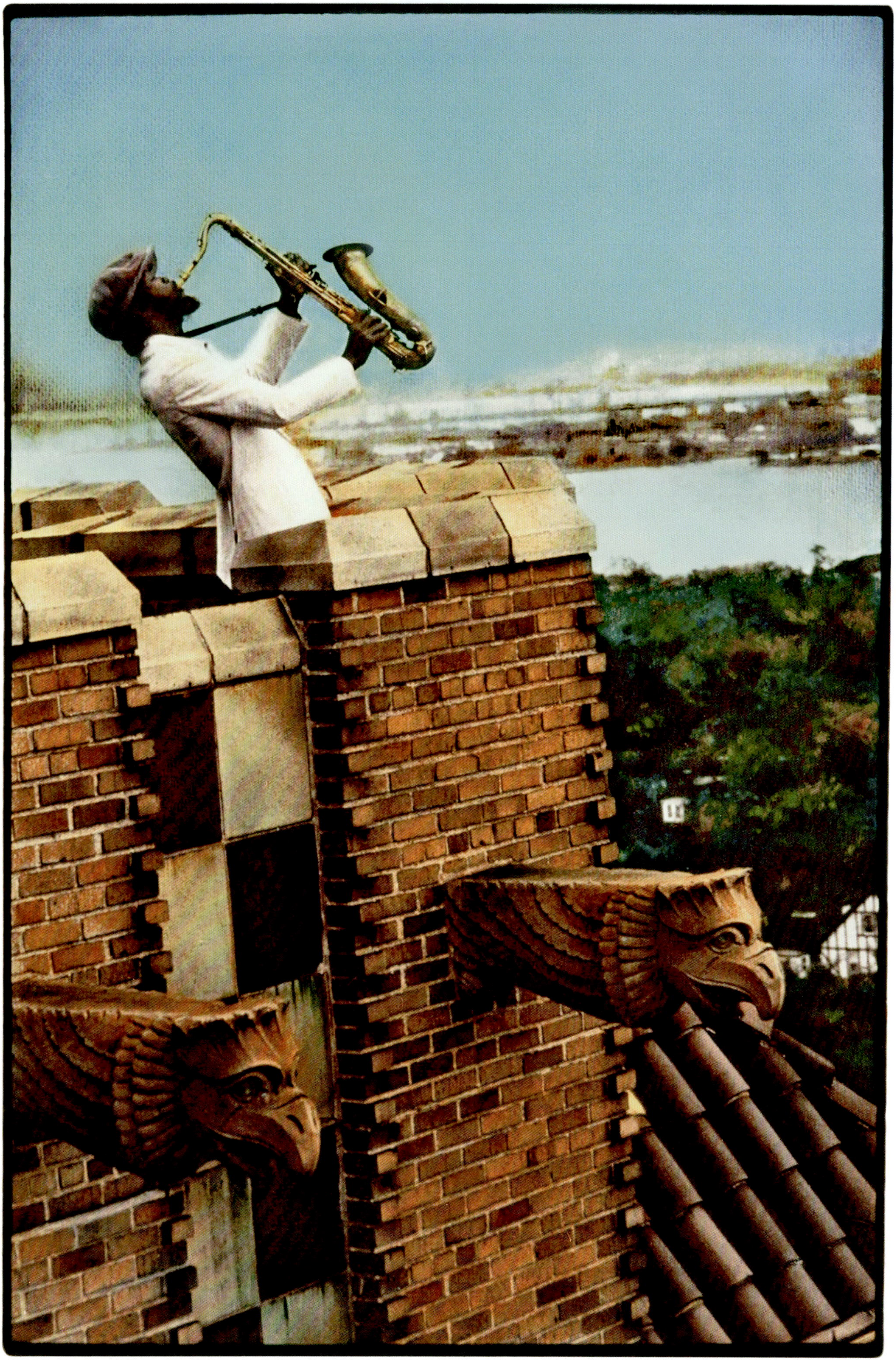

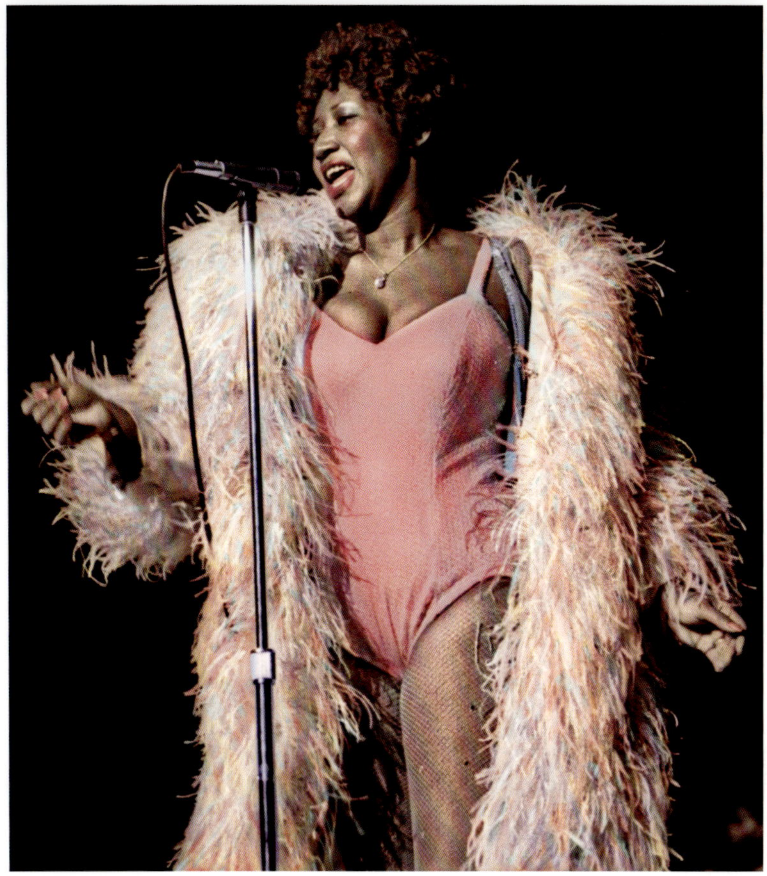

BARBARA WEINBERG BAREFIELD

Selected photographs, 1973–81
Digital prints, 2017
Courtesy the artist

Barbara Weinberg Barefield's photographs on view in *Sonic Rebellion* include a number of hand-tinted images she made for her 1979 photo book *Jazz Space Detroit.* After attending the John Sinclair Freedom Rally in December 1971, Barefield reached out to Leni and John Sinclair and began working with them at the *Ann Arbor Sun*, photographing and interviewing legendary musicians. She became art director for the *Detroit Free Press* Sunday magazine starting in 1976. In 1979, she and her husband, jazz musician Spencer Barefield, began collaborating on "Creative Music," an acclaimed concert series that ran for thirteen years at the Detroit Institute of Arts.

Faruq Z. Bey on the roof of the Kean Building, Detroit, 1979

Aretha Franklin, Ford Auditorium, Detroit, 1977

THE TERROR, BRUTALITY AND MURDER OF MY BROTHERS AND SISTERS IS THE SUFFERING OF BLACK PEOPLE. THEREFORE, NOT TO LET SUCH EVENTS CONTINUE I MUST MERCILESSLY DO AWAY WITH THE LOW-NATURED BEAST THAT BITES THE HAND THAT FEEDS IT.

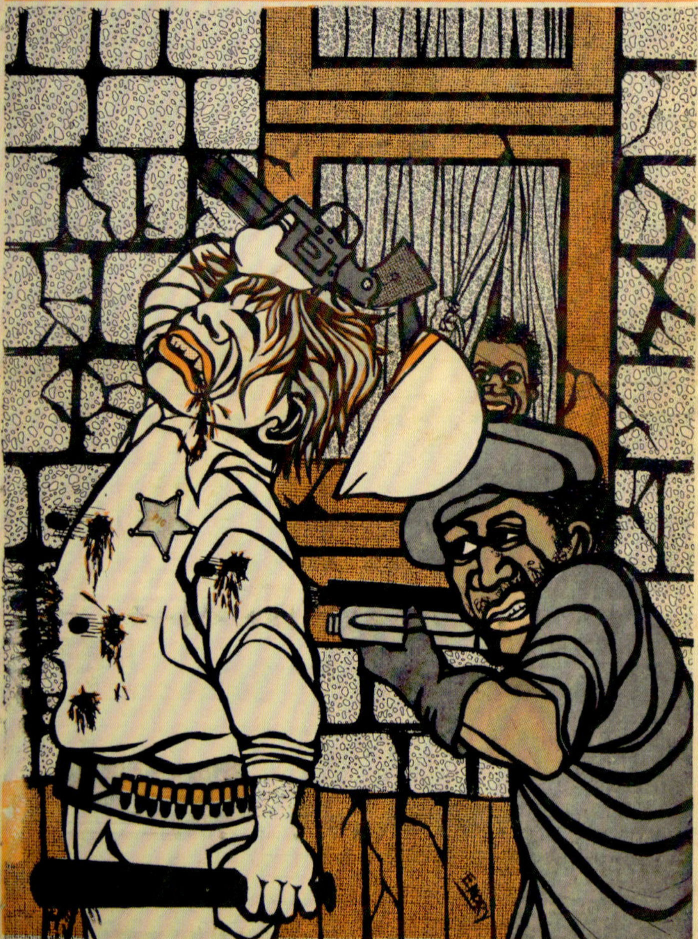

WE HAVE NO HANG UPS ABOUT REVOLUTIONARY VIOLENCE

THE BLACK PANTHER

25 cents

Black Community News Service

VOL. V, NO. 25 SATURDAY, DECEMBER 19, 1970

PUBLISHED WEEKLY THE BLACK PANTHER PARTY MINISTRY OF INFORMATION BOX 2967, CUSTOM HOUSE SAN FRANCISCO, CA 94126

GUERRILLA WAR IN THE U.S.A.

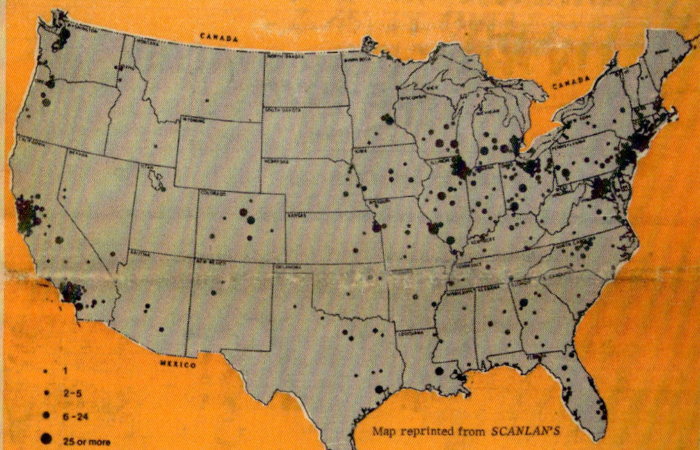

Map reprinted from *SCANLAN'S*

EDITORIAL

That there is a new wave of urban guerillas carrying out acts of "armed propaganda" inside the confines of this imperialist, fascist, racist decadent community called the United States, cannot be disputed.

Whether their ideologies or motivations differ, the techniques and the ultimate goal of destruction of the system is consistent.

Guerilla war is a radically different political reality from anything the United States has experienced. It would be incorrect for it to be misunderstood either by those who would wish to crush it and thereby attempt to curb the inevitable tide of revolution, or by those who would attempt reasonably to cope with it as a passing phase.

It is not unusual, or rather, it is in the interests of the oppressor, to deny the success, much less the reality to a guerilla movement opposing it. Batista, for example, spread continual rumors that Castro was smashed to smithereens when he wasn't; reports of Che Guevara's death in Bolivia were greatly exaggerated at least a dozen times before the C.I.A. could deliver a corpse to match the story; defeat of the Vietnamese has been reported daily, when in fact they have won the war and reports of the decline of the Black Panther Party has been Community News, when in fact our ranks and support is at its highest peak.

In order to keep the people in the communities of the U.S.A. in a perpetual state of confusion, emphasis is placed on the atrocities abroad and the true perpetrators of these atrocities, the U.S. imperialists, manage to hide under the covers and demean the significance of the present occurrences.

It is now getting to the point where it will not require the services of a computer to project a full scale civil war resulting from the rapidly multiplying attacks of sabotage and guerilla tactics. During March 1970 there were 62 guerilla actions against targets in 17 states. Each target was symbolic.

The administration has found it necessary to define these freedom fighters and their actions by descriptive labels such as "disrupters", "a small minority", "destructive activists", "small bands of destructionists", "acts of viciousness", "blackmail and terror", "assaults which terrorize" and everything else except the true fact that the people are rising up in anger.

With all the resources at the hands of the F.B.I., the C.I.A. and various other agencies the revolutionary spirit of the people cannot be crushed. The Pentagon Counter Intelligence Analysis Division has a subversive data bank with 1.5 million names. The Secret Service has indices of 100,000 radical names and extensive dossiers on 50,000 revolutionaries presumed to be dangerous, this includes fingerprint files, police records, medical and psy-

continued on next page

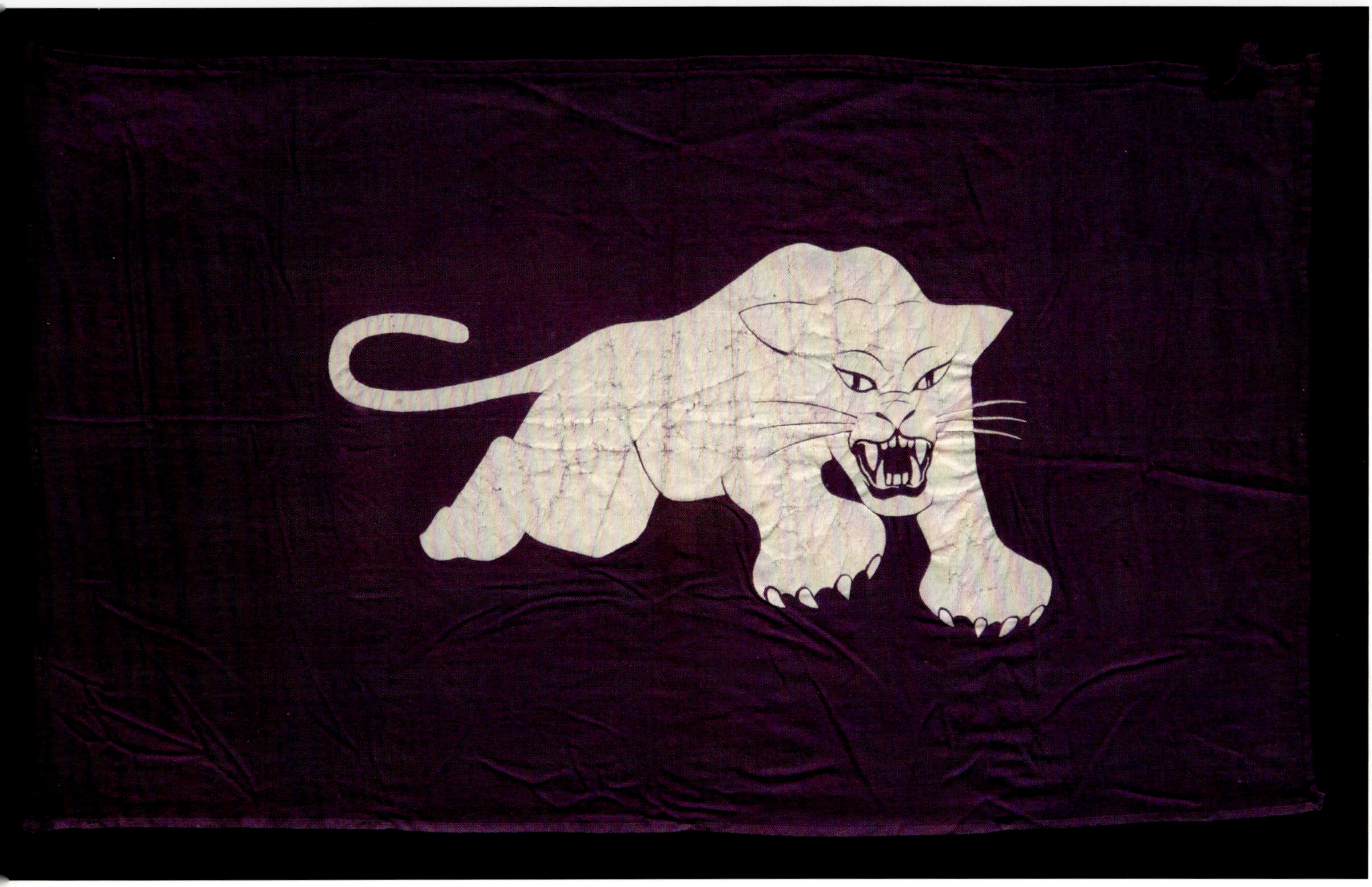

Left page:

THE BLACK PANTHER: BLACK COMMUNITY NEWS SERVICE

Founded by Huey P. Newton and Bobby Seale
Art direction and graphics by Emory Douglas

As Minister of Culture for the Black Panther Party, artist Emory Douglas played a vital role in shaping the party's cultural identity and spreading its message. Through poster art and illustrations in the Party's weekly newspaper, the *Black Panther*, Douglas's images of black men and women armed to fight for their rights became icons of Black Power, and he popularized imagery of police as pigs. Douglas's graphic style bears the influence of Charles White and Elizabeth Catlett, both African American artists he admires. The powerful directness of his imagery also embodies Black Arts Movement principles to communicate in a manner accessible to all members of the black community.

Vol. 5, No. 25 (December 19, 1970)
Private collection, New York

WHITE PANTHER PARTY

Black Panther Party cofounder Huey P. Newton once said that if white people wanted to support the Black Panthers, they could start a White Panther Party. In response, activists Pun Plamondon, John Sinclair, and Leni Sinclair did just that in 1968, forming the White Panthers, a far-left, antiracist, anticapitalist collective. Gary Grimshaw, its Minister of Culture, designed the Party flag as an inversion of the BPP flag by Emory Douglas. As Plamondon put it, the party used "culture and art, spearheaded by rock and roll, to bring about a revolutionary change in America." Party bands the MC5 and, subsequently, The Up embodied revolutionary energy and ideals in their live performances, and the *Ann Arbor Sun* functioned as the Party's newspaper. The WPP became the Rainbow People's Party circa 1970 and disbanded in 1973.

White Panther Party Flag
Courtesy the Ben Blackwell Collection

POLITICAL CONCERT POSTERS

John Sinclair, Leni Sinclair, and Gary Grimshaw formed the multidisciplinary collective Trans-Love Energies circa 1967. The group was a constant target of police harassment, and at one point, John Sinclair was sentenced for up to ten years in prison for possessing two joints of marijuana. The excessive sentence elicited national outrage over police and government efforts to silence oppositional voices. Leni Sinclair helmed the Free John Sinclair movement, a protracted legal battle and countercultural campaign culminating in the John Sinclair Freedom Rally (featuring an impressive lineup of musicians and speakers) and Sinclair's release three days later.

J. & S. Stoddard, International Solidarity Day,
Grande Ballroom, Oct. 2, 1970
Courtesy Greg Bosch

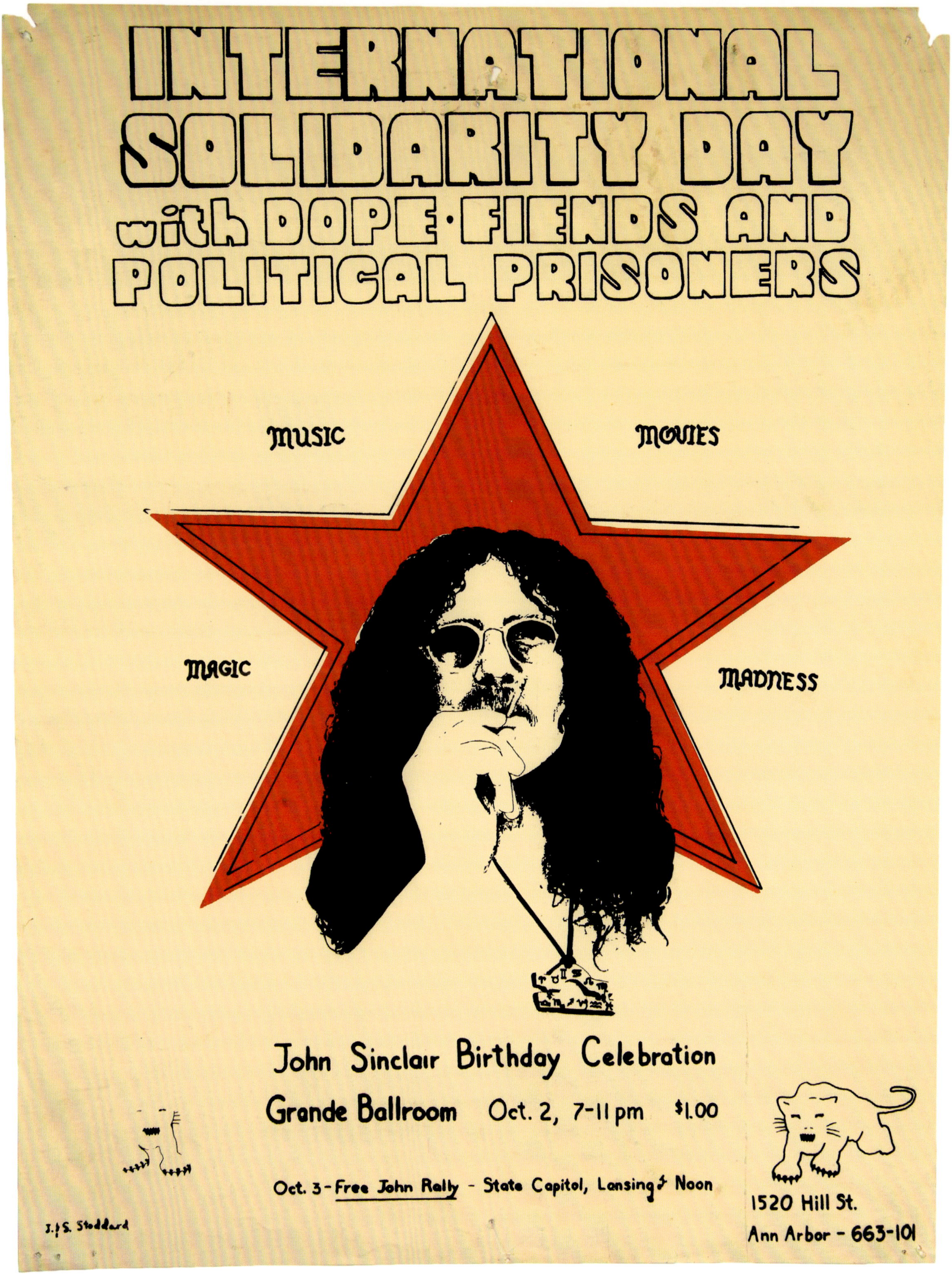
INTERNATIONAL SOLIDARITY DAY
with DOPE·FIENDS AND POLITICAL PRISONERS
MUSIC
MOVIES
MAGIC
MADNESS
John Sinclair Birthday Celebration
Grande Ballroom Oct. 2, 7-11 pm $1.00
Oct. 3 - Free John Rally - State Capitol, Lansing & Noon
1520 Hill St.
Ann Arbor - 663-101
J. & S. Stoddard

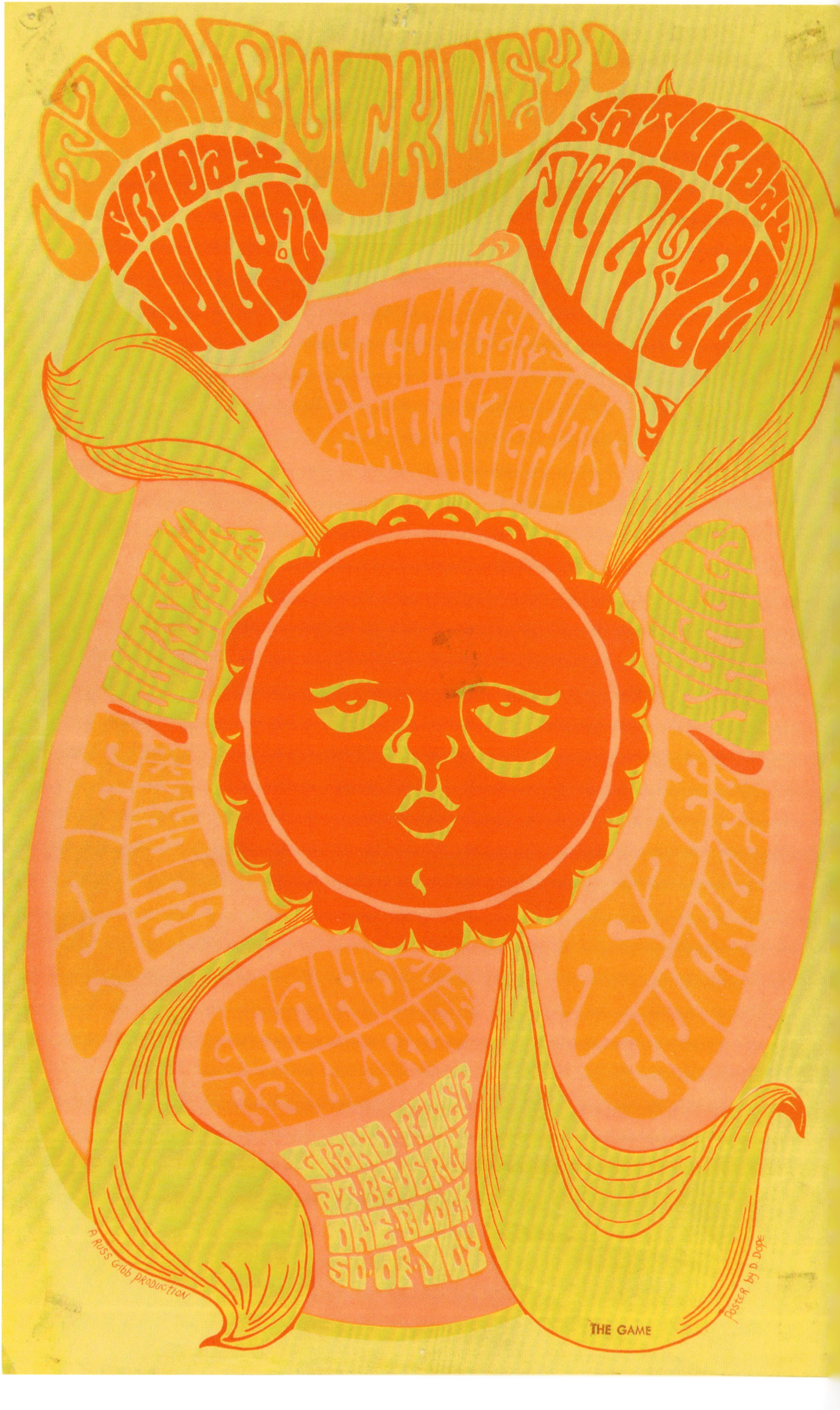
GRAND RIVER
AT BEVERLY
ONE BLOCK
SO. OF JOY
A RUSS GIBB PRODUCTION
THE GAME
POSTER by D. DOPE

1960S CONCERT POSTERS

"Uncle Russ" Gibb purchased the historic Grande Ballroom in 1966 after a trip to San Francisco convinced him Detroit needed a rock venue to rival the Fillmore. It opened on October 7, 1966, with Detroit garage bands the MC5 and The Chosen Few. The MC5 played weekly gigs there and recorded their first album live at the Grande in 1968. The Stooges also played regular gigs beginning in 1968, the Grande launching both bands to stardom. By the late 1960s it was one of the country's top venues. Early on, Rob Tyner of the MC5 introduced Gibb to artist Gary Grimshaw, who became the venue's principal poster artist and soon among the most sought-after poster artists in the country. This poster, by Detroit graphic artist "Donny Dope," advertises a Tim Buckley concert at the Grande taking place July 22, 1967, the night before the Rebellion broke out on 12th Street.

Donny Dope, Tim Buckley, Grande Ballroom, July 21–22, 1967
Courtesy Greg Bosch

MOTOWN BLACK FORUM 1970-1973

Motown founder Berry Gordy created the Black Forum label as a platform for Black thought leaders of the day, a place for their different, often opposing viewpoints. Between 1970 and 1973 the label released eight historic recordings of events, speeches, poetry, and music, serving as a record of the Black struggle and the need for a new reality. Stokely Carmichael's *Free Huey!* is a celebration of Black Panther Huey Newton's birthday and a demand for his release from jail. Journalist Wallace Terry's *Guess Who's Coming Home: Black Fighting Men Recorded Live in Vietnam* comprises interviews with soldiers on their experiences fighting two wars—one at home and one across the ocean. *Black Spirits* by Imamu Amiri Baraka and The Original Last Poets presents fourteen poets associated with the Black Arts Movement voicing struggles of Black America. Baraka's *It's Nation Time* explores African Visionary Music intent on inspiring and strengthening communities of African men and women living in the United States. *Elaine Brown* captures the Black Panther leader using her voice, through spoken word and music, to express pain and suffering in the Black community.

Imamu Amiri Baraka, The Original Last Poets,
Black Spirits, April 1972
Courtesy the Motown Museum

BLACK SPIRITS

FESTIVAL OF NEW BLACK POETS IN AMERICA

IMAMU AMIRI BARAKA (LE ROI JONES) □ THE ORIGINAL LAST POETS

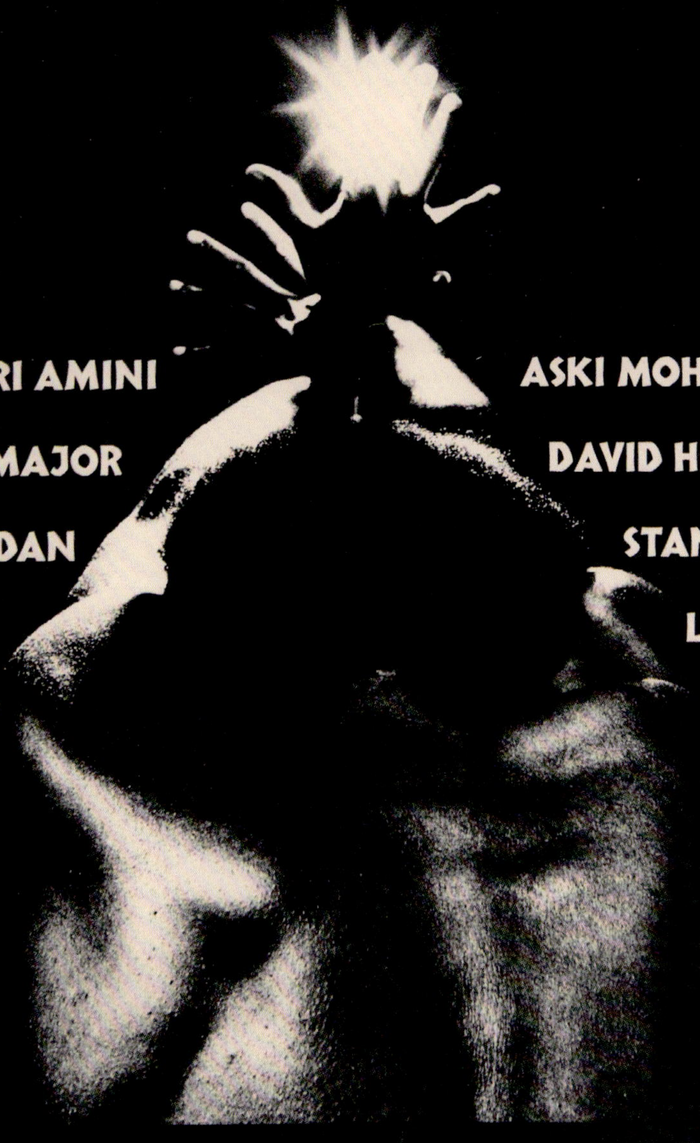

JOHARI AMINI

CLARENCE MAJOR

NORMAN JORDAN

KALI

JACKIE EARLEY

ASKI MOHAMMAD TOURE

DAVID HENDERSON

STANLEY CROUCH

LARRY NEAL

AMUS MOORE

BLACK FORUM

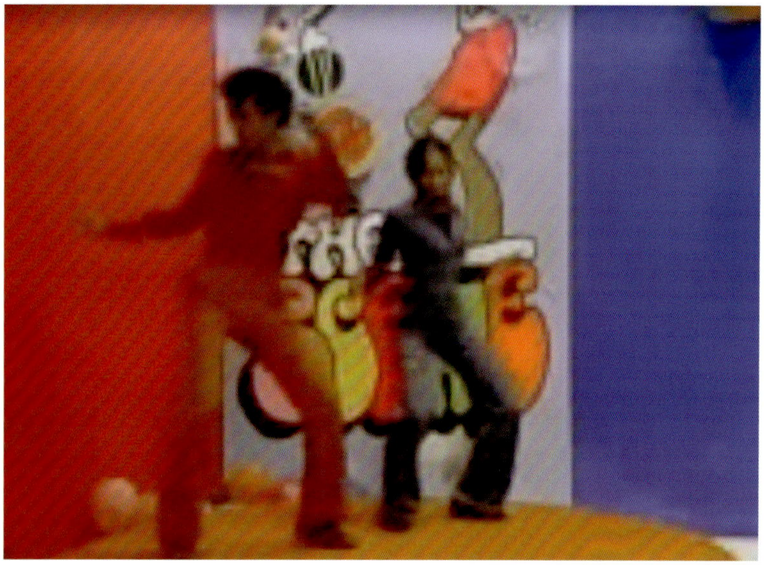

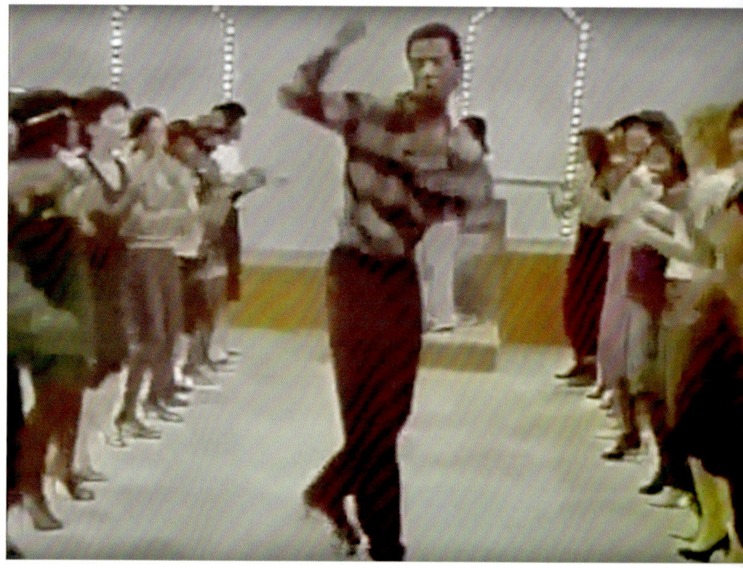

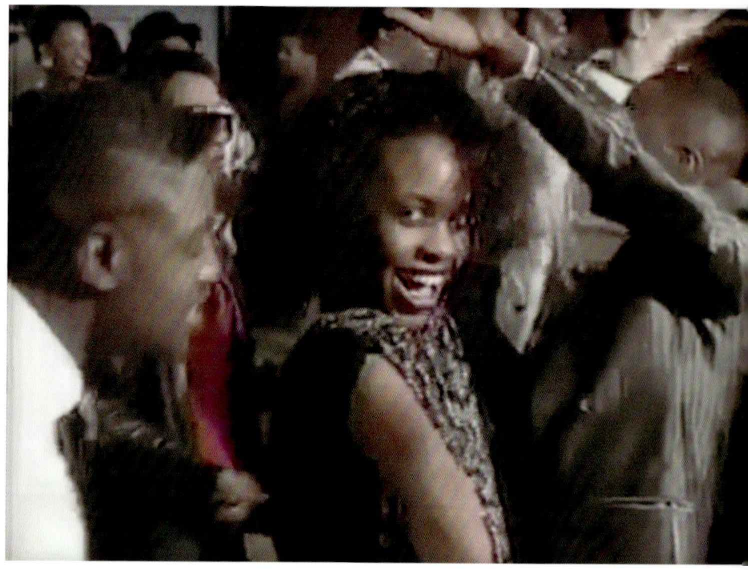

WGPR-TV

The Scene, 1975–87
The New Dance Show, 1988–95
Videos courtesy of Nat Morris, R.J. Watkins, and
the WGPR-TV Historical Society

WGPR-TV was the first black-owned television station in the country, signing on in 1975. For the next twenty years as an independent station, WGPR ran an array of programs geared primarily toward Detroit's urban black audiences. Among these were three popular music-dance shows: *The Scene*, *Contempo*, and *The New Dance Show*. Like the nationally-syndicated *Soul Train*, the shows featured popular music and dancers showing off their styles and moves. *The Scene*, hosted by Nat Morris, and *The New Dance Show*, hosted by R.J. Watkins both had long runs, together spanning two generations of Detroiters. The shows were produced on custom stage sets inside the WGPR studios on East Jefferson Avenue. Young Detroiters came into the studio to dance and be seen on TV. Hosts Morris and Watkins worked the crowd in the studio and at home, playing not only national music but also cutting-edge local music like early techno.

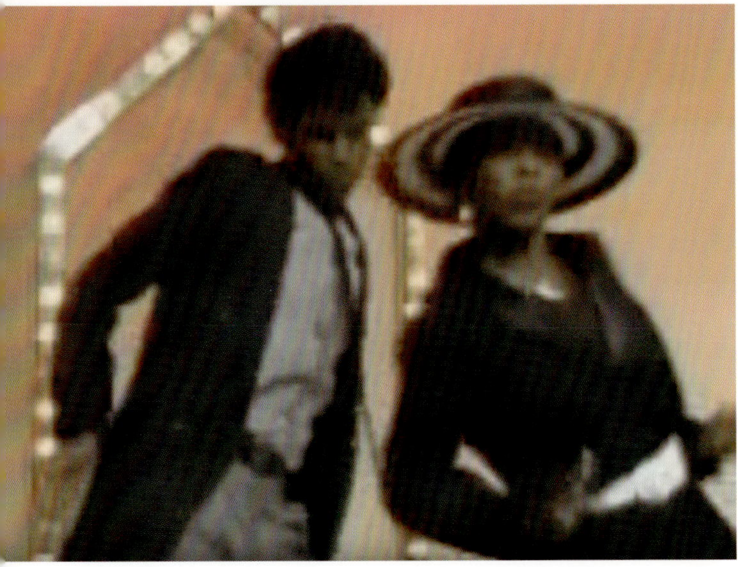

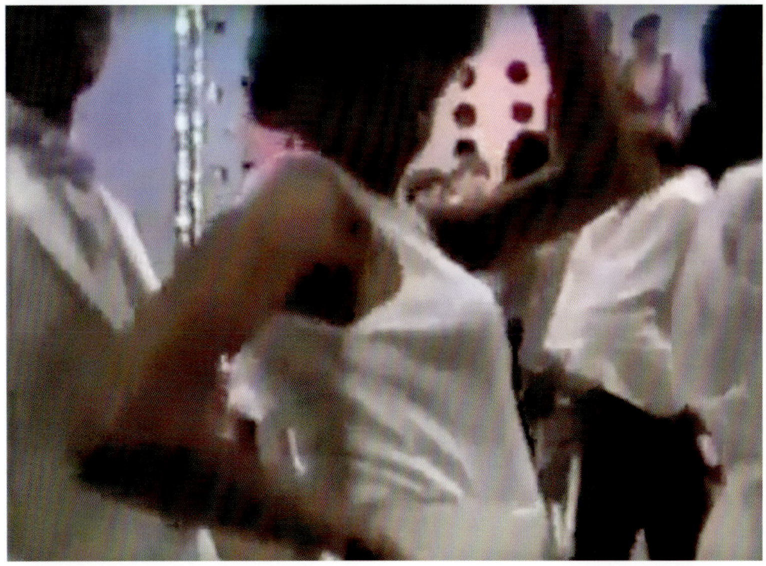

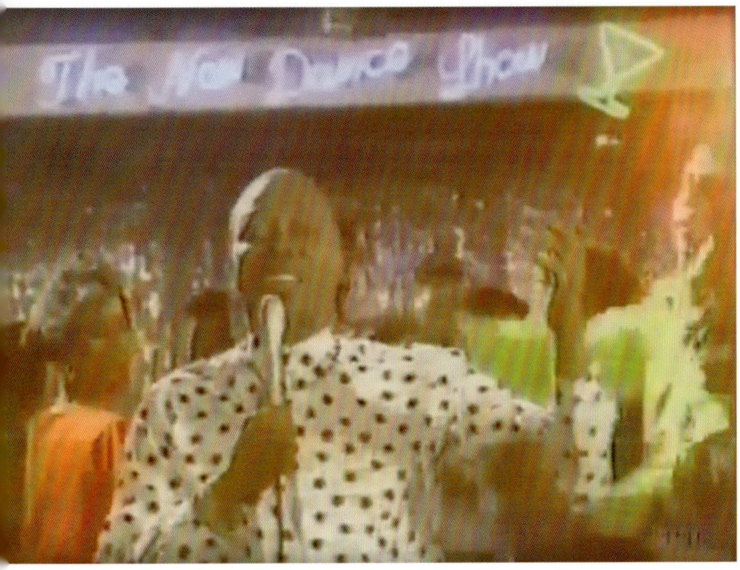
The New Dance Show

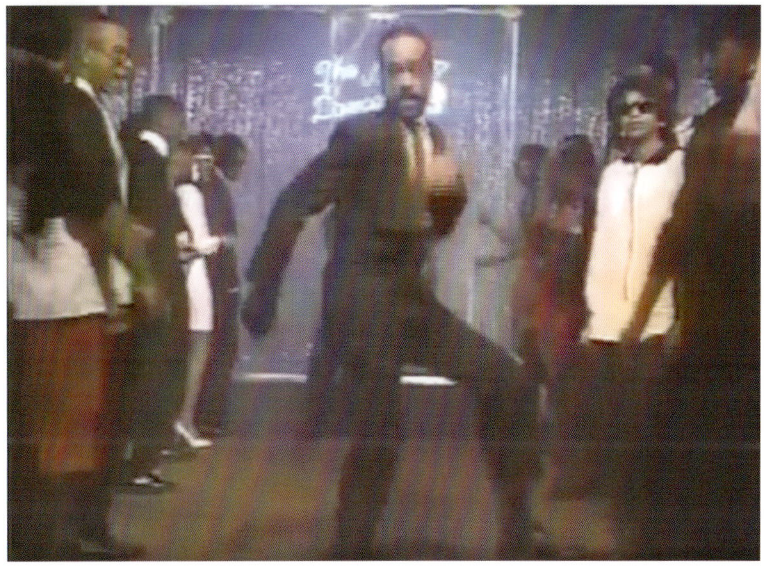

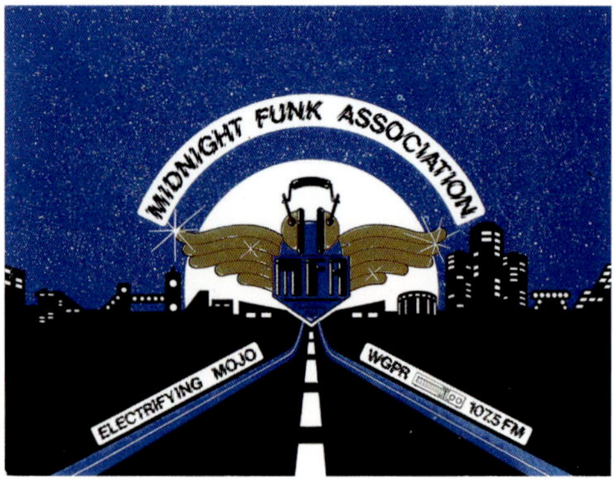

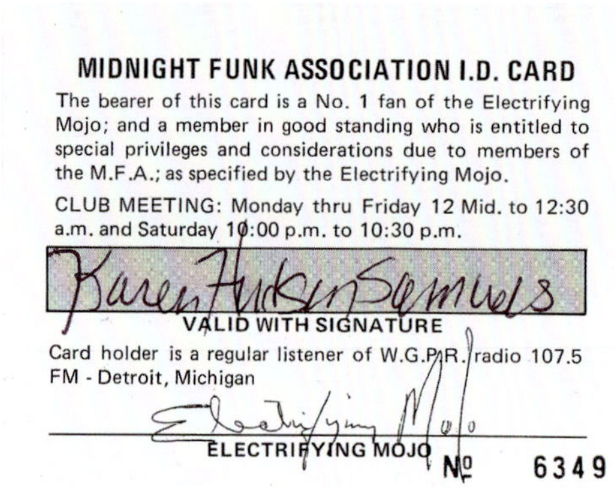

MIDNIGHT FUNK ASSOCIATION I.D. CARD

The bearer of this card is a No. 1 fan of the Electrifying Mojo; and a member in good standing who is entitled to special privileges and considerations due to members of the M.F.A.; as specified by the Electrifying Mojo.

CLUB MEETING: Monday thru Friday 12 Mid. to 12:30 a.m. and Saturday 10:00 p.m. to 10:30 p.m.

Karen Hudson Samuels

VALID WITH SIGNATURE

Card holder is a regular listener of W.G.P.R. radio 107.5 FM - Detroit, Michigan

Electrifying Mojo

ELECTRIFYING MOJO Nº 6349

"Midnight Funk Association" ID card, courtesy Karen Hudson Samuels

THE ELECTRIFYING MOJO

"All members of the Midnight Funk Association, please rise." With these words cult radio personality The Electrifying Mojo summoned a legion of devoted fans throughout metro Detroit. His nightly show ran on WGPR from 1977 to 1982 and on various stations through the 1990s. Mojo famously played what he liked, not what established radio formats demanded. His mixes ranged from George Clinton to Kraftwerk, Prince to the B-52s to Cybotron, and he played deep cuts and entire albums, not just the hits. The show's eclecticism and extended temporality were hugely influential to Detroit techno, as were Mojo's visionary, sci-fi persona, his positivity, and messages of solidarity. Each show began with "the landing of the mothership," his descent to Earth, inspired by Parliament's 1975 album *Mothership Connection.*

Courtesy The Electrifying Mojo and WGPR-TV Historical Society

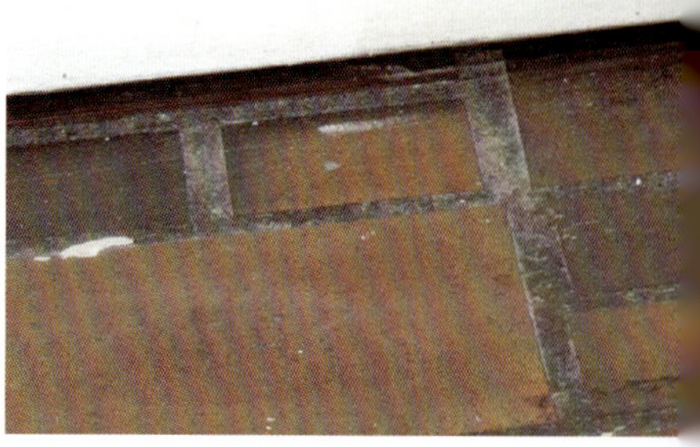

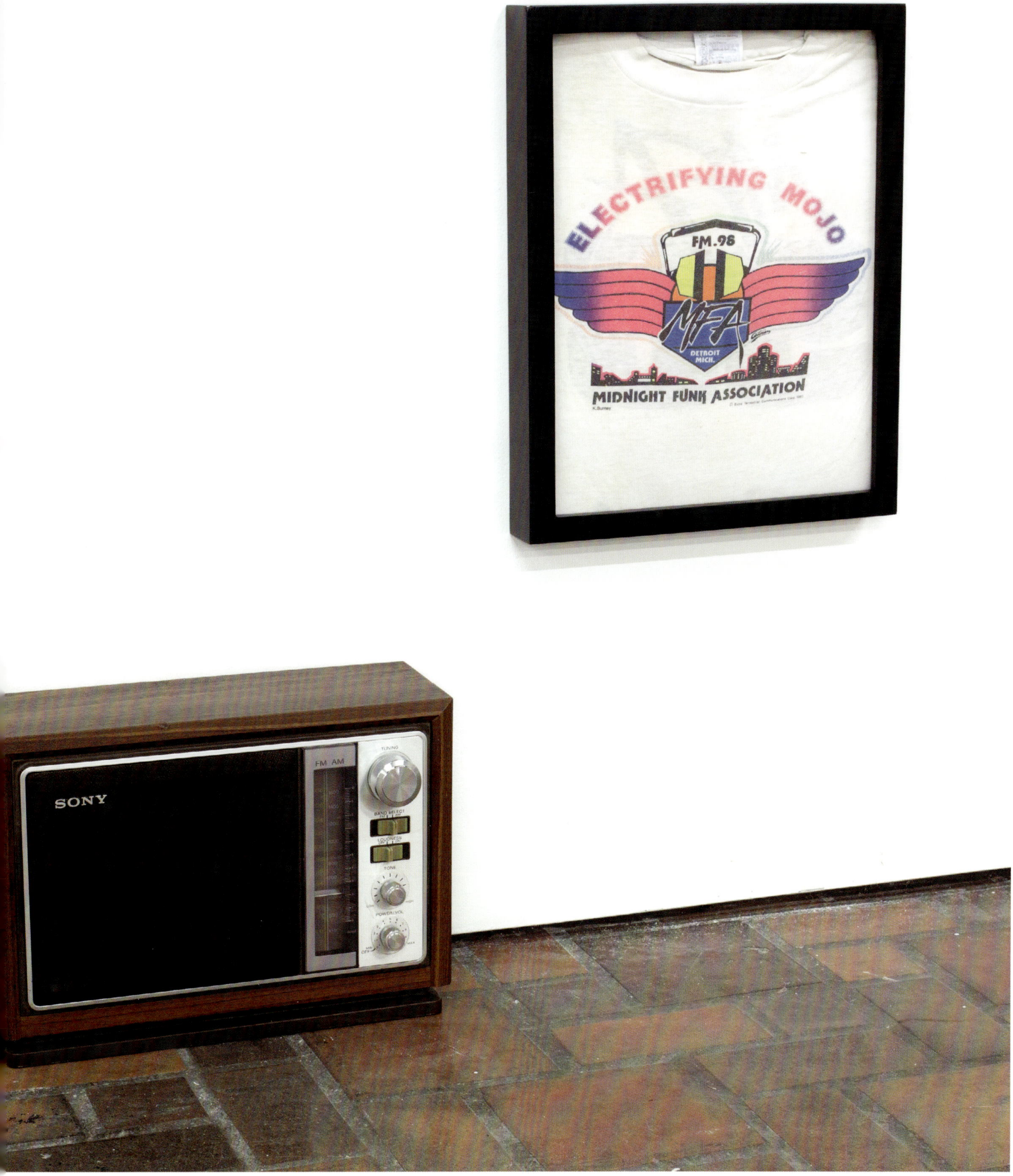
ELECTRIFYING MOJO
FM.98
MFA
DETROIT MICH.
MIDNIGHT FUNK ASSOCIATION
SONY
FM AM
TUNING
TONE

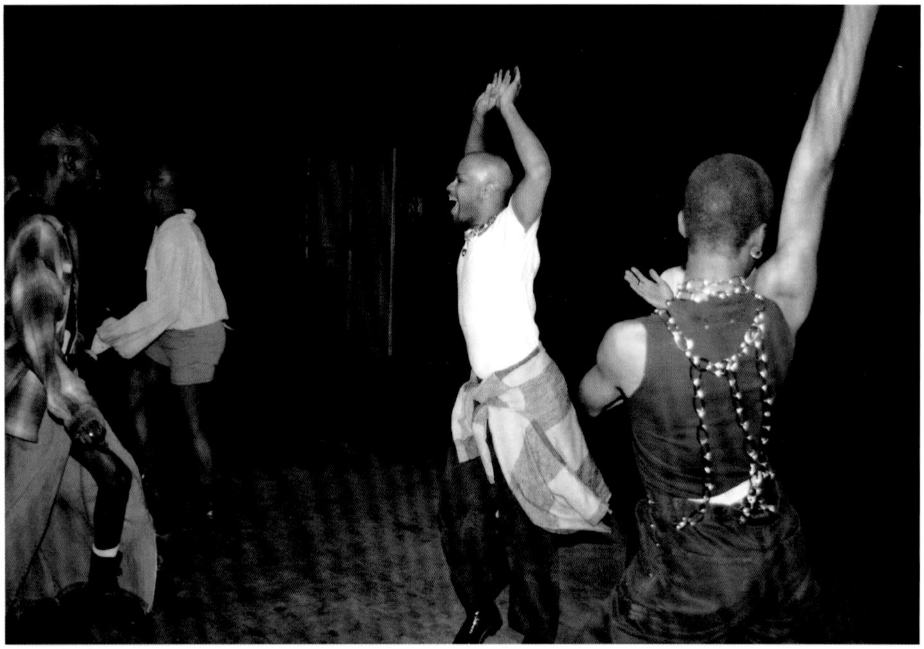
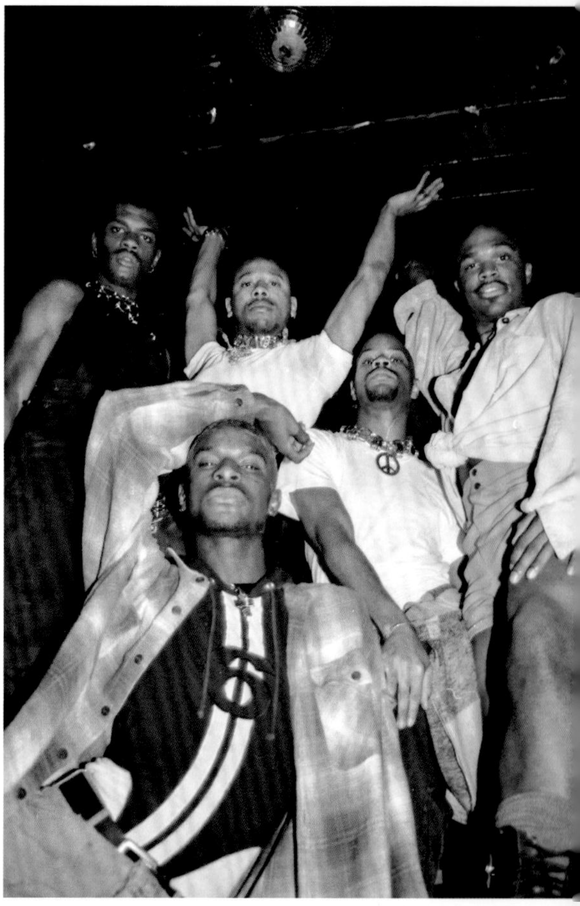
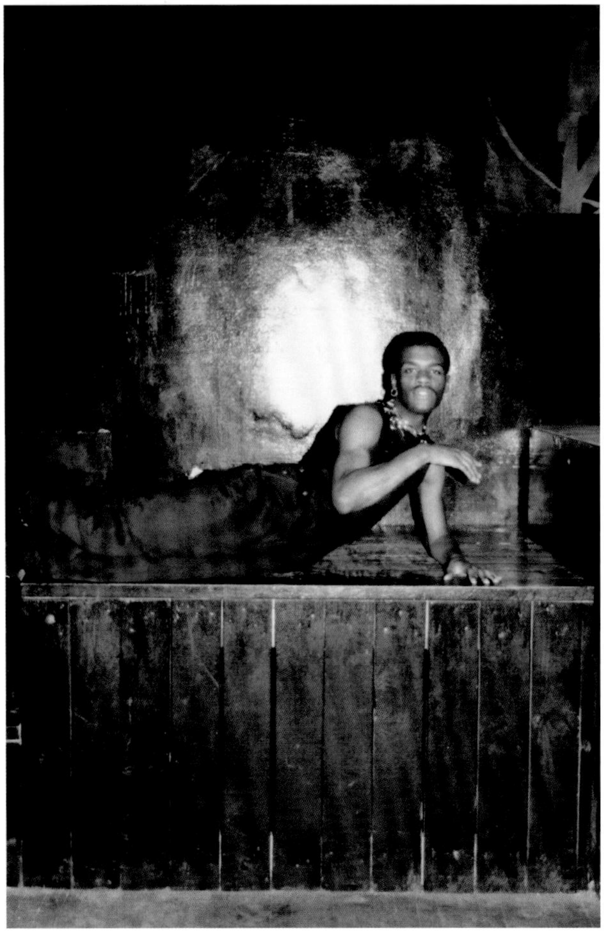
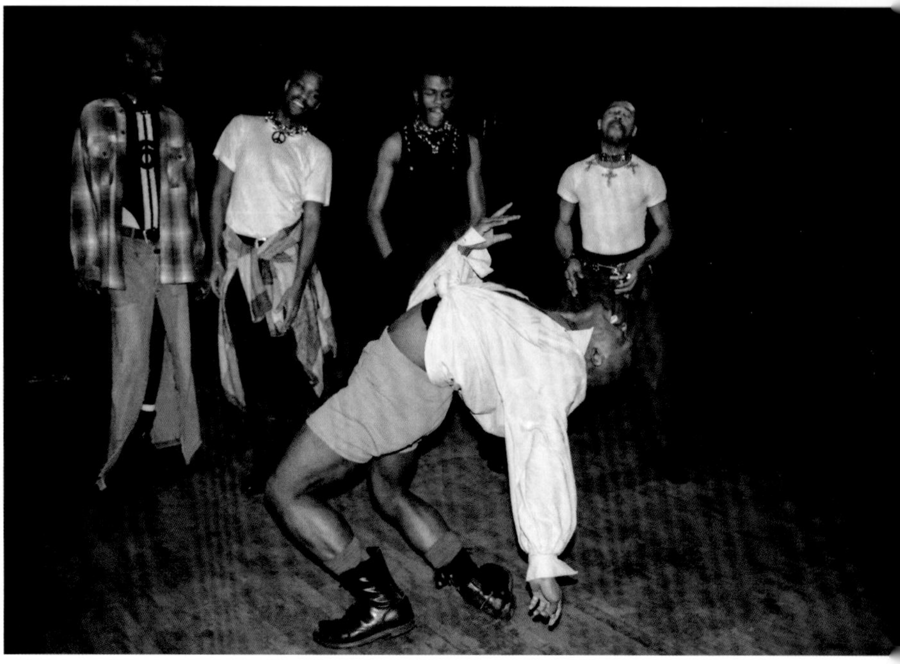

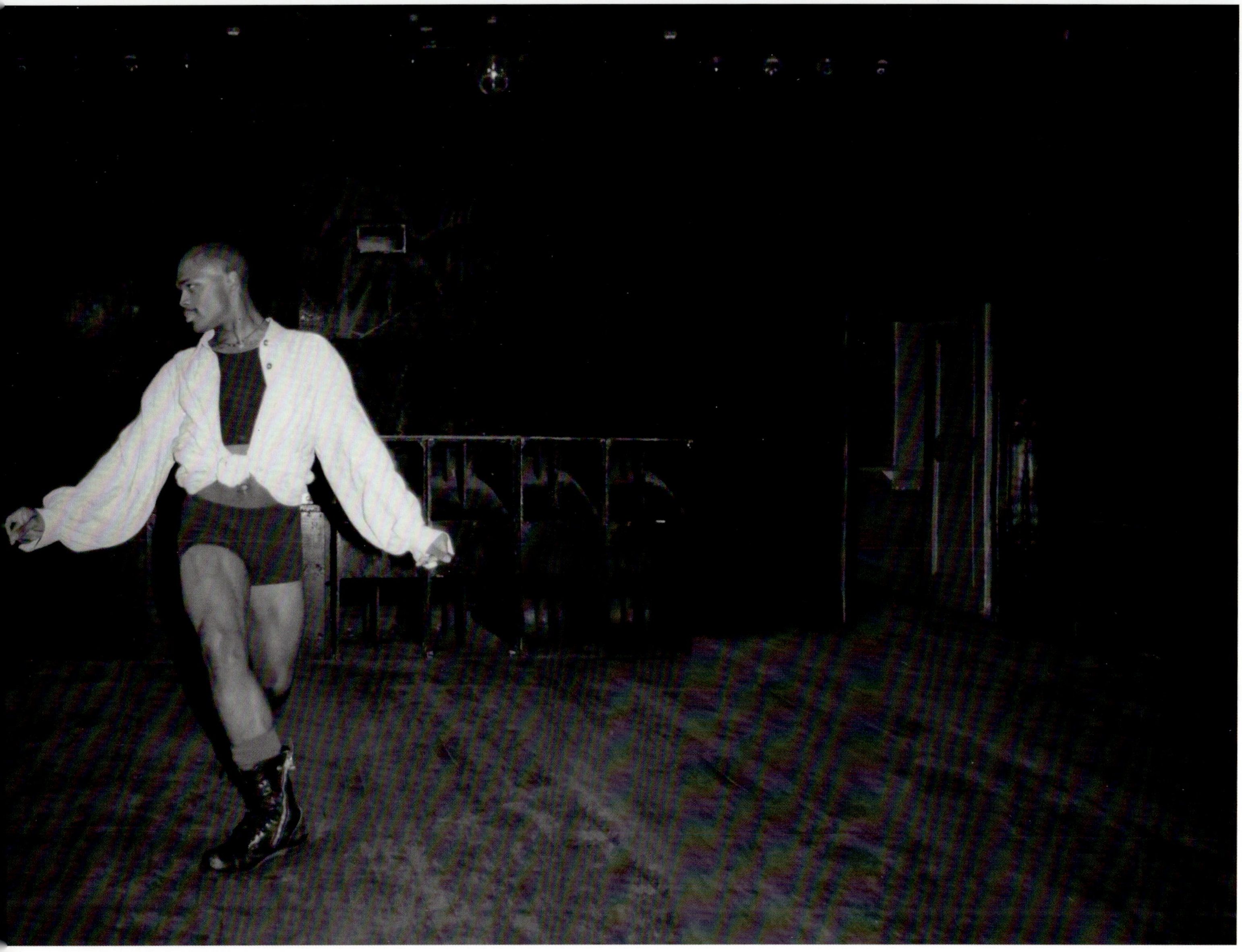

CHRISTOPHER CUSHMAN

Heaven/House of Charles, FIERCE! collection, 1994
Digital prints, 2017
Courtesy the artist

Heaven was an after-hours club at Seven Mile Road and Woodward where legendary DJ Ken Collier spun dance music every Saturday from the late 1980s through the mid-1990s. Collier stands beside The Electrifying Mojo as one of the most influential figures supporting original Detroit techno. Heaven was central to Detroit's black gay community, and Christopher Cushman's photos show the energy and sense of freedom on its dance floor. His pictures are among the only such images, as the club did not typically allow photography because some of its patrons were not publicly out. These were published in the premier issue of *Kick Magazine* with permission from Collier and the dancers.

DERRICK MAY

Ensoniq Mirage Sampler-Synth and Transmat labels
Circa 1986–88

Electronic musician and producer Derrick May pioneered Detroit Techno as one of the Belleville Three. His early releases, including the landmark tracks "Nude Photo" and "Strings of Life," became major club hits and strongly influenced burgeoning electronic music cultures, especially in Europe. This is the sampler May used to produce those classic tracks, which he released on Transmat, the influential techno label he founded in 1986.

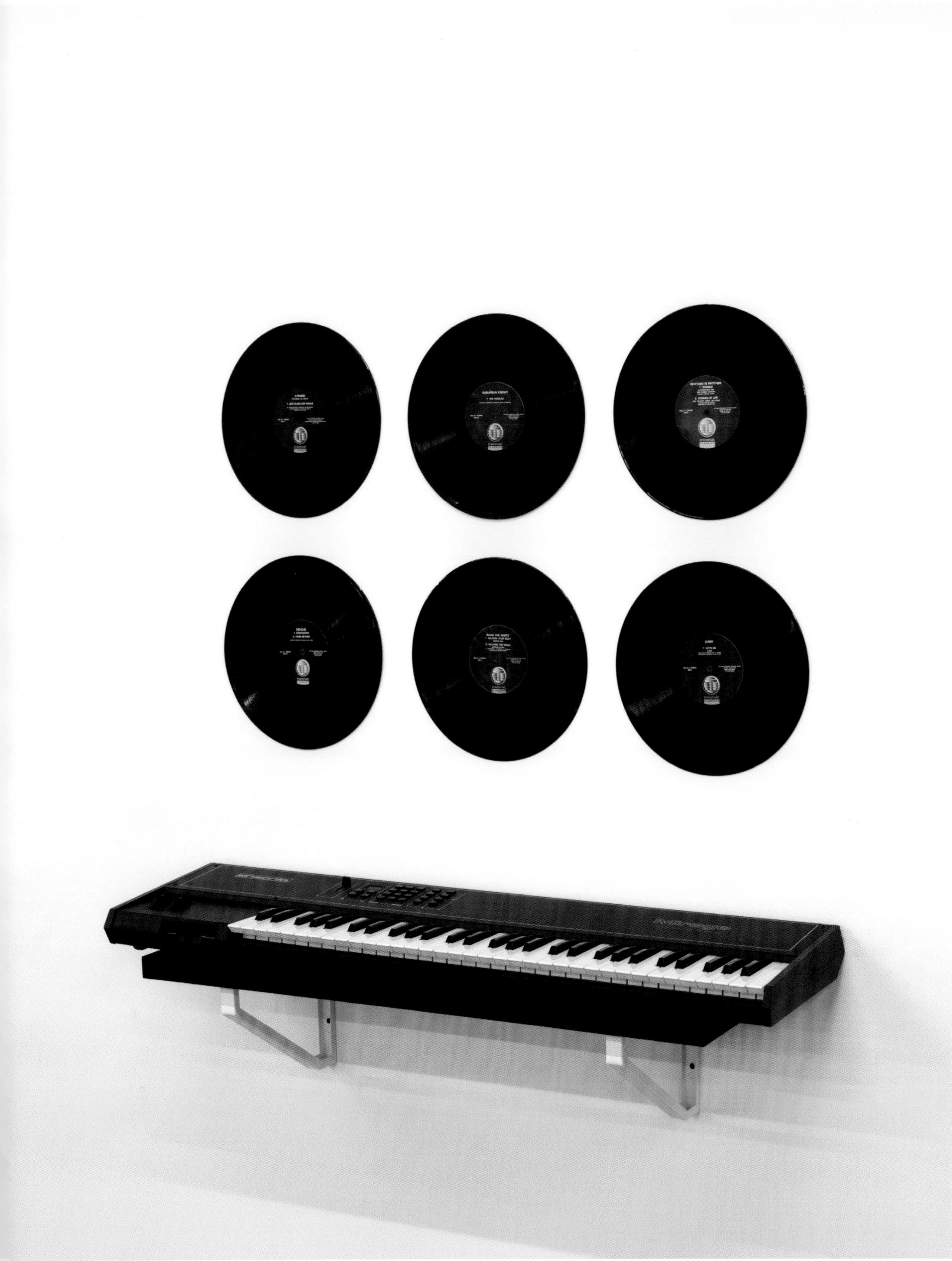

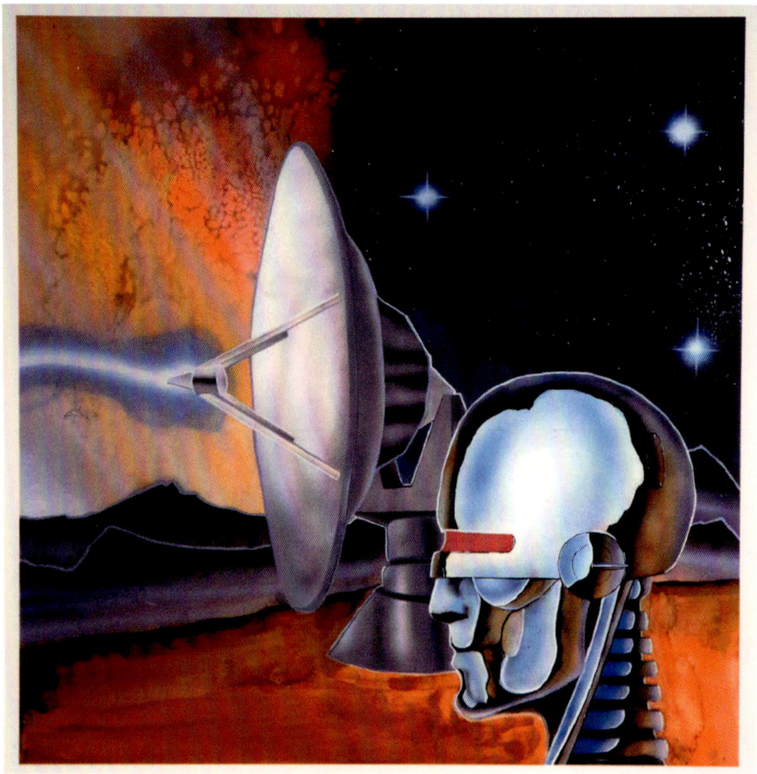

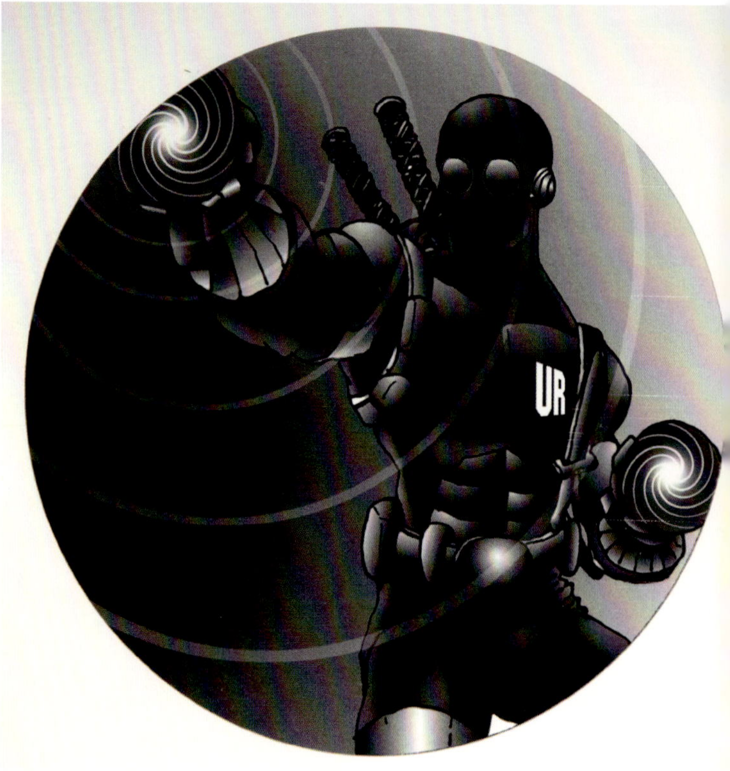

A. QADIM HAQQ AND ALAN OLDHAM

With an aesthetic and outlook based in Afro-Futurism, artists Abdul Haqq and Alan Oldham have been foundational in creating the visual imagery of Detroit techno. Over the last twenty-eight years, Haqq has produced cover art and label concepts for Juan Atkins, Drexciya, Transmat (Derrick May), and other artists, drawing inspiration from science fiction, comics, ancient mythology, and fantasy. Oldham's work focuses on pop culture and urbanism, influenced by 1970s and 1980s Marvel Comics, pop artists like Roy Lichtenstein, and Jean-Michel Basqiuat. Oldham also produces techno music under the name DJ-T1000, and both artists were original member of Detroit's influential, politically oriented techno collective Underground Resistance.

Top:
Haqq, *Classics* (Model 500, R&S Records), 1993
Haqq, *Analog Assassin* (Underground Resistance, UR), 2002

Right page:
Oldham, *Social Housing* (Marquis Hawkes, Houndstouth), 2016

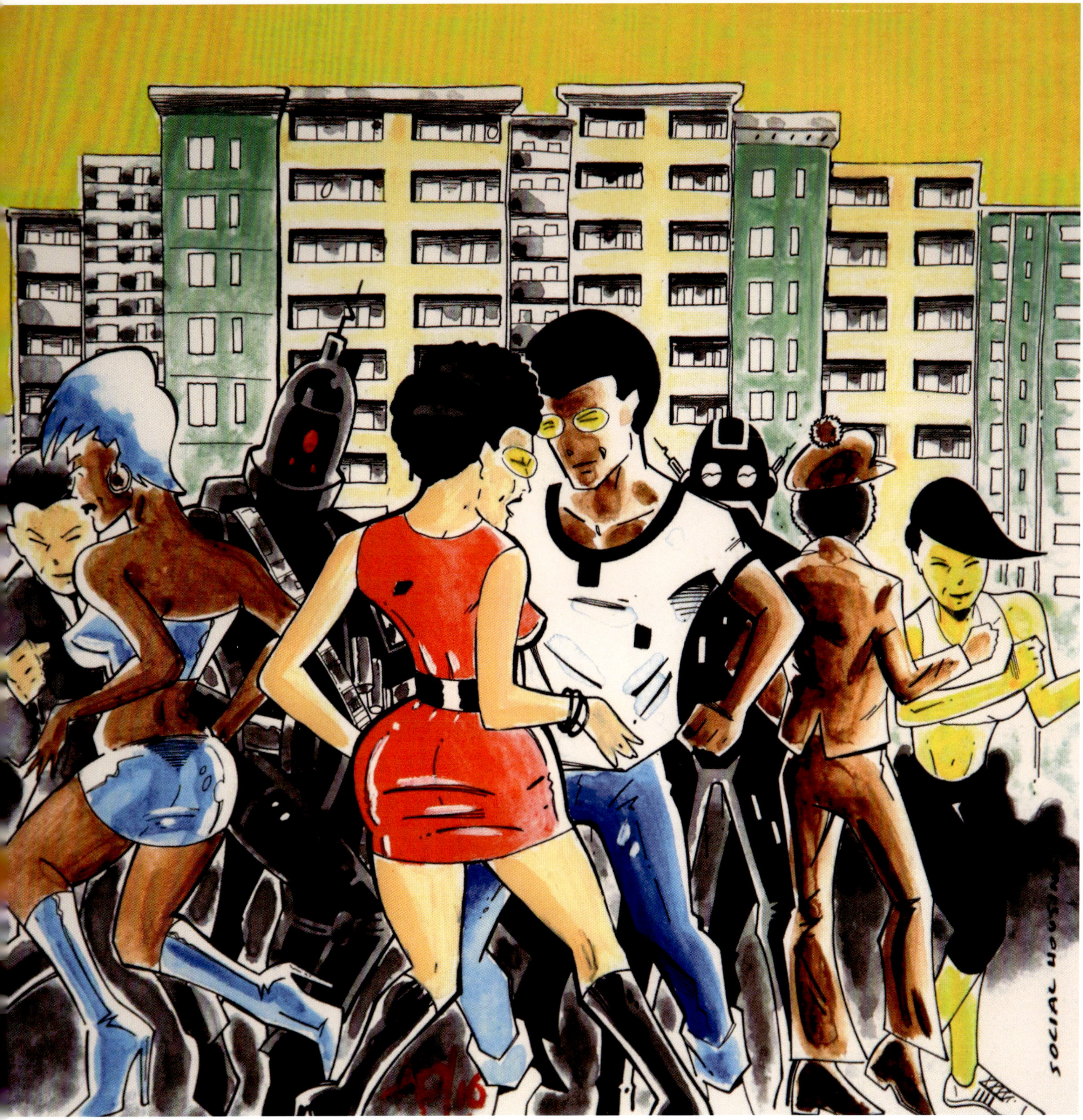
SOCIAL

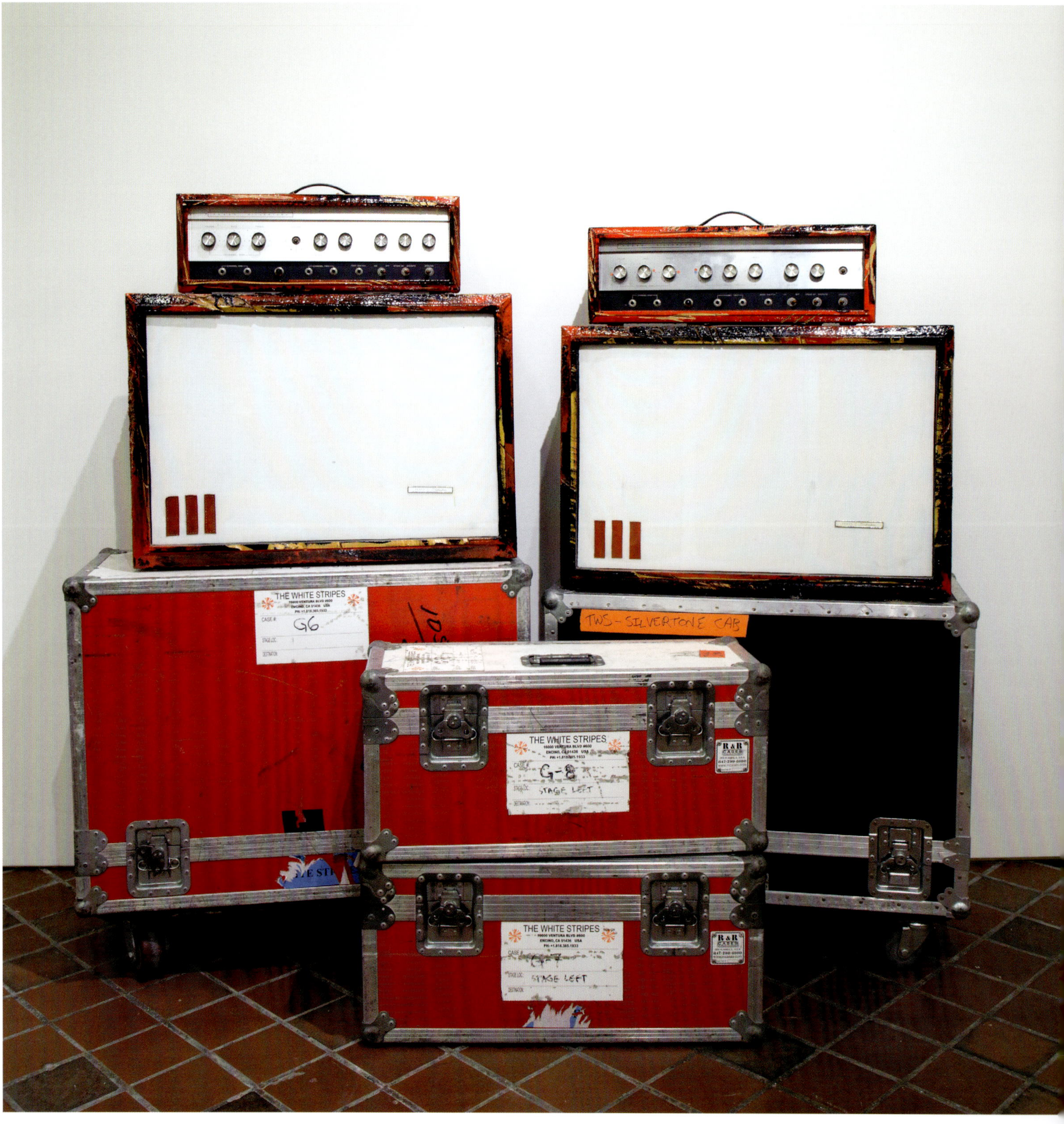
THE WHITE STRIPES
G6
TWS - SILVERTONE CAB
THE WHITE STRIPES
G-8
STAGE LEFT
THE WHITE STRIPES
STAGE LEFT

GORDON NEWTON

Deconstructed Amplifiers, 2003
Wood, electrical components, paint, resin, cardboard, cloth
Courtesy Third Man Records, Cass Corridor

In 2003, Jack White commissioned Cass Corridor artist Gordon Newton to deconstruct his vintage 1960s Silvertone and Fender guitar amplifiers. Newton attacked the amps with saws, covered them with red and black paint, constructed miniature cardboard chairs to sit inside newly created crevices, and sealed it all with multiple coats of gloss resin. Master upholsterer Brian Muldoon then replaced the original silver-thread grill cloths with clean white fabric to cover the speaker frames. The White Stripes debuted the amps live at Detroit's Masonic Temple in 2003 and continued using them until disbanding in 2007. Simultaneously functional music equipment and a sculptural artwork, the amplifiers harness the legacy of punk and D.I.Y. art in Detroit.

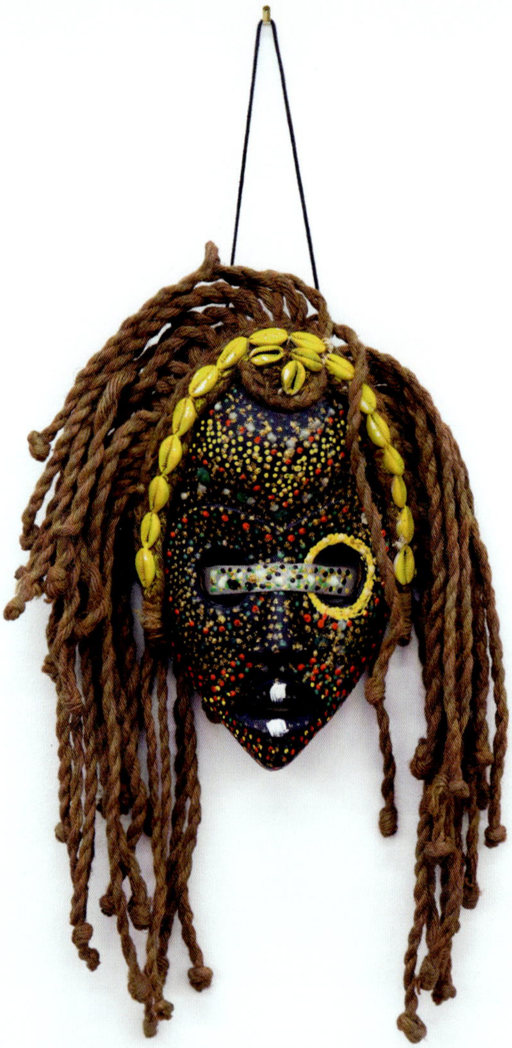

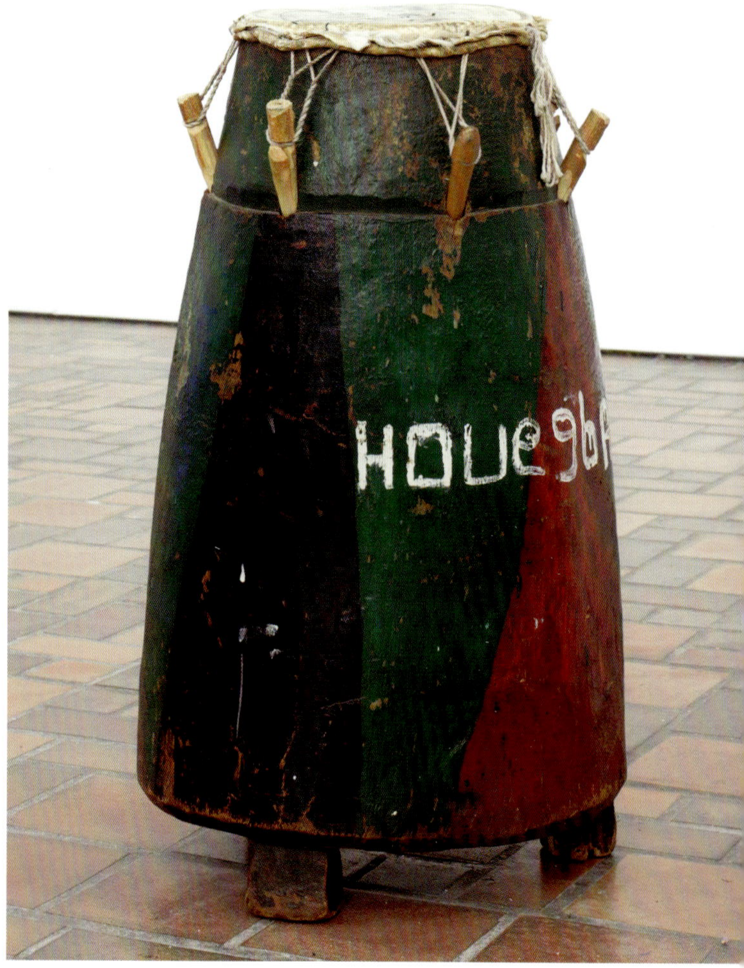

EFE BES

Modified drum from Ghana and mask
Wood, acrylic paint, beads, yarn, duct tape
Courtesy the artist

Detroit native, drummer and visual artist Efe Bes harnesses the music and material culture of Africa. Whether performing solo or with other musicians, using one drum or finely-tuned array, his music relocates the drum from the background to the foreground, developing irresistible rhythms and subtle melodies that move people. He sees his work as connecting people of the African diaspora with ancestral African forms. "If you don't embrace your culture, no one will embrace you," he has said, "and the easiest way to embrace your culture is through your music, through your creations… that's the thing keeping us together, the African people." He performs wearing African masks he modifies, and also exhibits these masks as art objects.

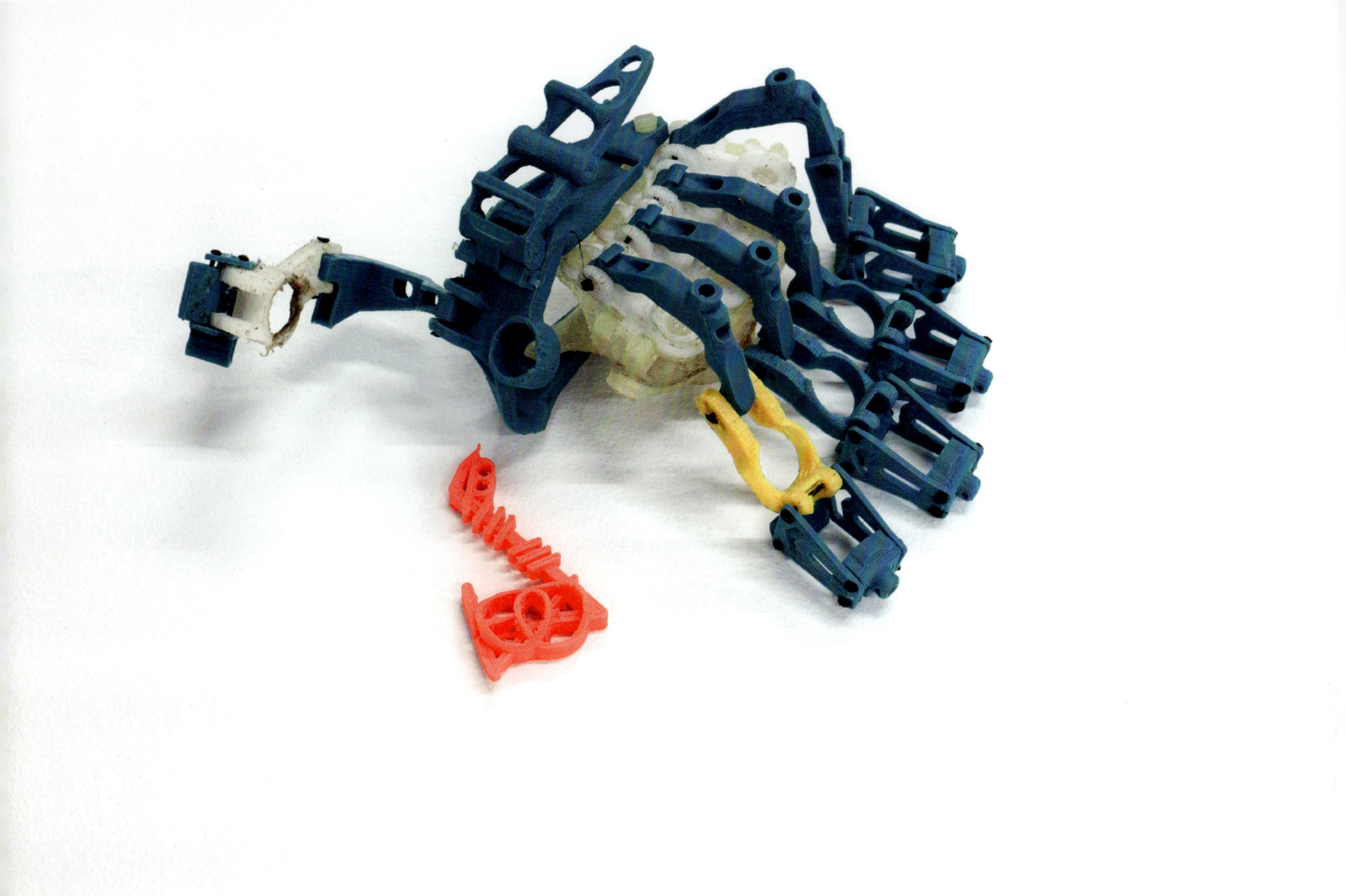

ONYX ASHANTI

3D-printed glove and beatjazz icon
Courtesy the artist

Musician, programmer, 3D print designer, writer, performer, and inventor Onyx Ahsanti has spent the last few years creating a multidimensional concept called beatjazz. He designed this glove with open-source CAD software, 3D printed it, and wired it with motion-sensing Arduinos linked to computers, which he straps to his body during his performances, merging man and machine, the biological and the electronic.

STERLING TOLES

Resurget Cineribus
2017
LP Cover Layouts
Courtesy the artist

Sterling Toles is a music producer and multidisciplinary artist raised on Detroit's east side. His 2017 LP *Resurget Cineribus* revisits the 1967 Detroit Rebellion through the life of his father, Dennis Edward Toles. The album mixes sound clips from archival news coverage of the rioting with audio of Dennis discussing his life, recorded in the mid-2000s. At the time, Dennis was caught in a circular trap, selling heroin to put himself through methadone treatment. Someone had recently thrown a Molotov cocktail through his living room window, and his house caught on fire. For Sterling, who was already making music from the archival reportage in which blazes figure prominently, the image of fire helped him connect the two events. He began to understand his father's life as ensnared in the same historical conditions of racial oppression and violence that had given rise to the '67 Rebellion and persist today in different forms.

In the album, Toles interweaves audio from these two stories, using the sound of a door shutting to structure the narrative temporality. The artist-designed record cover features an image of Dennis Toles with a door collaged over his face. The door opens to reveal an accordion-folded set of images from Detroit '67. The album's title, *Resurget Cinerbius*, comes from Detroit's two-part motto, first adopted when the French settlement burned down in 1805: "Speramus Meliora. Resurget Cineribus." Translated from Latin, this motto reads: "We hope for better things. It will arise form the ashes." Exploring his own familial history and that of the city through sound and memory, Toles leads us on a quest for "better things" through times of trouble.

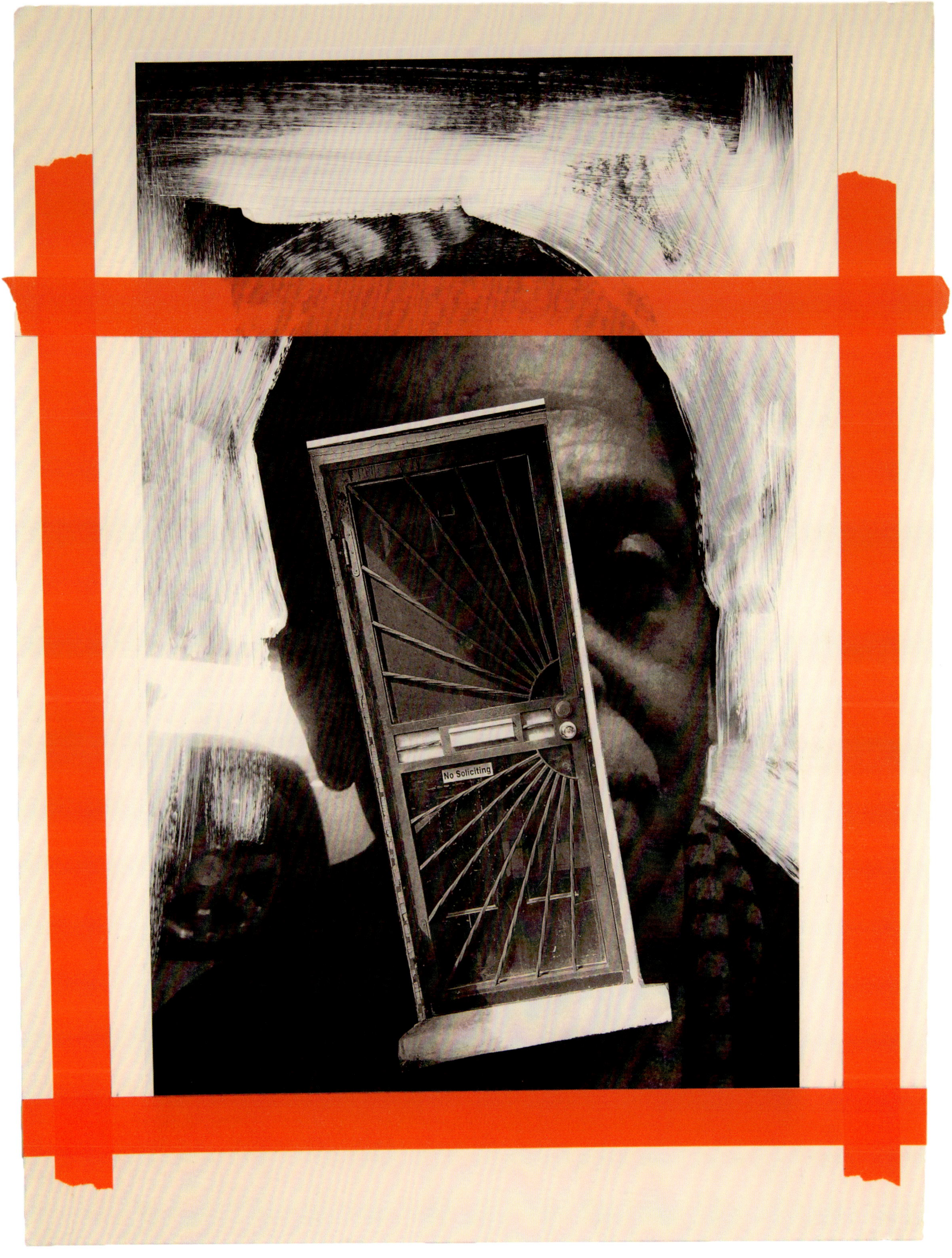
No Soliciting

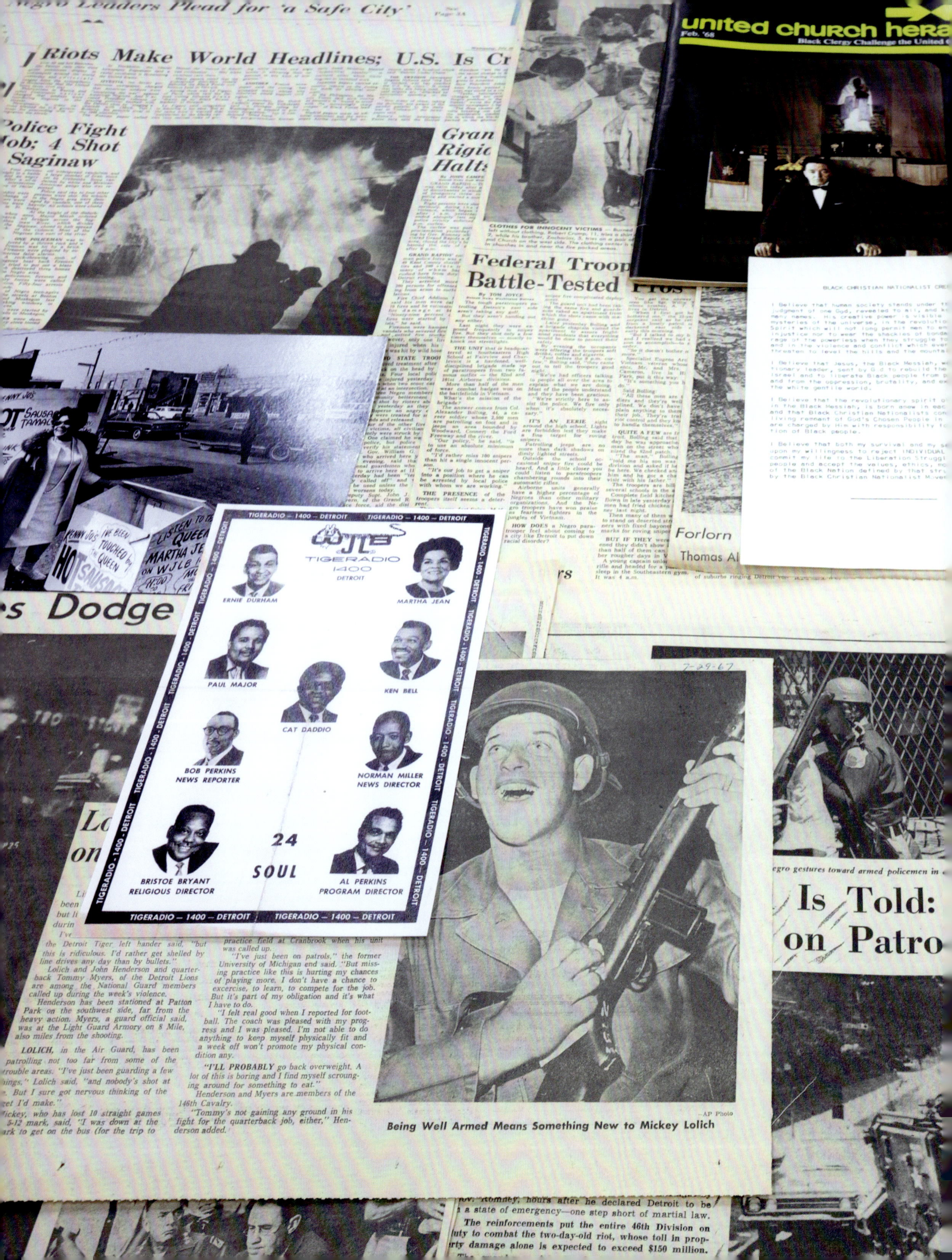
Riots Make World Headlines; U.S. Is Cr
Police Fight
Saginaw
Federal Troop
Battle-Tested
By TOM JOYCE
united church hera
Feb. '68
BLACK CHRISTIAN NATIONALIST CRE
Forlorn
Thomas Al
Dodge
TIGERADIO — 1400 — DETROIT
WJLB
TIGERADIO
1400
DETROIT
ERNIE DURHAM
MARTHA JEAN
PAUL MAJOR
KEN BELL
CAT DADDIO
BOB PERKINS
NEWS REPORTER
NORMAN MILLER
NEWS DIRECTOR
24
SOUL
BRISTOE BRYANT
RELIGIOUS DIRECTOR
AL PERKINS
PROGRAM DIRECTOR
LISTEN TO THE QUEEN
MARTHA JE
ON WJLB
7-29-67
the Detroit Tiger left hander said, "but this is ridiculous. I'd rather get shelled by line drives any day than by bullets."
Lolich and John Henderson and quarterback Tommy Myers, of the Detroit Lions are among the National Guard members called up during the week's violence.
Henderson has been stationed at Patton Park on the southwest side, far from the heavy action. Myers, a guard official said, was at the Light Guard Armory on 8 Mile, also miles from the shooting.
LOLICH, in the Air Guard, has been patrolling not too far from some of the trouble areas. "I've just been guarding a few things," Lolich said, "and nobody's shot at me. But I sure got nervous thinking of the
practice field at Cranbrook when his unit was called up.
"I've just been on patrols," the former University of Michigan end said. "But missing practice like this is hurting my chances of playing more. I don't have a chance to excercise, to learn, to compete for the job. But it's part of my obligation and it's what I have to do.
"I felt real good when I reported for football. The coach was pleased with my progress and I was pleased. I'm not able to do anything to keep myself physically fit and a week off won't promote my physical condition any.
"I'LL PROBABLY go back overweight. A lot of this is boring and I find myself scrounging around for something to eat."
Henderson and Myers are members of the 146th Cavalry.
"Tommy's not gaining any ground in his fight for the quarterback job, either," Henderson added.
—AP Photo
Being Well Armed Means Something New to Mickey Lolich
Is Told:
on Patro
a state of emergency—one step short of martial law.
The reinforcements put the entire 46th Division on duty to combat the two-day-old riot, whose toll in property damage alone is expected to exceed $150 million.

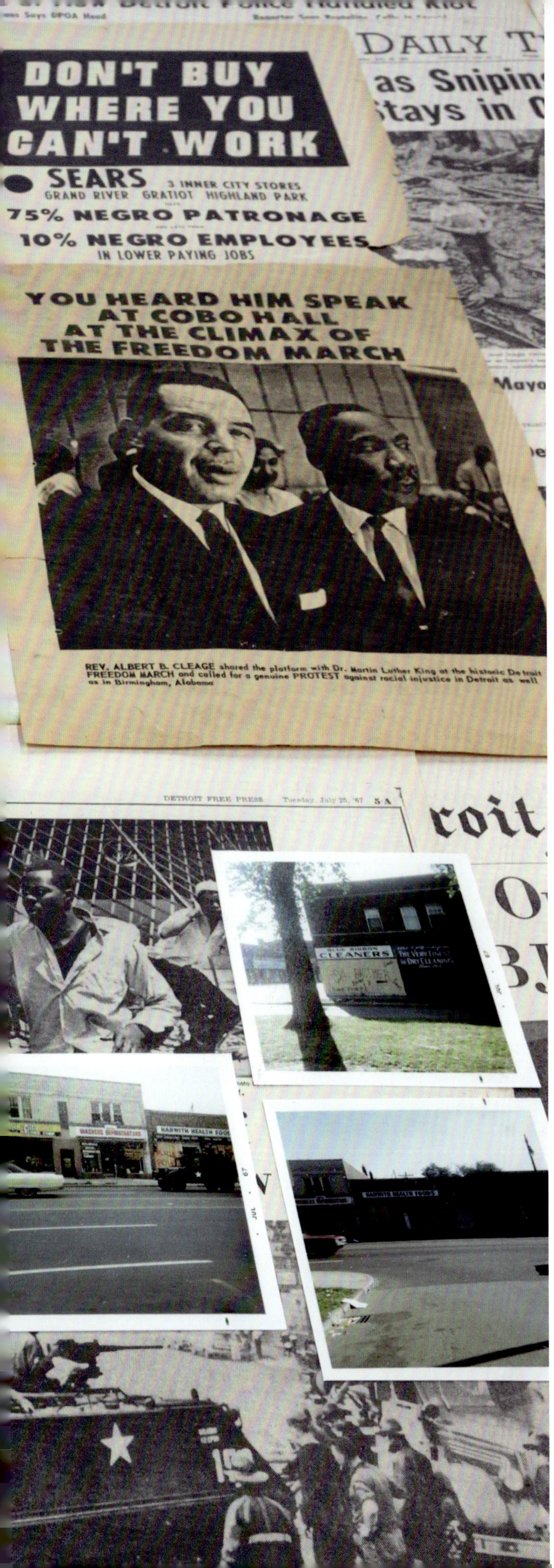

DETROIT 1967

Materials courtesy Ben Blackwell, T.M. Caldwell, Khalid el-Hakim / Black History 101 Mobile Museum, Morry Greener, Marsha Music, Martha Jean the Queen Legacy Committee, Shrine of the Black Madonna, Kathy Thayer

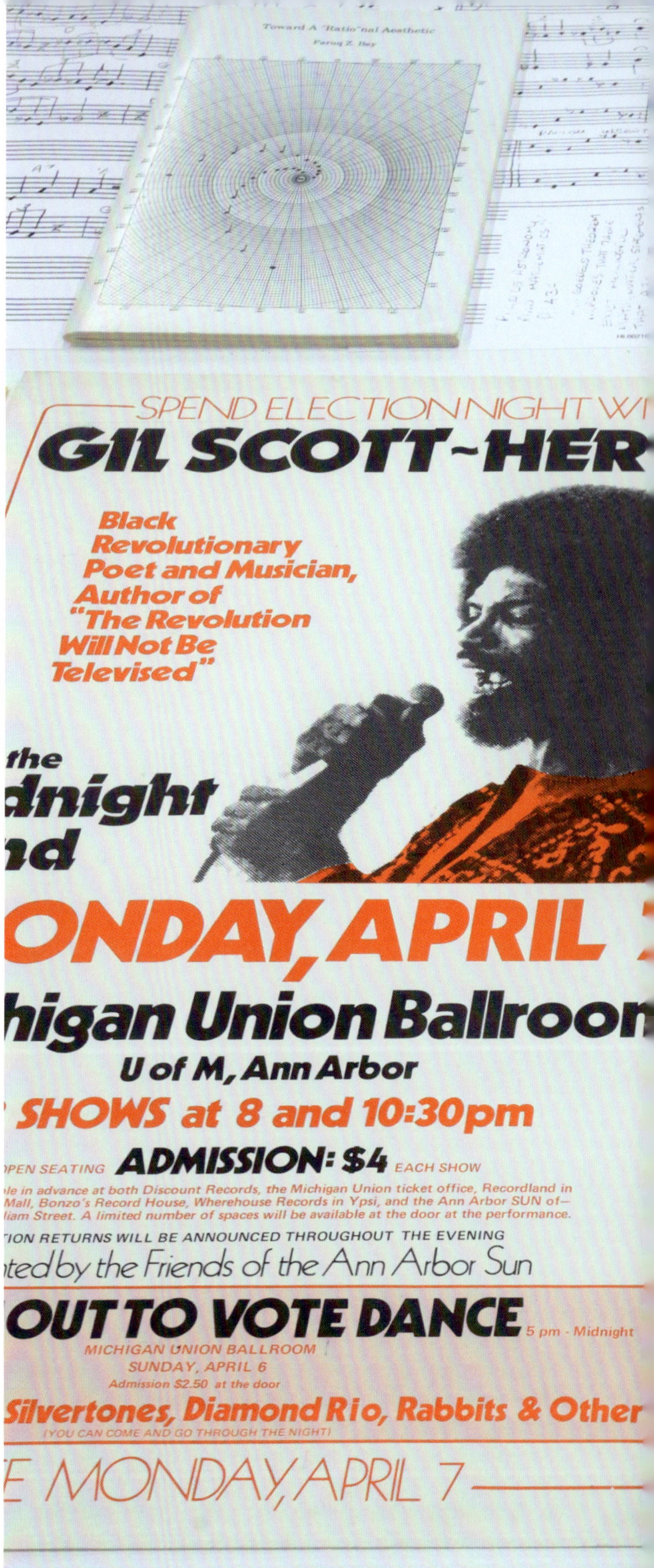

BLACK ARTS, FREE JAZZ, AND NEW DIRECTIONS IN ROCK

Materials courtesy Khalid el-Hakim / Black History 101 Mobile Museum, Morry Greener, Craig Huckaby, Bobby Hackney / Death, Mike Khoury / Entropy Stereo Recordings, MAHS Museum, VC Lamont Veasey / Black Merda

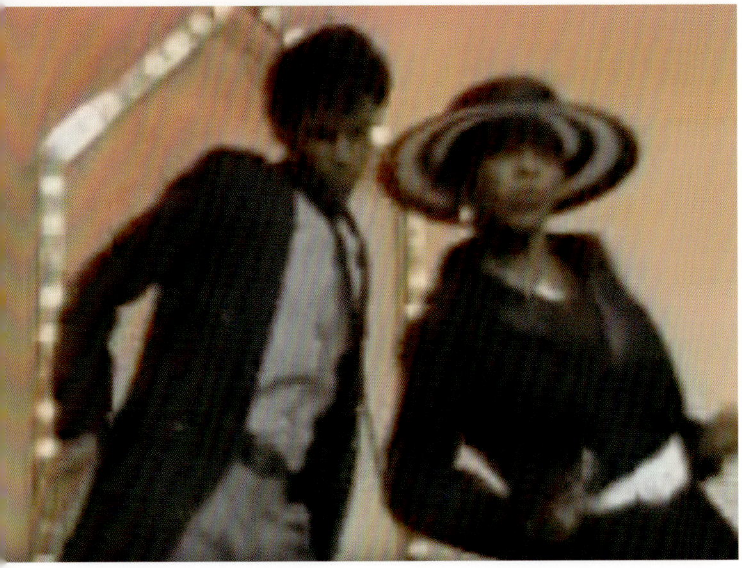

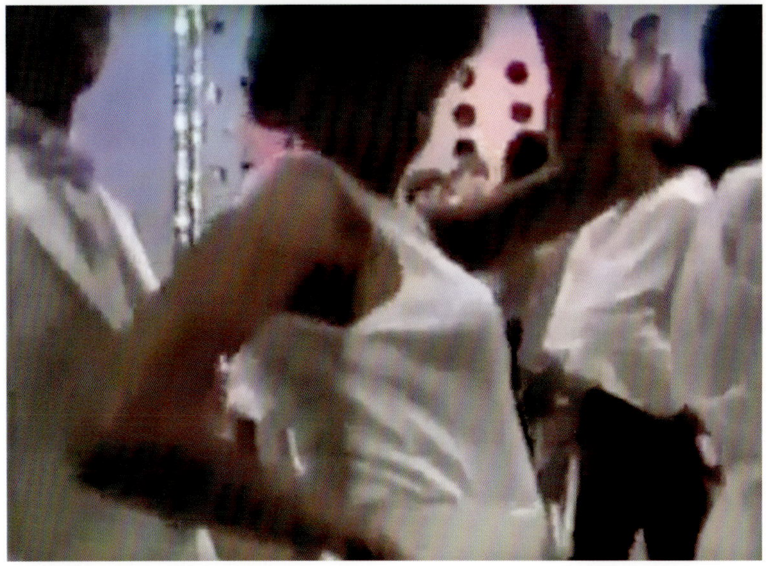

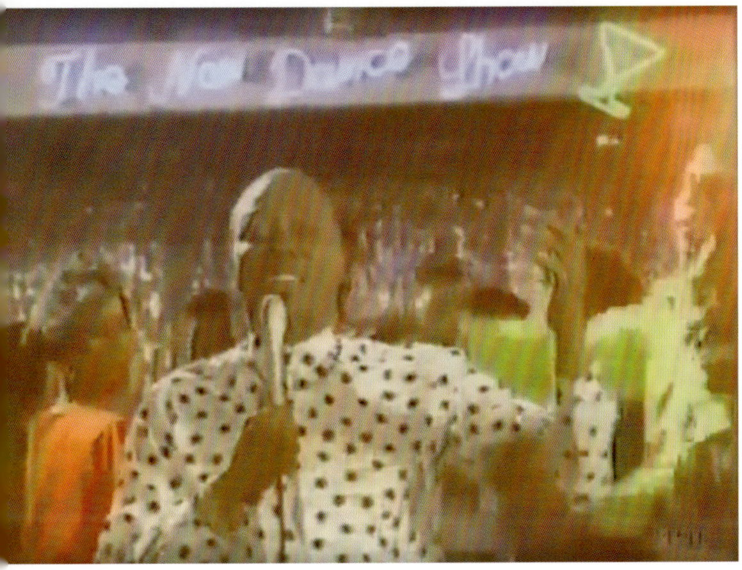
The New Dance Show

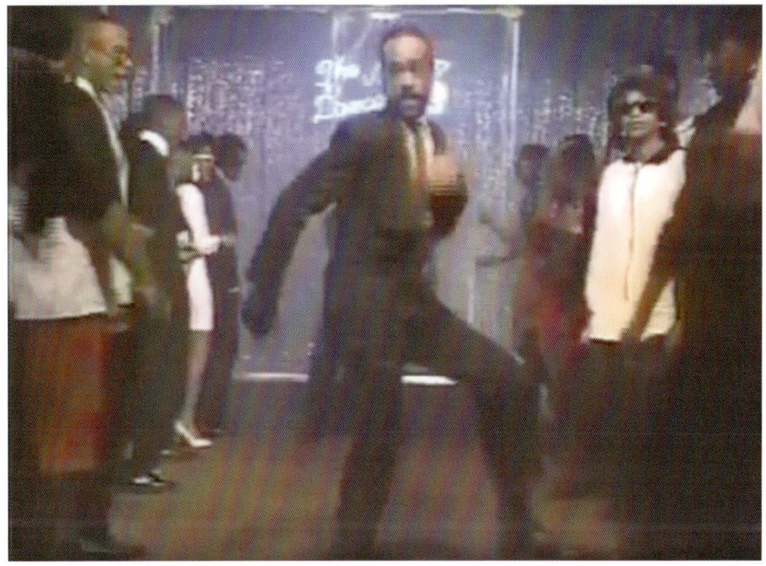

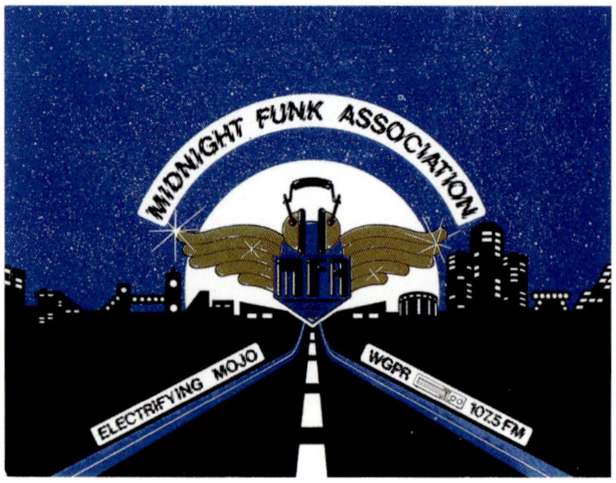

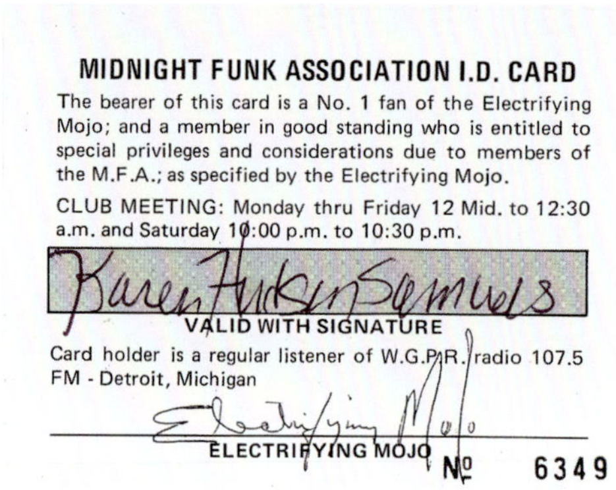
MIDNIGHT FUNK ASSOCIATION I.D. CARD

The bearer of this card is a No. 1 fan of the Electrifying Mojo; and a member in good standing who is entitled to special privileges and considerations due to members of the M.F.A.; as specified by the Electrifying Mojo.

CLUB MEETING: Monday thru Friday 12 Mid. to 12:30 a.m. and Saturday 10:00 p.m. to 10:30 p.m.

Karen Hudson Samuels

VALID WITH SIGNATURE

Card holder is a regular listener of W.G.P.R. radio 107.5 FM - Detroit, Michigan

Electrifying Mojo

ELECTRIFYING MOJO Nº 6349

"Midnight Funk Association" ID card, courtesy Karen Hudson Samuels

THE ELECTRIFYING MOJO

"All members of the Midnight Funk Association, please rise." With these words cult radio personality The Electrifying Mojo summoned a legion of devoted fans throughout metro Detroit. His nightly show ran on WGPR from 1977 to 1982 and on various stations through the 1990s. Mojo famously played what he liked, not what established radio formats demanded. His mixes ranged from George Clinton to Kraftwerk, Prince to the B-52s to Cybotron, and he played deep cuts and entire albums, not just the hits. The show's eclecticism and extended temporality were hugely influential to Detroit techno, as were Mojo's visionary, sci-fi persona, his positivity, and messages of solidarity. Each show began with "the landing of the mothership," his descent to Earth, inspired by Parliament's 1975 album *Mothership Connection*.

Courtesy The Electrifying Mojo and WGPR-TV Historical Society

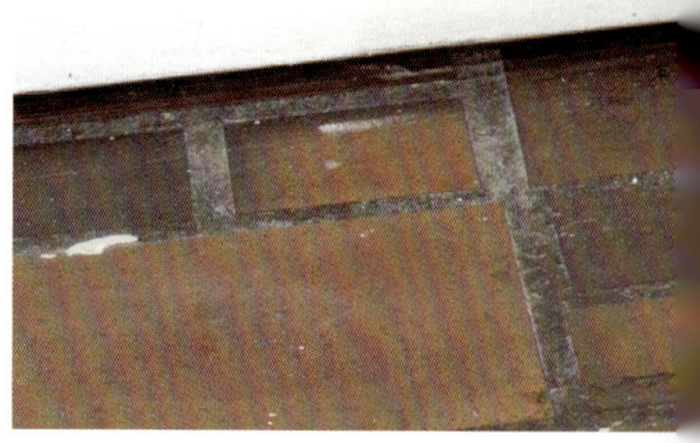

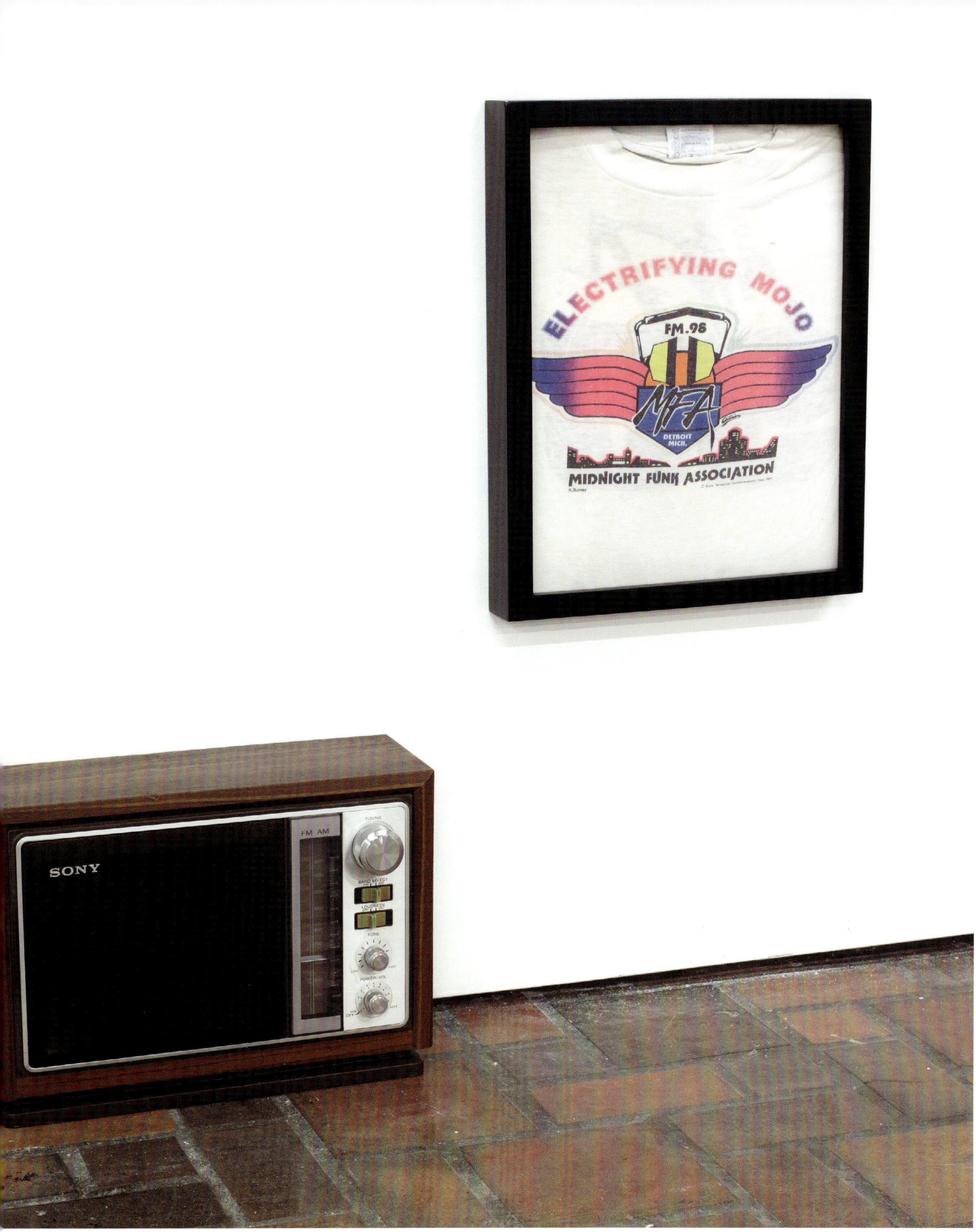
ELECTRIFYING MOJO
FM.98
MFA
DETROIT MICH.
MIDNIGHT FUNK ASSOCIATION
SONY
FM AM
TUNING
TONE

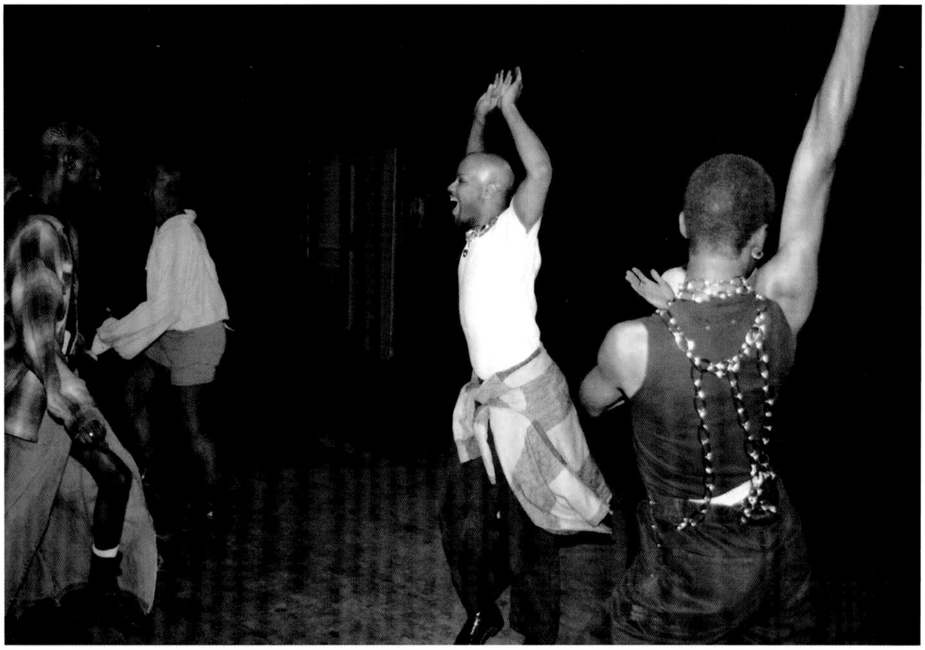
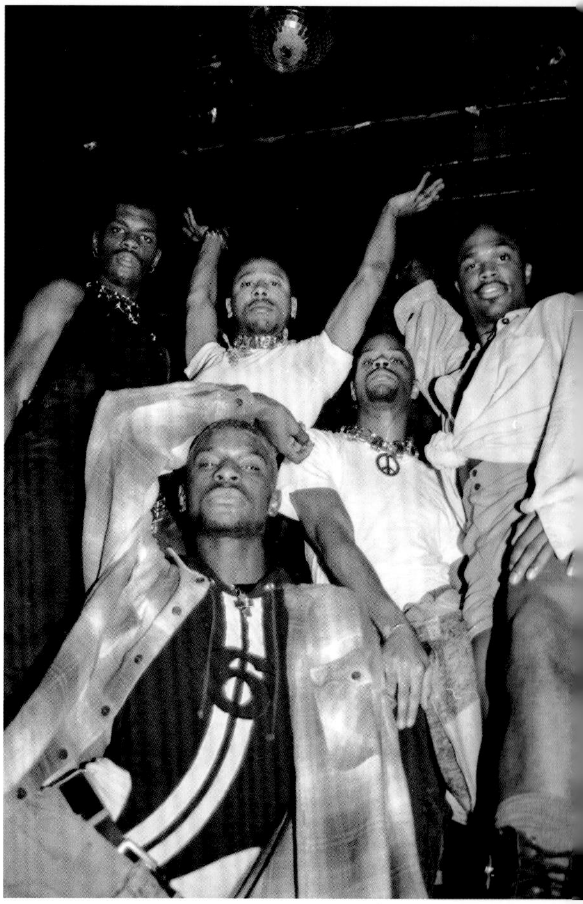
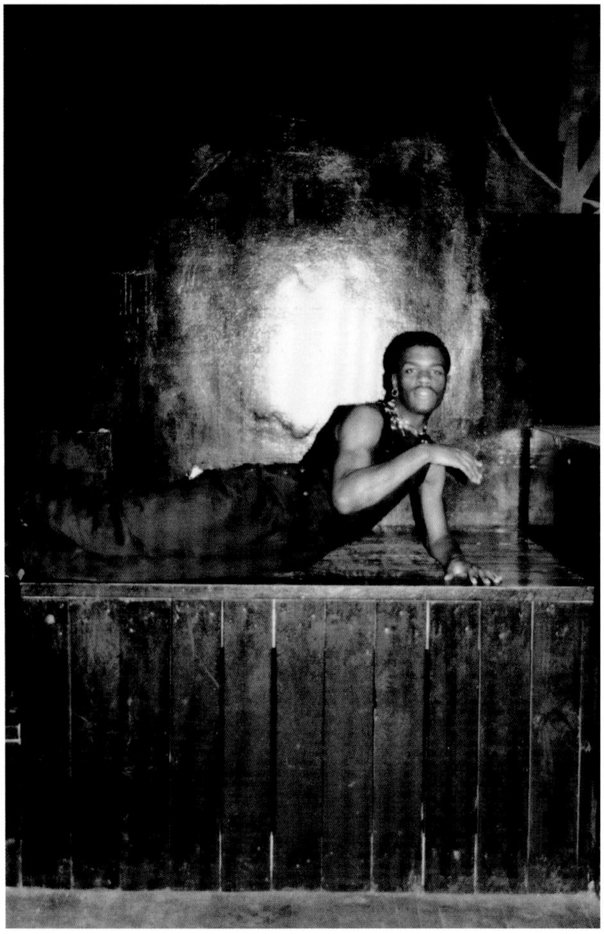
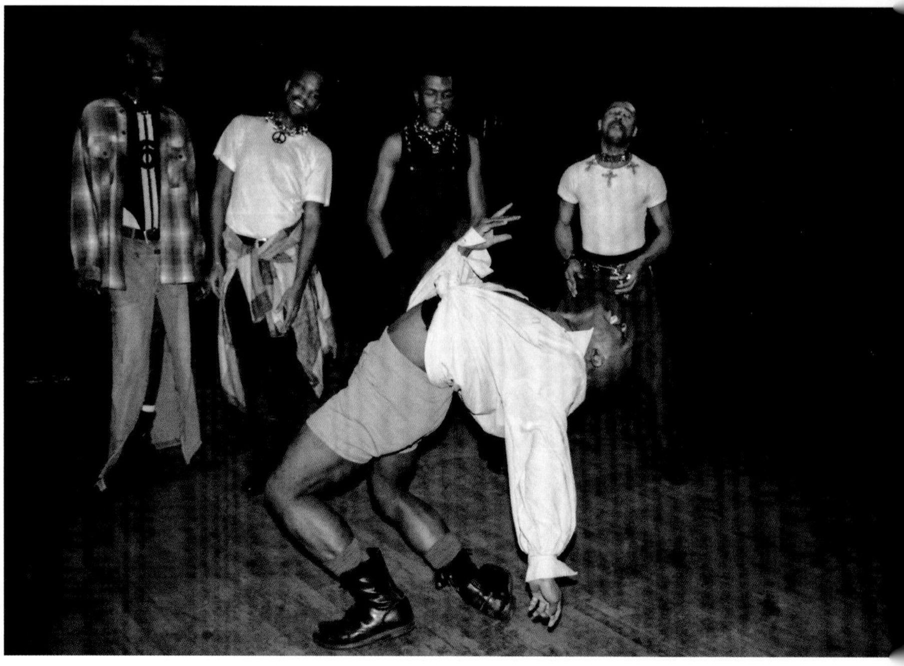

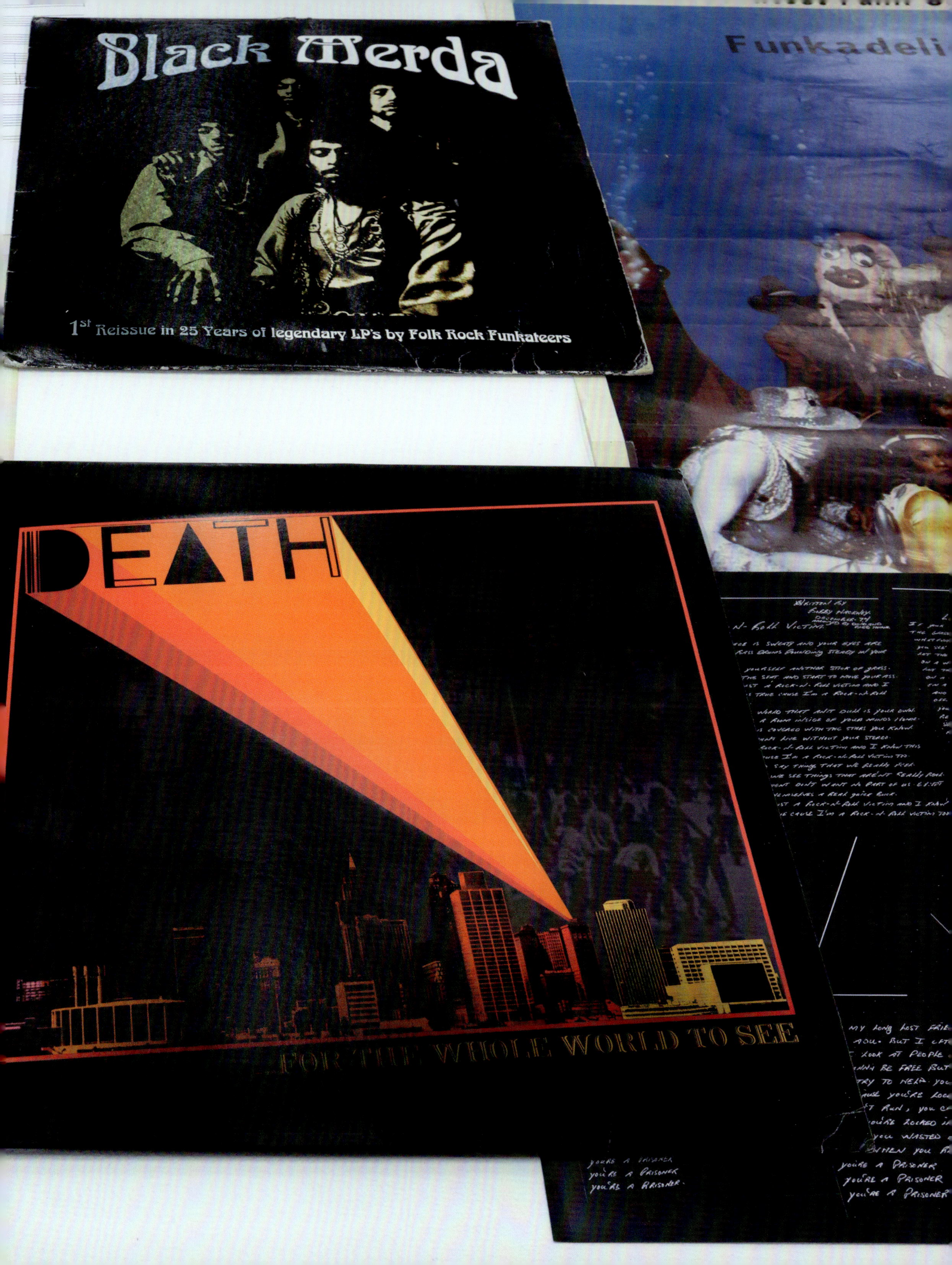
Black Merda
1st Reissue in 25 Years of legendary LP's by Folk Rock Funkateers
DEATH
FOR THE WHOLE WORLD TO SEE
you're a Prisoner
you're a Prisoner
you're a Prisoner

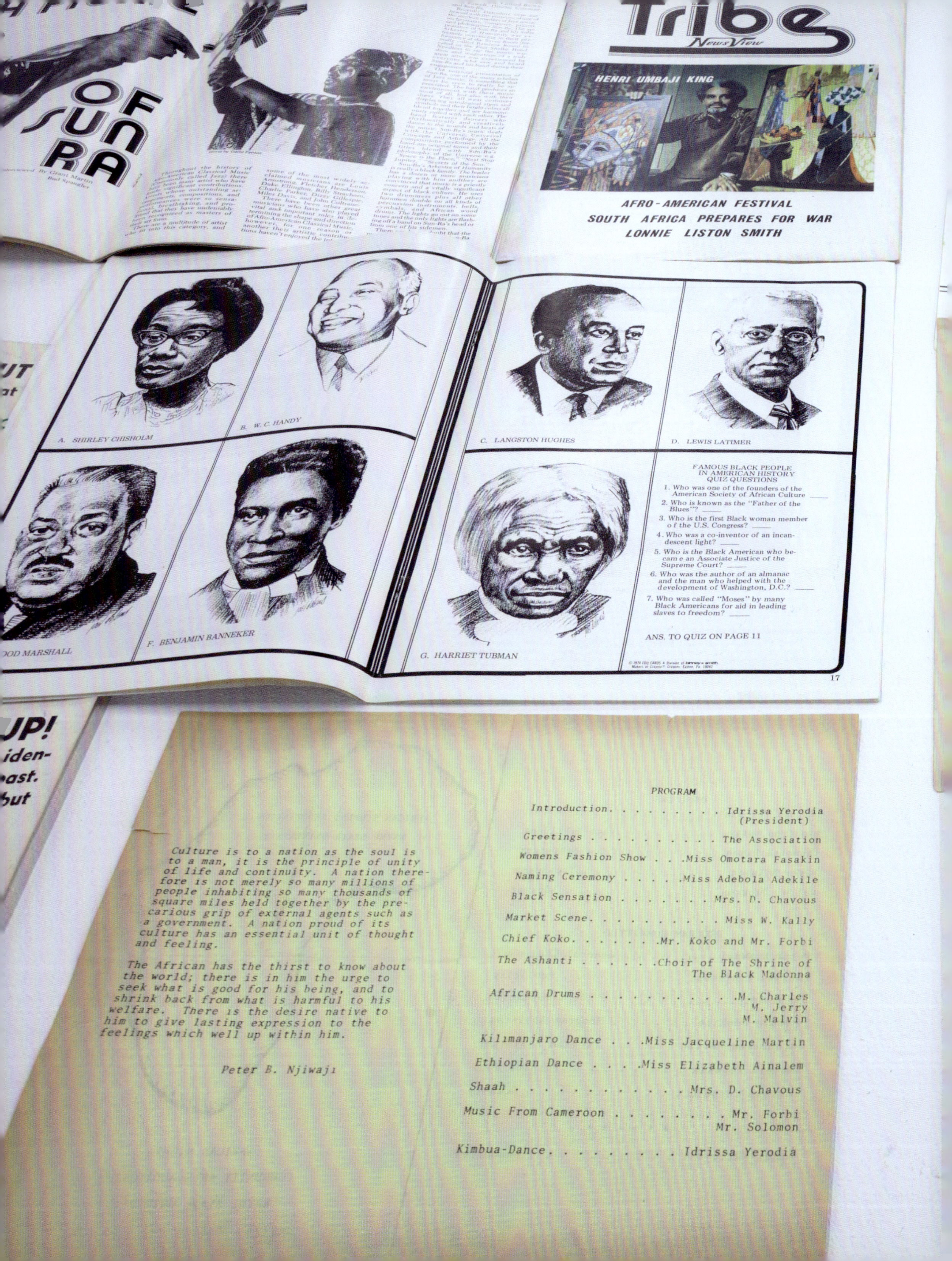
OF SUN RA
Interviewed By Grant Martin
Bud Spangler
Tribe
News View
HENRI UMBAJI KING
AFRO-AMERICAN FESTIVAL
SOUTH AFRICA PREPARES FOR WAR
LONNIE LISTON SMITH
A. SHIRLEY CHISHOLM
B. W. C. HANDY
C. LANGSTON HUGHES
D. LEWIS LATIMER
OOD MARSHALL
F. BENJAMIN BANNEKER
G. HARRIET TUBMAN
FAMOUS BLACK PEOPLE IN AMERICAN HISTORY QUIZ QUESTIONS
1. Who was one of the founders of the American Society of African Culture ____
2. Who is known as the "Father of the Blues"? ____
3. Who is the first Black woman member of the U.S. Congress? ____
4. Who was a co-inventor of an incandescent light? ____
5. Who is the Black American who became an Associate Justice of the Supreme Court? ____
6. Who was the author of an almanac and the man who helped with the development of Washington, D.C.? ____
7. Who was called "Moses" by many Black Americans for aid in leading slaves to freedom? ____
ANS. TO QUIZ ON PAGE 11
17
Culture is to a nation as the soul is to a man, it is the principle of unity of life and continuity. A nation therefore is not merely so many millions of people inhabiting so many thousands of square miles held together by the precarious grip of external agents such as a government. A nation proud of its culture has an essential unit of thought and feeling.
The African has the thirst to know about the world; there is in him the urge to seek what is good for his being, and to shrink back from what is harmful to his welfare. There is the desire native to him to give lasting expression to the feelings which well up within him.
Peter B. Njiwaji
PROGRAM
Introduction. . . . . Idrissa Yerodia (President)
Greetings . . . . The Association
Womens Fashion Show . . .Miss Omotara Fasakin
Naming Ceremony . . . . .Miss Adebola Adekile
Black Sensation . . . . Mrs. D. Chavous
Market Scene. . . . . Miss W. Kally
Chief Koko. . . . . . .Mr. Koko and Mr. Forbi
The Ashanti . . . . . .Choir of The Shrine of The Black Madonna
African Drums . . . . .M. Charles
M. Jerry
M. Malvin
Kilimanjaro Dance . . .Miss Jacqueline Martin
Ethiopian Dance . . . .Miss Elizabeth Ainalem
Shaah . . . . Mrs. D. Chavous
Music From Cameroon . . . . Mr. Forbi
Mr. Solomon
Kimbua-Dance. . . . . Idrissa Yerodia

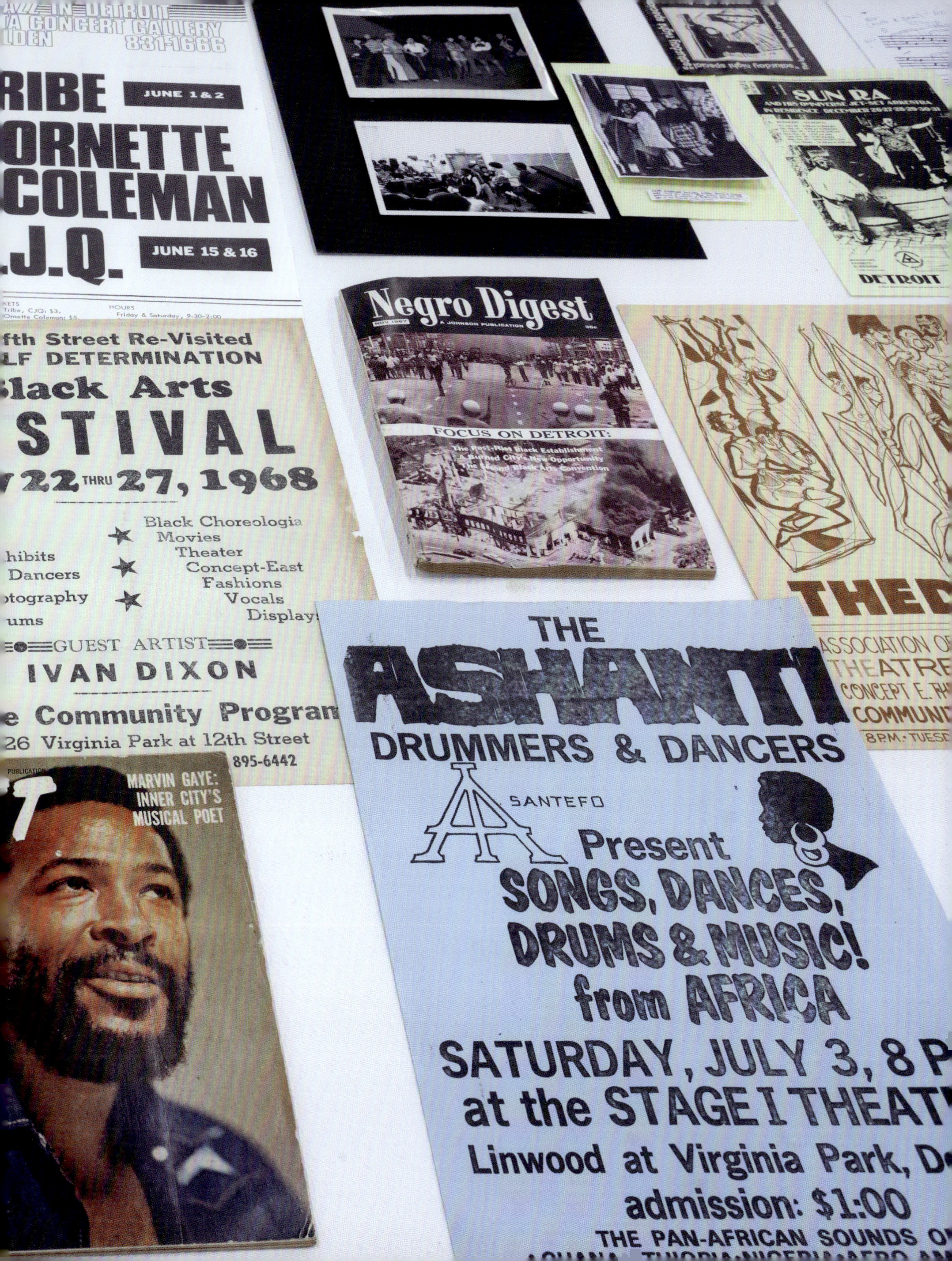

TRIBE
JUNE 1 & 2
ORNETTE COLEMAN
C.J.Q.
JUNE 15 & 16
831-1666
Negro Digest
A JOHNSON PUBLICATION
FOCUS ON DETROIT:
The Post-Riot Black Establishment
A Burned City's New Opportunity
The Second Black Arts Convention
SUN RA
DETROIT
Street Re-Visited
DETERMINATION
Black Arts
STIVAL
22 THRU 27, 1968
Black Choreologia
Movies
Theater
Concept-East
Fashions
Vocals
Displays
Dancers
hibits
otography
ums
GUEST ARTIST
IVAN DIXON
Community Program
26 Virginia Park at 12th Street
895-6442
MARVIN GAYE:
INNER CITY'S
MUSICAL POET
THE
ASHANTI
DRUMMERS & DANCERS
SANTEFO
Present
SONGS, DANCES,
DRUMS & MUSIC!
from AFRICA
SATURDAY, JULY 3, 8 P
at the STAGE I THEAT
Linwood at Virginia Park, D
admission: $1:00
THE PAN-AFRICAN SOUNDS O
ASSOCIATION OF
THEATRE
CONCEPT E. TH
COMMUNIT
8 PM · TUES

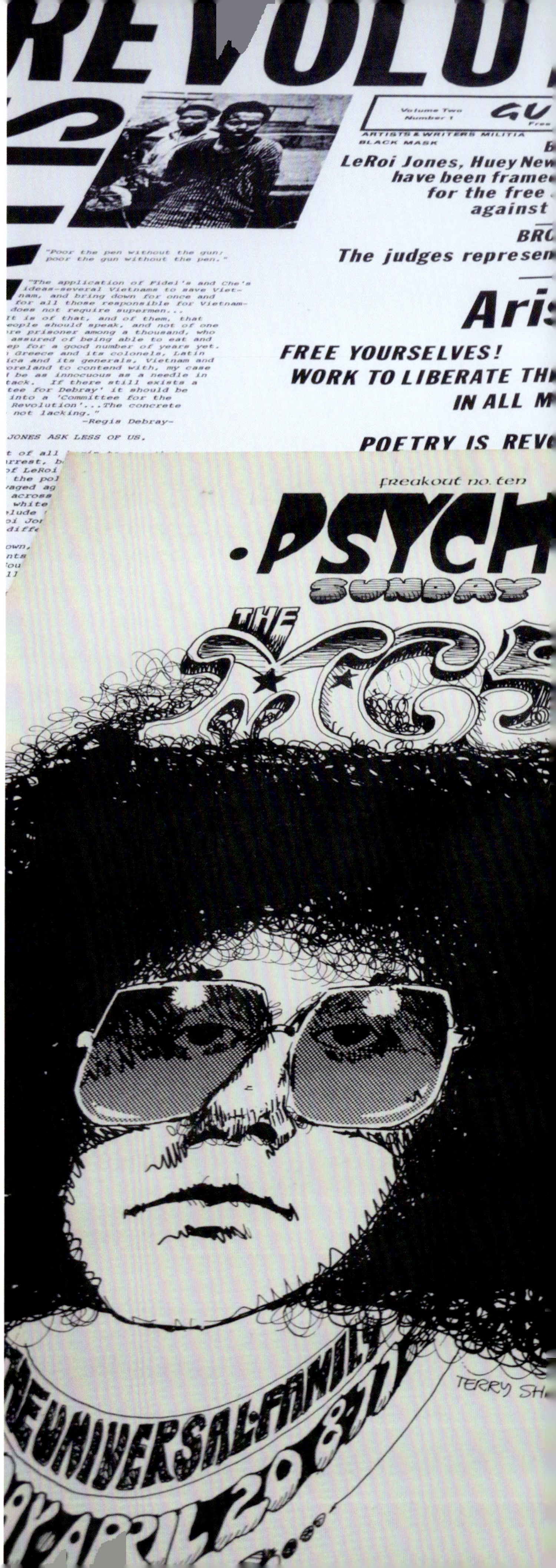

1960S-70S
RADICAL CULTURAL POLITICS

Materials courtesy Black & Red Books, Ben Blackwell, Khalid el-Hakim/Black History 101 Mobile Museum, Morry Greener, Hello Records, and Peter Werbe

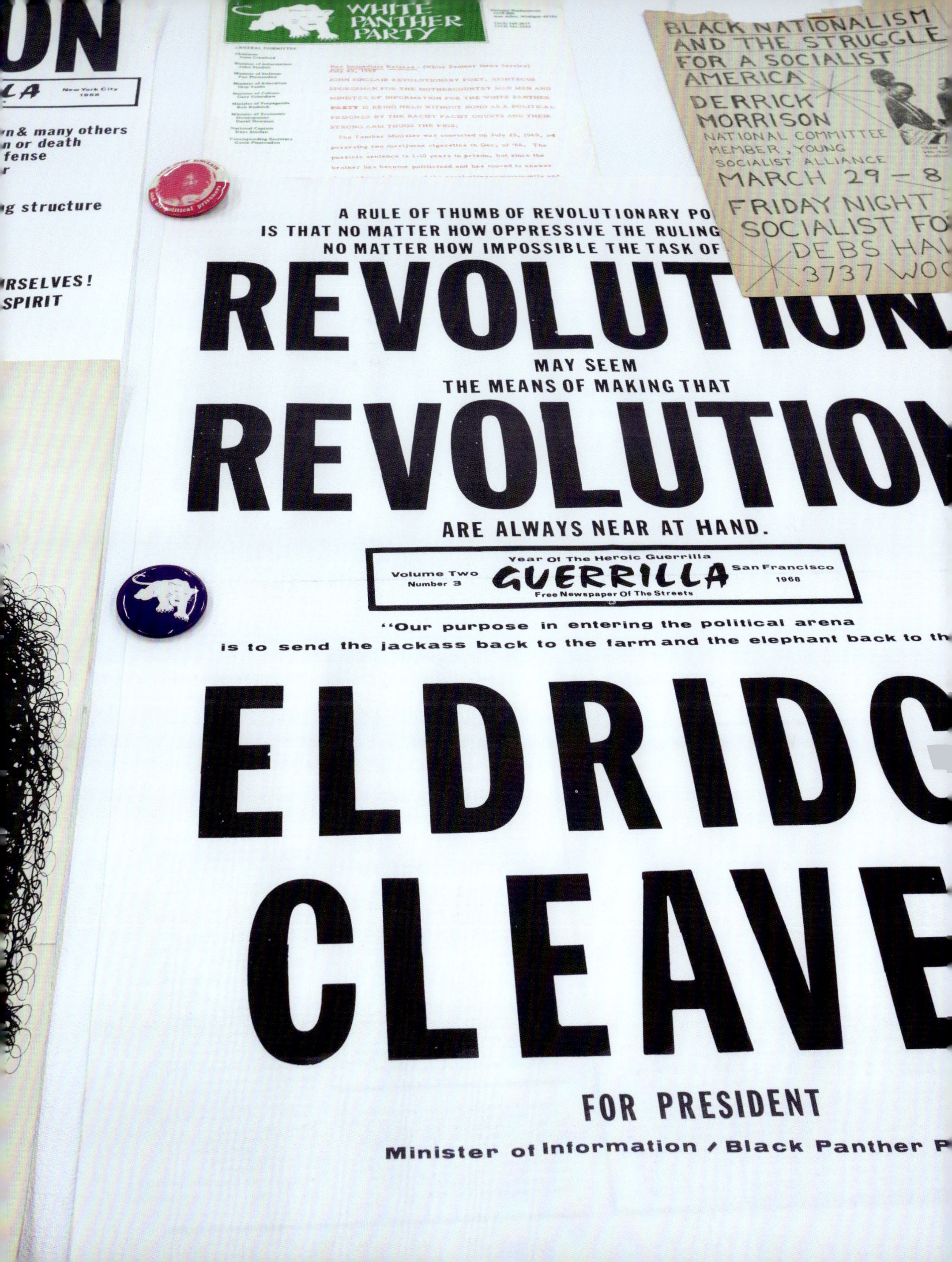
WHITE PANTHER PARTY
BLACK NATIONALISM AND THE STRUGGLE FOR A SOCIALIST AMERICA
DERRICK MORRISON
NATIONAL COMMITTEE MEMBER, YOUNG SOCIALIST ALLIANCE
MARCH 29 – 8
FRIDAY NIGHT SOCIALIST FO
DEBS HA
3737 WO
A RULE OF THUMB OF REVOLUTIONARY PO
IS THAT NO MATTER HOW OPPRESSIVE THE RULING
NO MATTER HOW IMPOSSIBLE THE TASK OF
REVOLUTI
MAY SEEM
THE MEANS OF MAKING THAT
REVOLUTIO
ARE ALWAYS NEAR AT HAND.
Year Of The Heroic Guerrilla
Volume Two Number 3
GUERRILLA
Free Newspaper Of The Streets
San Francisco 1968
"Our purpose in entering the political arena
is to send the jackass back to the farm and the elephant back to th
ELDRIDG
CLEAVE
FOR PRESIDENT
Minister of Information / Black Panther P
New York City 1968
n & many others
n or death
fense
g structure
RSELVES!
SPIRIT

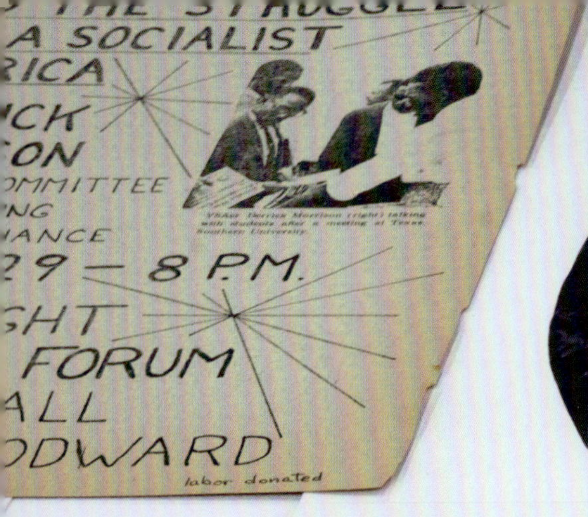

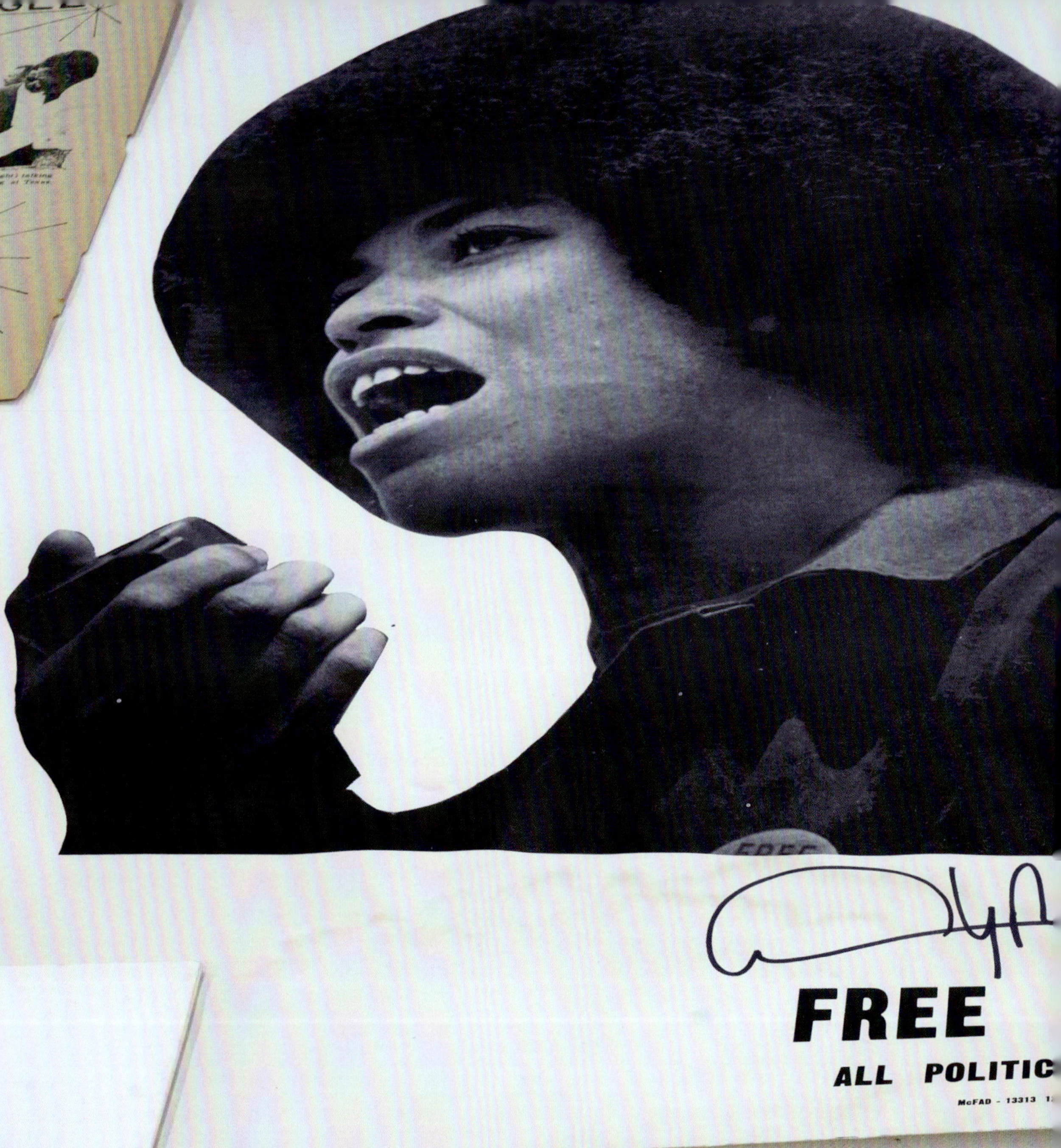

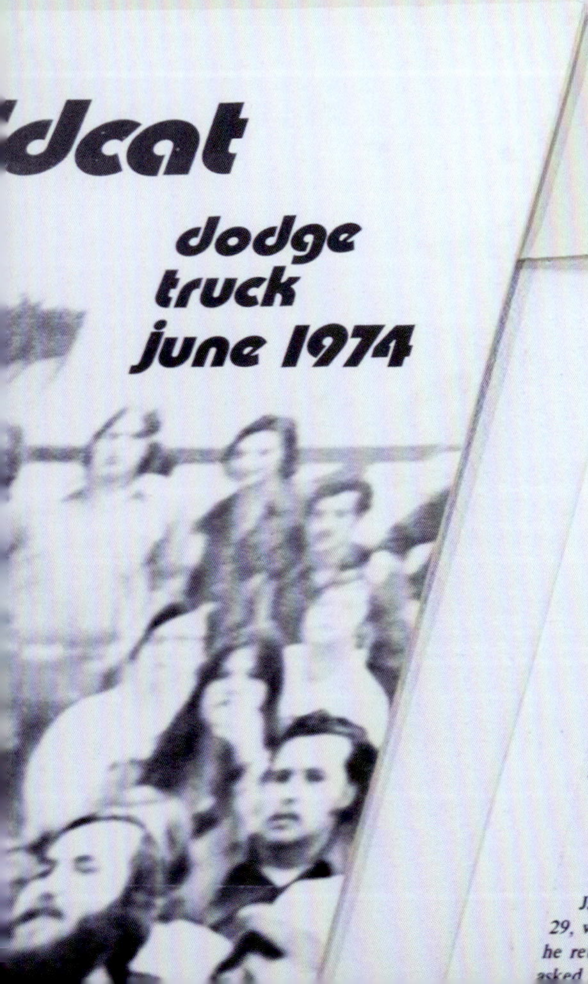

James Johnson is not a worldly man, but he is a man of honor, a gentle man, a man with pride, a man with respect for himself and his fellow men, He is an exceptionally quiet man, one who usually keeps to himself. He is not a man whom you would generally see at parties or in bars. A man who, until now, was without violence in his life. But what circumstances caused a man, much like you and me, a man know for his extreme kindness, to now be charged with the shooting deaths of three men?

James Johnson had beer employed at the Eldon Avenue Gear and Axle Plant for two years. Like other Black workers there, he had to put up with the daily harassments by racist foremen, the lack of proper safety conditions, and the backbreaking and dangerous work. In addition, James was singled out for special harassment because of the fact that he rarely laughed or smiled while on the job. He would be put on certain jobs and given no instruction. Then the foremen would stand around watching him. hoping that he would make a mistake so that they could fire him. But James rarely, if ever, made mistakes on the job. So the supervisors evidently decided that since he was not dumb, he must be a potential troublemaker, and they kept him under constant surveillance.

In May of 1970, James was involved in an automobile accident. His car was a total loss, and the back, neck, and head injuries which he suffered as a result of the accident caused him to undergo treatment twice a week. Because of the seriousness of his injuries, James Johnson's doctor advised him not to go back to work. When James went to get his insurance papers and to tell Chrysler Corporation details of these injuries

he was sent to anovercrowded "Industrial Clinc" where he was hardly even examined. And, in the same way that Chrysler did Sister Mamie Williams, which by ordering her off her hospital bed sent her to her death, they sent James a telegram ordering him back to work immediately. They refused to give him disability payments for the five days he was off the job. Then they sent him a registered letter stating that his insurance had been cancelled. From that time on he was forced to work without any insurance whatsoever.

But James Johnson is you and me. What drove James Johnson to the breaking point?

James was scheduled for vacation on June 1, 1970. The date was posted on the bulletin board. On May 29, which was a Friday, James had "his" foreman sign his time card, and left on vacation after work. When he returned to work on schedule, he noticed that his time card had been pulled from the rack. When he asked the foreman why, the foreman would just shrug his shoulders and walk away. James was forced to

Joh
day
U.S
"ju
poi

JAM

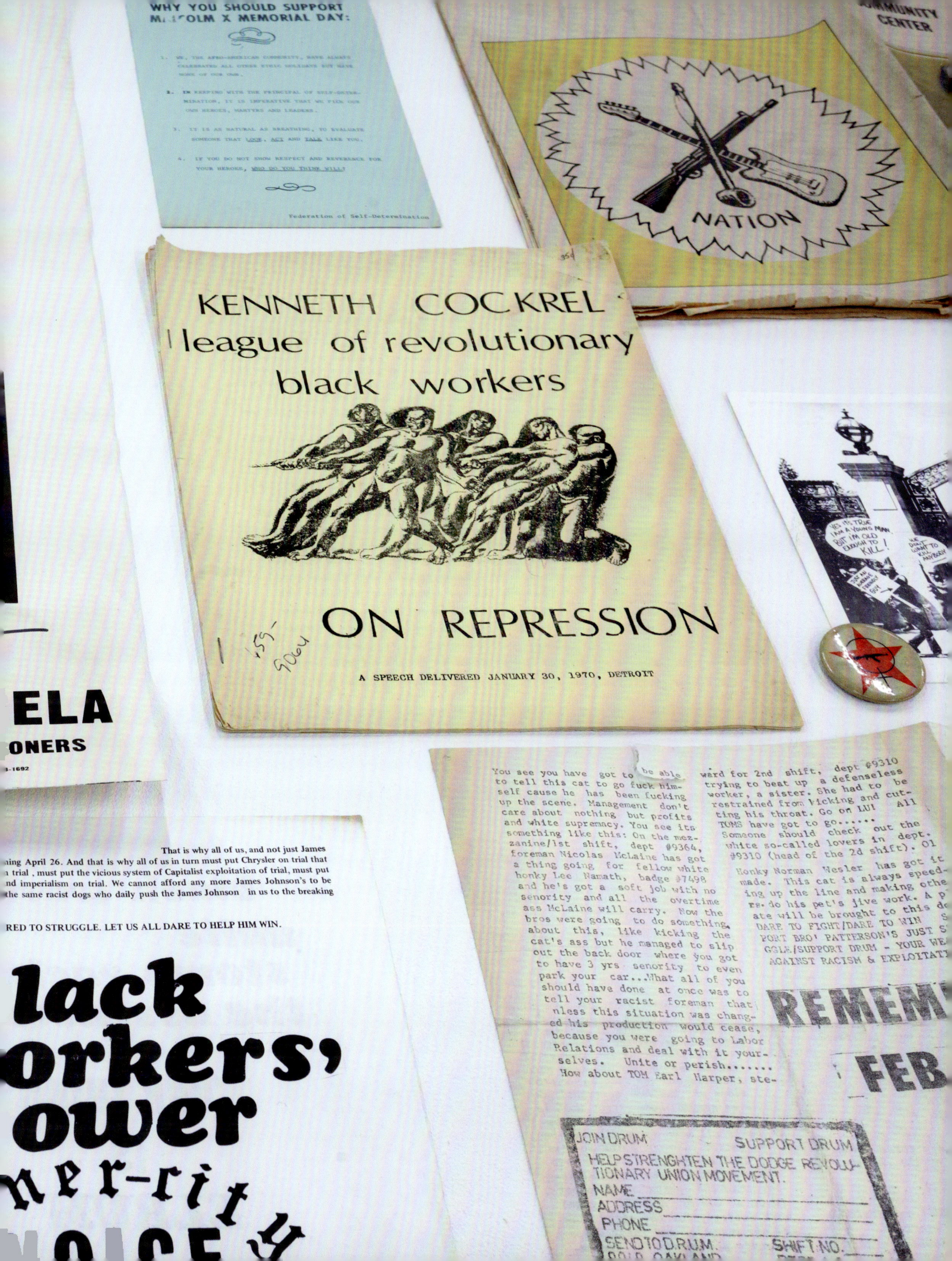

WHY YOU SHOULD SUPPORT
MALCOLM X MEMORIAL DAY:
Federation of Self-Determination
NATION
KENNETH COCKREL
league of revolutionary
black workers
ON REPRESSION
A SPEECH DELIVERED JANUARY 30, 1970, DETROIT
ELA
ONERS
That is why all of us, and not just James
ning April 26. And that is why all of us in turn must put Chrysler on trial that
n trial , must put the vicious system of Capitalist exploitation of trial, must put
nd imperialism on trial. We cannot afford any more James Johnson's to be
the same racist dogs who daily push the James Johnson in us to the breaking
RED TO STRUGGLE. LET US ALL DARE TO HELP HIM WIN.
lack
orkers'
ower
You see you have got to be able
to tell this cat to go fuck him-
self cause he has been fucking
up the scene. Management don't
care about nothing but profits
and white supremacy. You see its
something like this: On the mez-
zanine/1st shift, dept #9364,
foreman Nicolas McLaine has got
a thing going for fellow white
honky Lee Namath, badge #7498
and he's got a soft job with no
senority and all the overtime
ass McLaine will carry. Now the
bros were going to do something
about this, like kicking the
cat's ass but he managed to slip
out the back door where you got
to have 3 yrs senority to even
park your car...What all of you
should have done at once was to
tell your racist foreman that
nless this situation was chang-
ed his production would cease,
because you were going to Labor
Relations and deal with it your-
selves. Unite or perish.......
How about TOM Earl Harper, ste-
ward for 2nd shift, dept #9310
trying to beat up a defenseless
worker, a sister. She had to be
restrained from kicking and cut-
ting his throat. Go on LU! All
TOMS have got to go......
Someone should check out the
white so-called lovers in dept.
#9310 (head of the 2d shift). Ol
Honky Norman Wesler has got it
made. This cat is always speed-
ing up the line and making othe
rs do his pet's jive work.
DARE TO FIGHT/DARE TO WIN
AGAINST RACISM & EXPLOITAT
REMEM
FEB
JOIN DRUM
SUPPORT DRUM
HELP STRENGHTEN THE DODGE REVOLU-
TIONARY UNION MOVEMENT.
NAME
ADDRESS
PHONE
SEND TO D.R.U.M.
SHIFT NO.

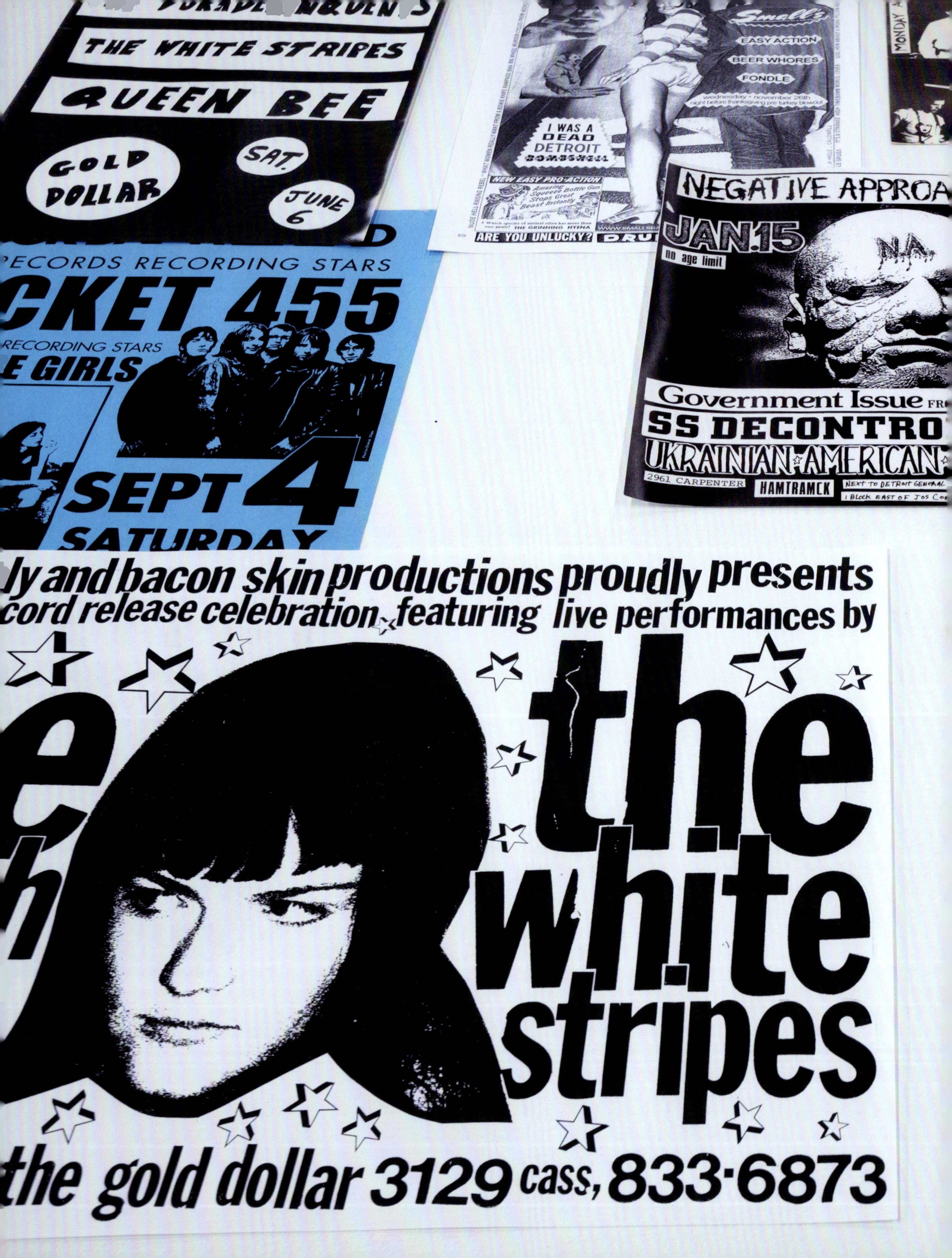
THE WHITE STRIPES
QUEEN BEE
GOLD DOLLAR
SAT.
JUNE 6
ECORDS RECORDING STARS
CKET 455
RECORDING STARS
E GIRLS
SEPT 4
SATURDAY
EASY ACTION
BEER WHORES
FONDLE
wednesday • november 26th
night before thanksgiving pre turkey blowout
I WAS A DEAD DETROIT BOMBSHELL
NEW EASY PRO-ACTION
Amazing Squeeze Bottle Gun Stops Great Beast Instantly
ARE YOU UNLUCKY?
NEGATIVE APPROA
JAN.15
no age limit
N.A.
Government Issue
SS DECONTRO
UKRAINIAN AMERICAN
2961 CARPENTER
HAMTRAMCK
NEXT TO DETROIT GENERAL
1 BLOCK EAST OF JOS CON
MONDAY
ly and bacon skin productions proudly presents
cord release celebration featuring live performances by
the white stripes
the gold dollar 3129 cass, 833-6873

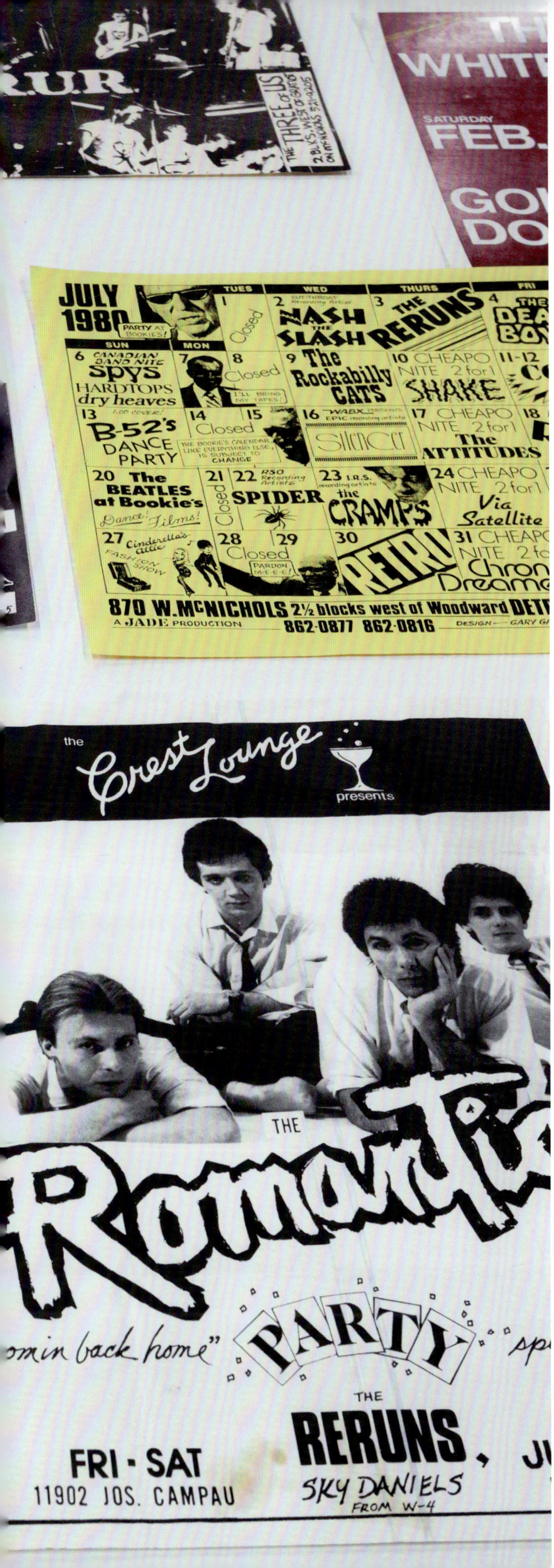

GARAGE AND PUNK FLYERS

Courtesy Ben Blackwell and T. M. Caldwell

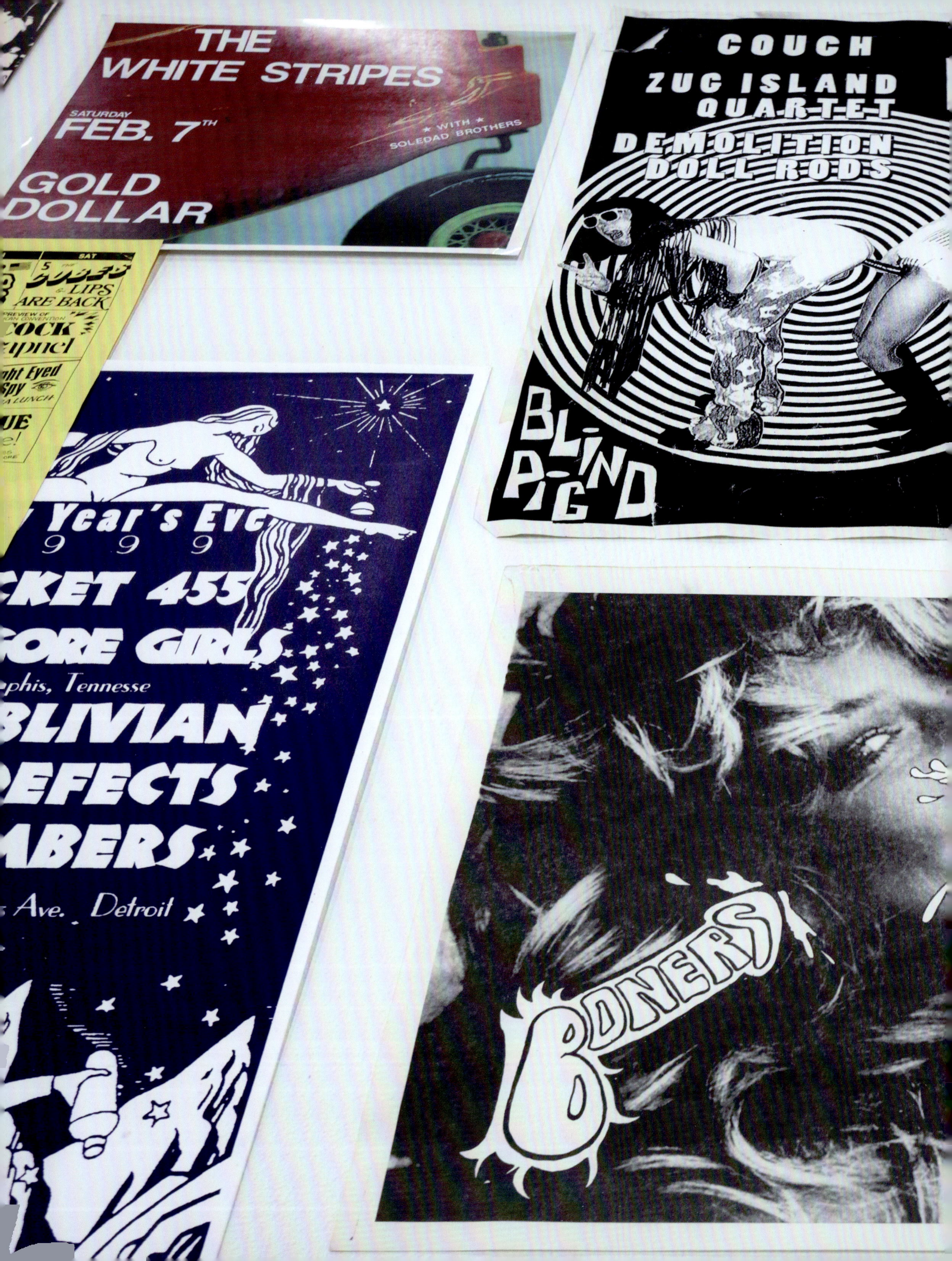
THE WHITE STRIPES
SATURDAY
FEB. 7TH
★ WITH ★
SOLEDAD BROTHERS
GOLD DOLLAR
COUCH
ZUG ISLAND QUARTET
DEMOLITION DOLL RODS
BLIND PIG
LIPS ARE BACK
Year's Eve
9 9 9
CKET 455
CORE GIRLS
phis, Tennessee
BLIVIAN
DEFECTS
ABERS
Ave. Detroit
BONERS

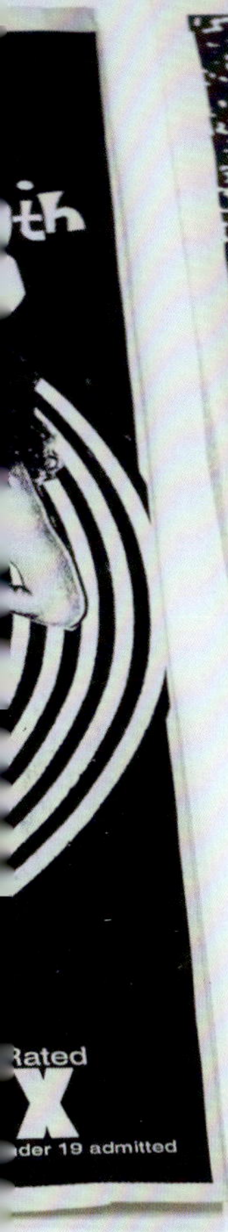
Rated
X

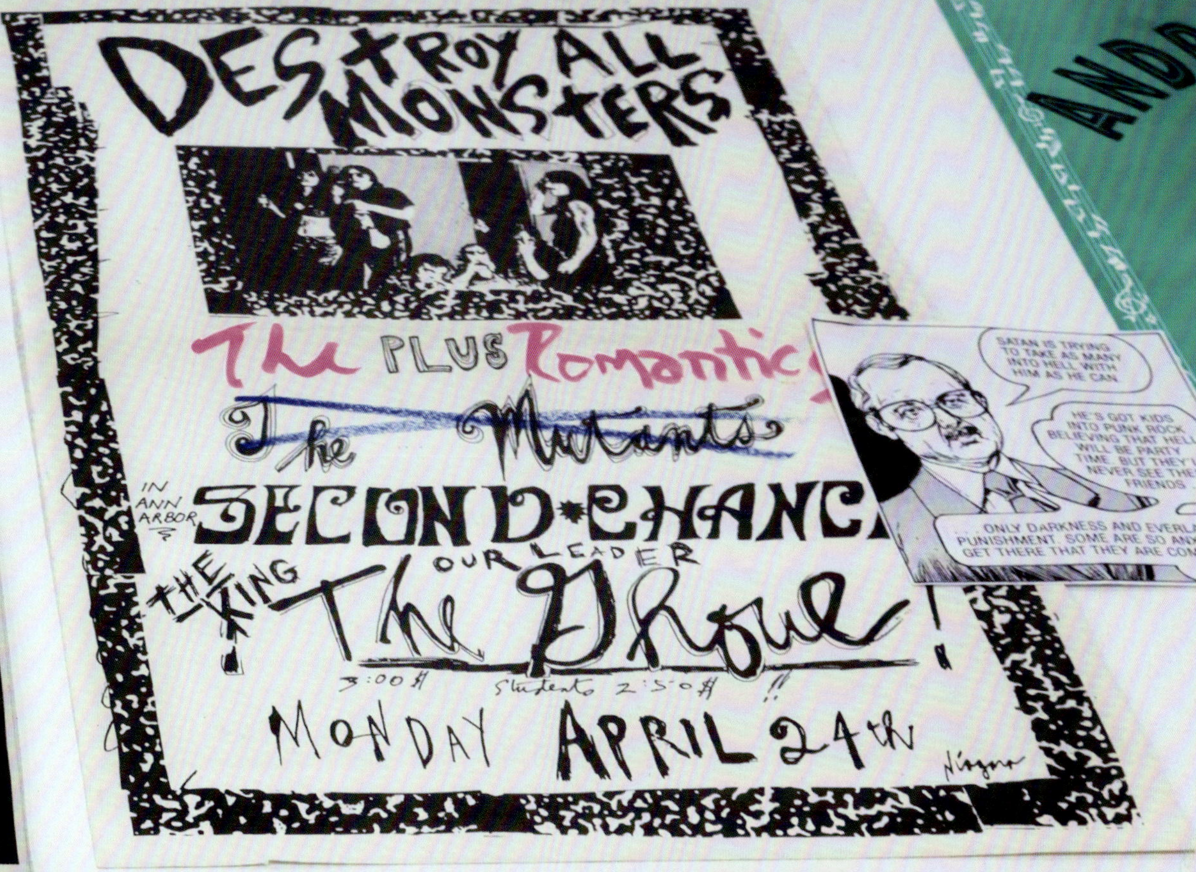
DESTROY ALL MONSTERS
The PLUS Romantics
The Mutants
IN ANN ARBOR
SECOND CHANC
THE KING OUR LEADER
MONDAY APRIL 24th
SATAN IS TRYING TO TAKE AS MANY INTO HELL WITH HIM AS HE CAN
HE'S GOT KIDS INTO PUNK ROCK BELIEVING THAT HELL WILL BE PARTY TIME. BUT THEY'LL NEVER SEE THEIR FRIENDS . . .
. . . ONLY DARKNESS AND EVERLASTING PUNISHMENT. SOME ARE SO ANXIOUS TO GET THERE THAT THEY ARE COMMITTING SUICIDE.

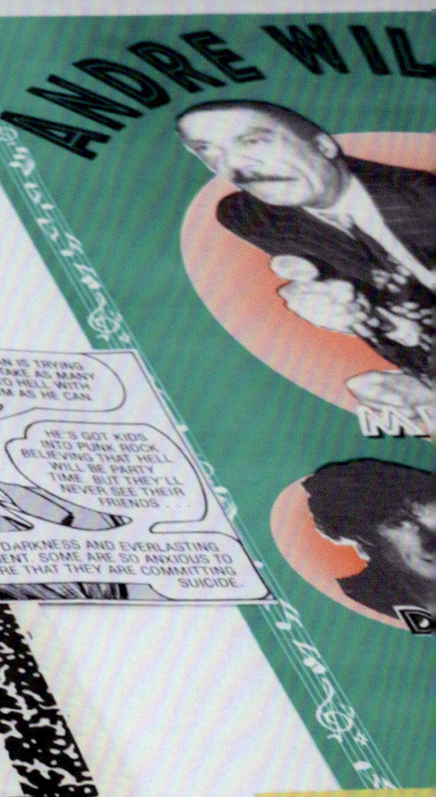
ANDRE WIL

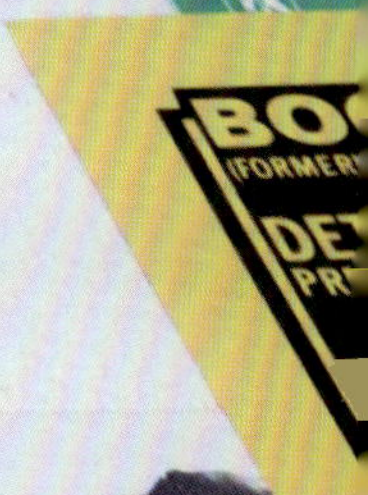

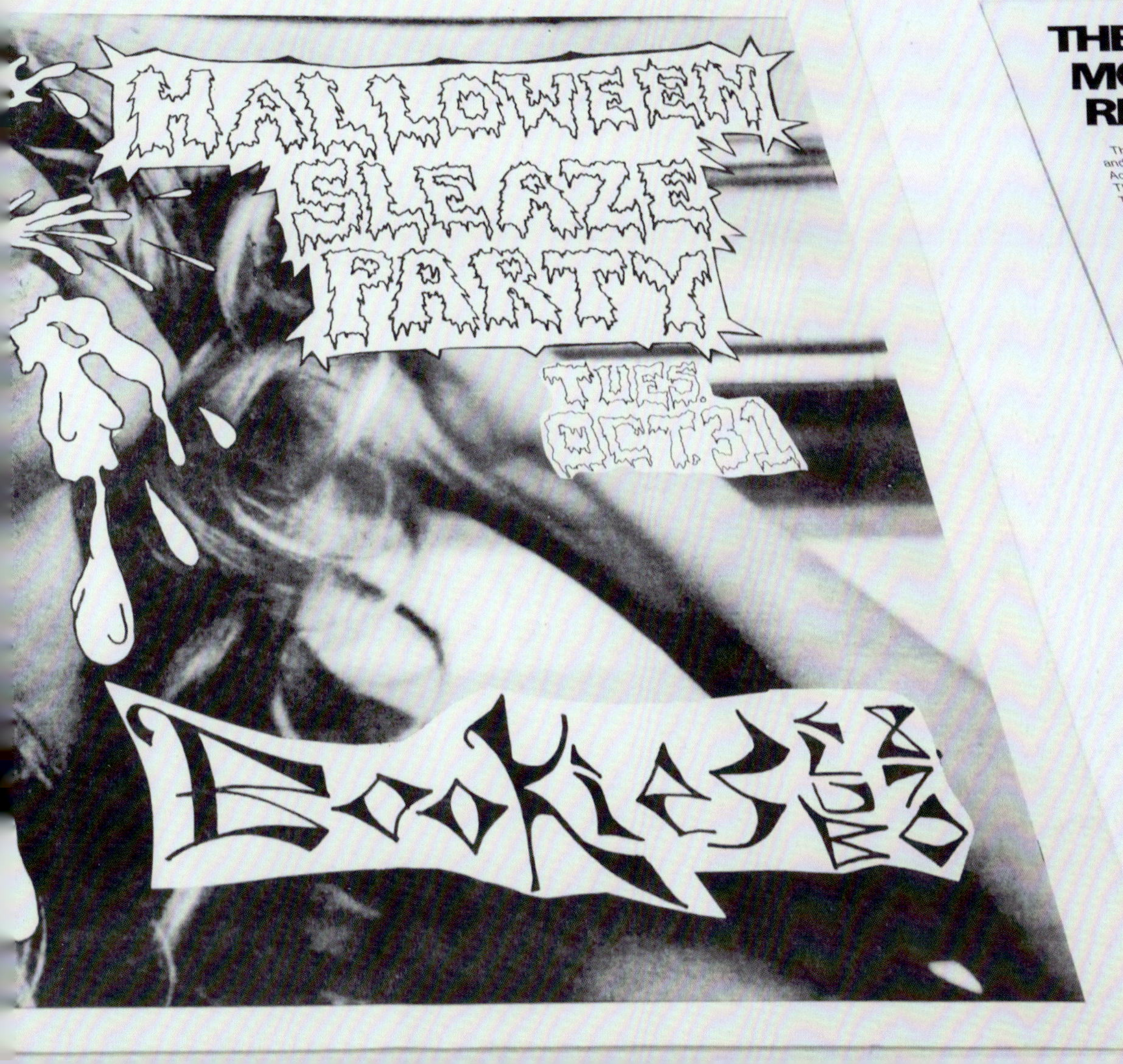
HALLOWEEN
SLEAZE
PARTY
TUES. OCT 31

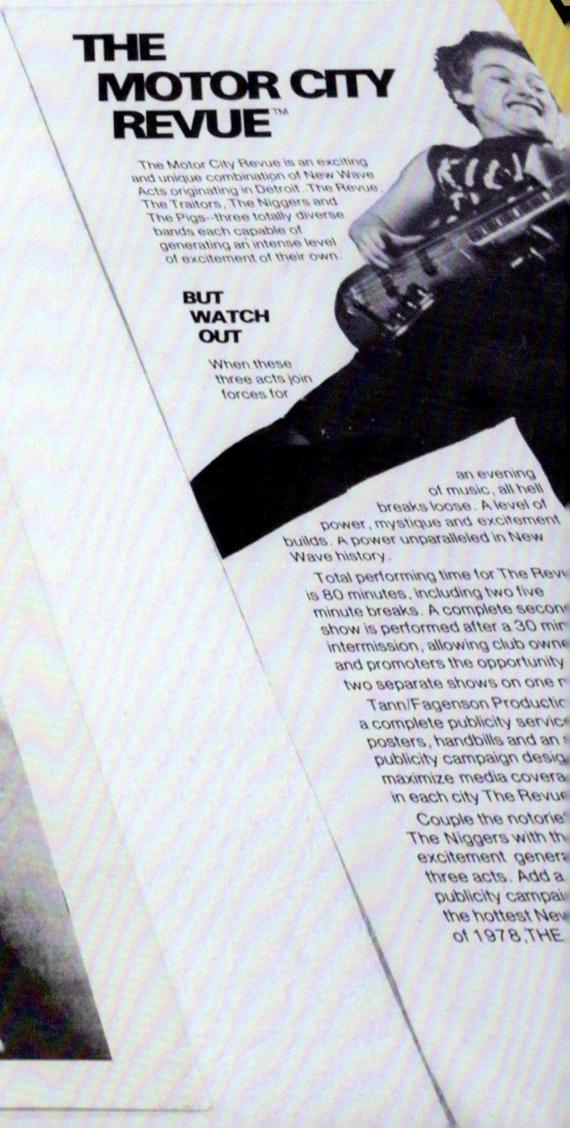
THE MOTOR CITY REVUE™
The Motor City Revue is an exciting and unique combination of New Wave Acts originating in Detroit. The Revue, The Traitors, The Niggers and The Pigs--three totally diverse bands each capable of generating an intense level of excitement of their own.
BUT WATCH OUT
When these three acts join forces for an evening of music, all hell breaks loose. A level of power, mystique and excitement builds. A power unparalleled in New Wave history.
Total performing time for The Rev
is 80 minutes, including two five
minute breaks. A complete secon
show is performed after a 30 mi
intermission, allowing club own
and promoters the opportunity
two separate shows on one
Tann/Fagenson Productio
a complete publicity servic
posters, handbills and an
publicity campaign desig
maximize media covera
in each city The Revue
Couple the notorie
The Niggers with th
excitement gener
three acts. Add a
publicity campa
the hottest Ne
of 1978, THE

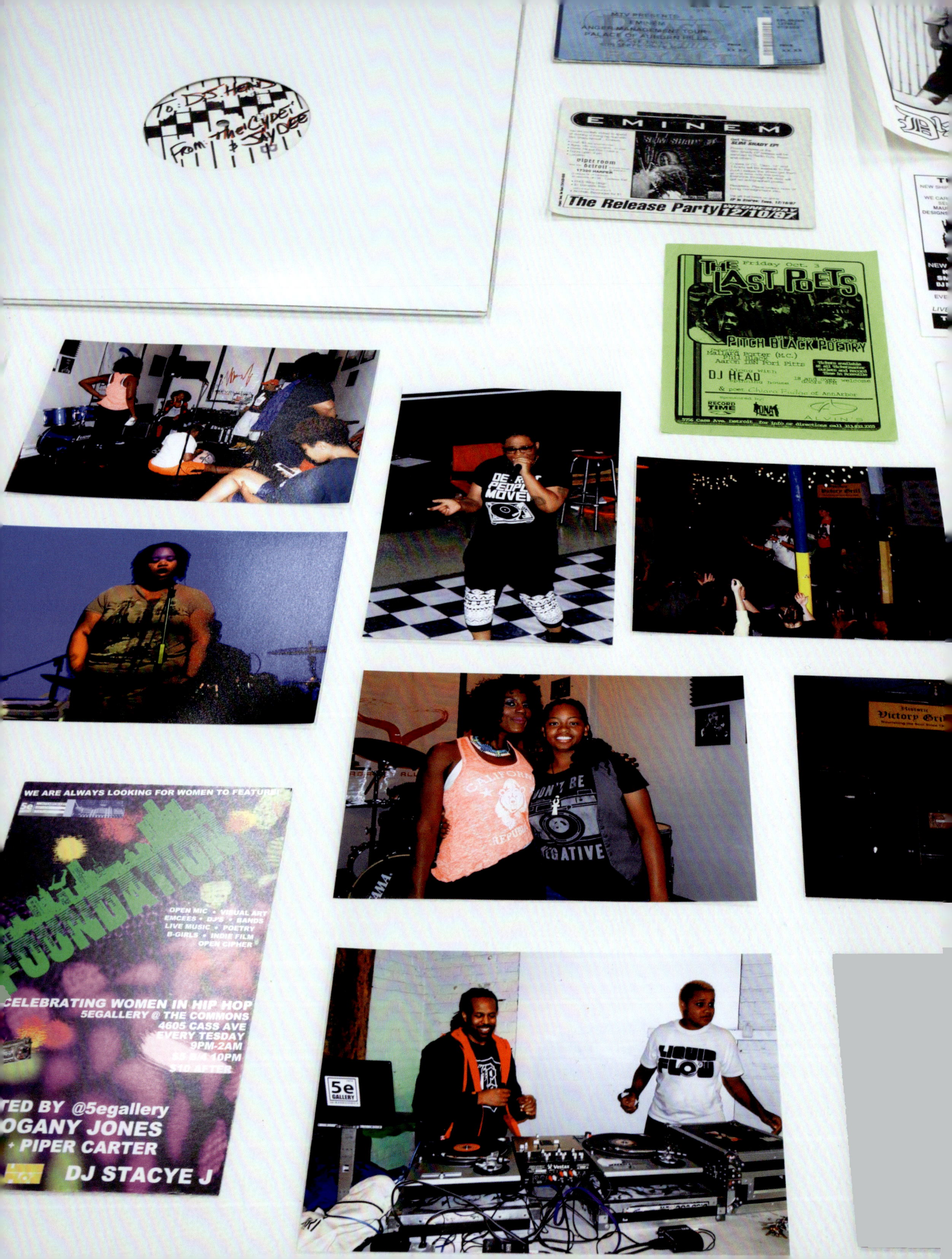

MTV PRESENTS
EMINEM
ANGER MANAGEMENT TOUR
PALACE OF AUBURN HILLS
To: DJ Head
From: The Cyde! & Jay Dee
EMINEM
The Release Party
WEDNESDAY 12/10/97
Friday Oct. 3
THE LAST POETS
PITCH BLACK POETRY
DJ HEAD
WE ARE ALWAYS LOOKING FOR WOMEN TO FEATURE!
FOUNDATION
OPEN MIC • VISUAL ART
EMCEES • DJ'S • BANDS
LIVE MUSIC • POETRY
B-GIRLS • INDIE FILM
OPEN CIPHER
CELEBRATING WOMEN IN HIP HOP
5EGALLERY @ THE COMMONS
4605 CASS AVE
EVERY TESDAY
9PM-2AM
$5 B4 10PM
$10 AFTER
TED BY @5egallery
OGANY JONES
+ PIPER CARTER
DJ STACYE J
5e GALLERY
Historic Victory Grill

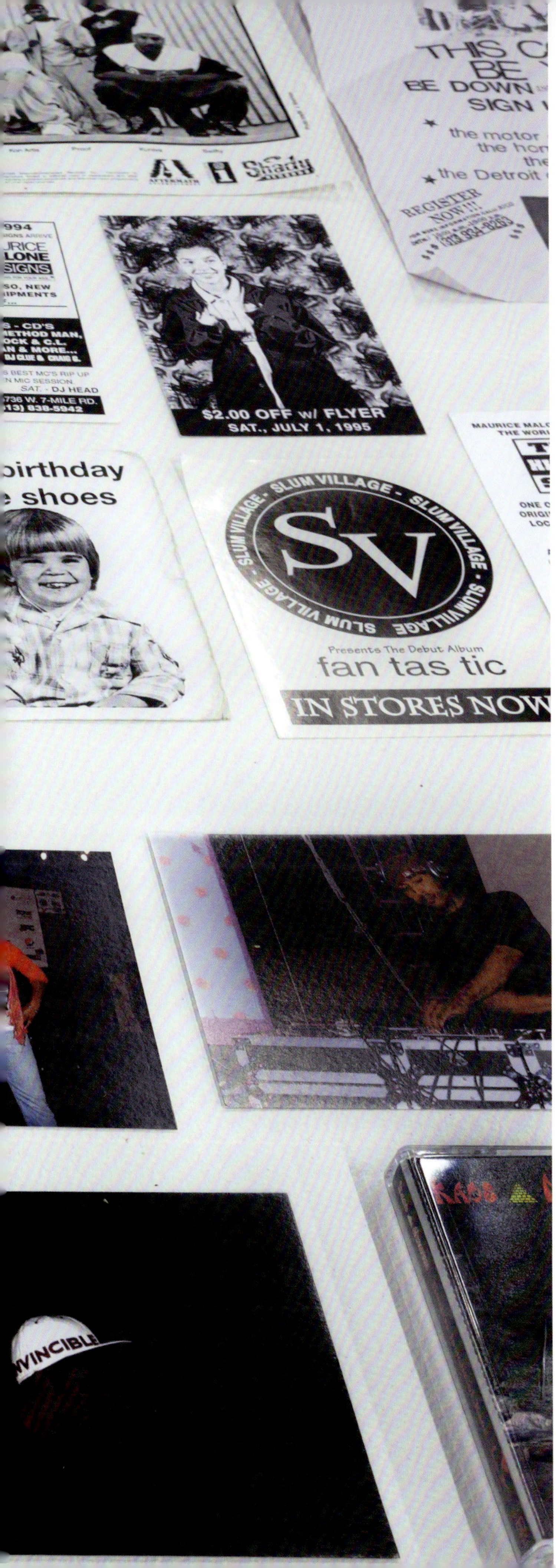

DETROIT RAP/HIP HOP

Materials from the collections of DJ Babe, DJ Dez, DJ Head, DJ Los, Kellie Hay and Rebekah Farrugia, Miz Korona

Selections curated with Miz Korona

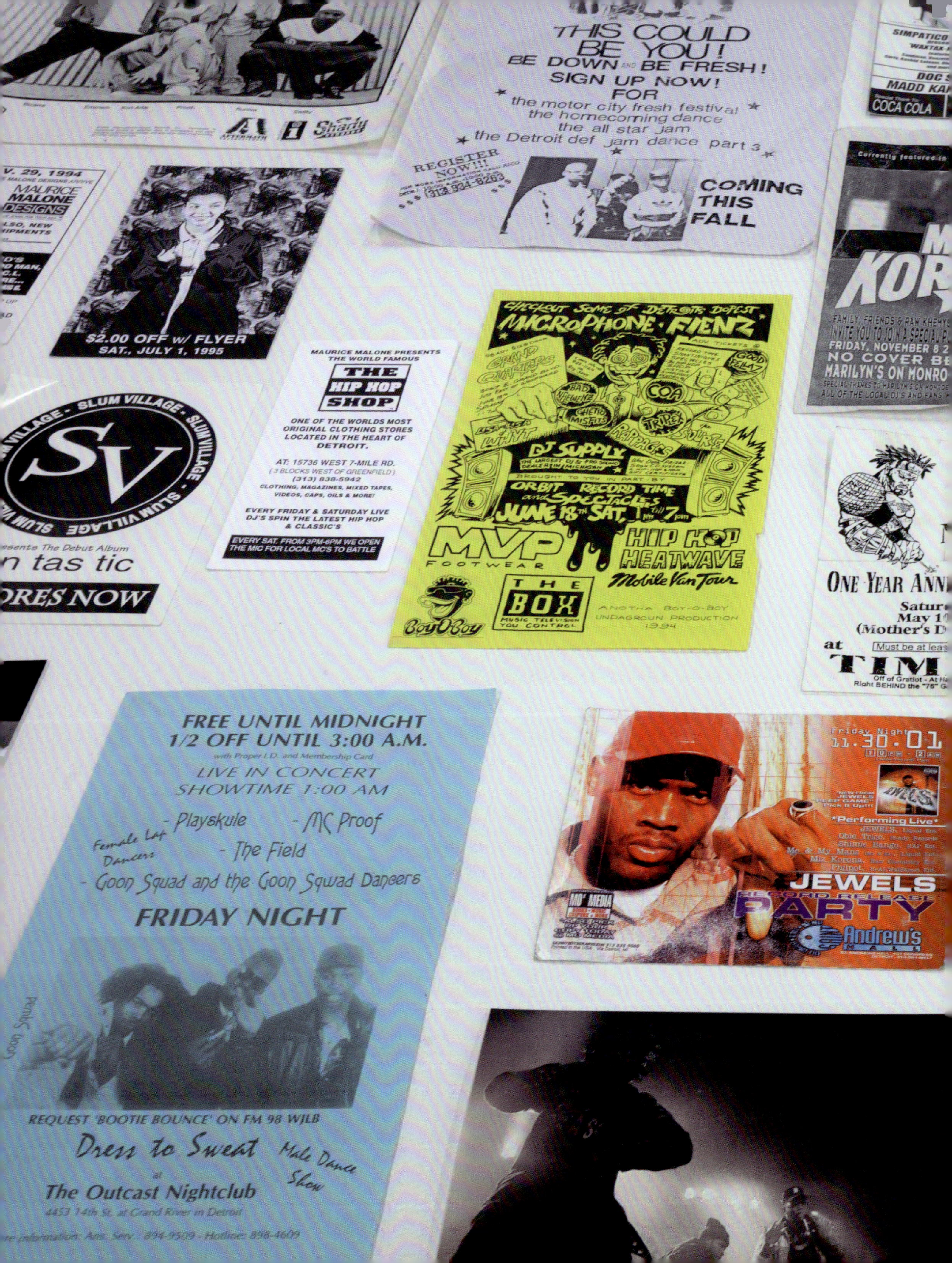
THIS COULD BE YOU!
BE DOWN AND BE FRESH!
SIGN UP NOW!
FOR
the motor city fresh festival
the homecoming dance
the all star jam
the Detroit def jam dance part 3
REGISTER NOW!!!
COMING THIS FALL
SIMPATICO
MADD KAP
COCA COLA
MAURICE MALONE DESIGNS
$2.00 OFF w/ FLYER
SAT., JULY 1, 1995
MAURICE MALONE PRESENTS THE WORLD FAMOUS
THE HIP HOP SHOP
ONE OF THE WORLDS MOST ORIGINAL CLOTHING STORES LOCATED IN THE HEART OF DETROIT.
AT: 15736 WEST 7-MILE RD.
(3 BLOCKS WEST OF GREENFIELD)
(313) 838-5942
CLOTHING, MAGAZINES, MIXED TAPES, VIDEOS, CAPS, OILS & MORE!
EVERY FRIDAY & SATURDAY LIVE DJ'S SPIN THE LATEST HIP HOP & CLASSIC'S
EVERY SAT. FROM 3PM-6PM WE OPEN THE MIC FOR LOCAL MC'S TO BATTLE
CHECKOUT SOME OF DETROIT'S DOPEST
MICROPHONE FIENZ
DJ SUPPLY
ORBIT RECORD TIME
JUNE 18TH SAT.
MVP FOOTWEAR
HIP HOP HEATWAVE
Mobile Van Tour
THE BOX
MUSIC TELEVISION YOU CONTROL
Boy O Boy
ANOTHA BOY-O-BOY UNDAGROUN PRODUCTION 1994
FAMILY, FRIENDS & RAW KHEMYS
FRIDAY, NOVEMBER 8
NO COVER
MARILYN'S ON MONRO
SLUM VILLAGE
SV
Presents The Debut Album
Fan tas tic
STORES NOW
ONE YEAR ANNI
(Mother's D
FREE UNTIL MIDNIGHT
1/2 OFF UNTIL 3:00 A.M.
with Proper I.D. and Membership Card
LIVE IN CONCERT
SHOWTIME 1:00 AM
- Playskule - MC Proof
Female Lap Dancers
- The Field
- Goon Squad and the Goon Sqwad Dancers
FRIDAY NIGHT
Goon Squad
REQUEST 'BOOTIE BOUNCE' ON FM 98 WJLB
Dress to Sweat
Male Dance Show
at
The Outcast Nightclub
4453 14th St. at Grand River in Detroit
Friday Night
11.30.01
Performing Live
JEWELS
Obie Trice
Mix Korona
Philpot
JEWELS
RECORD RELEASE
PARTY
Andrew's Hall

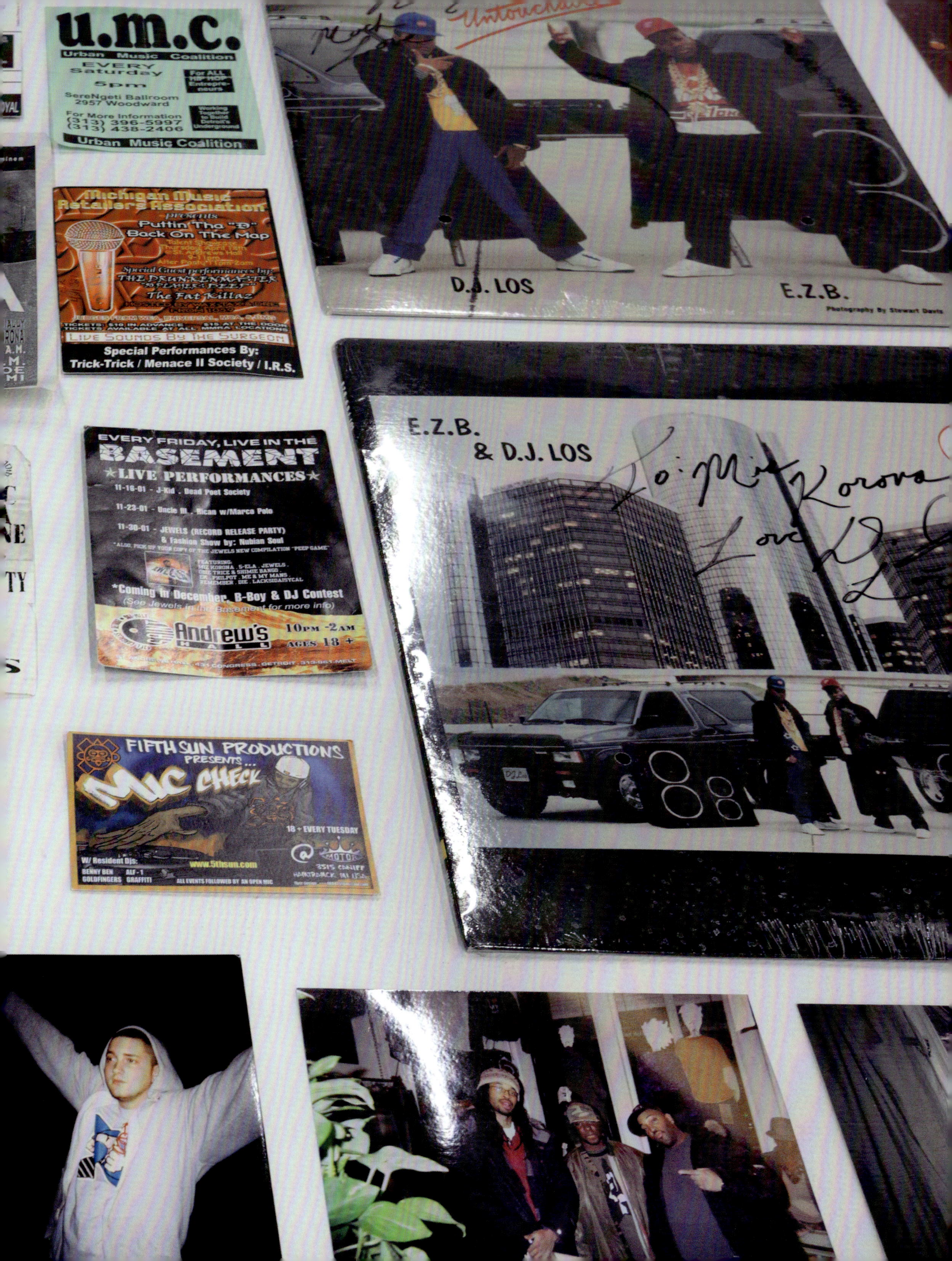
u.m.c.
Urban Music Coalition
EVERY Saturday 5pm
For ALL HIP HOP Entrepreneurs
SereNgeti Ballroom 2957 Woodward
For More Information (313) 396-5997 (313) 438-2406
Working Together to Build Detroit's Underground
Urban Music Coalition
Michigan Music Retailers Association
presents
Puttin Tha "D" Back On The Map
The Fat Killaz
Live Sounds By The Surgeon
Special Performances By:
Trick-Trick / Menace II Society / I.R.S.
EVERY FRIDAY, LIVE IN THE BASEMENT
LIVE PERFORMANCES
11-16-01 - J-Kid . Dead Poet Society
11-23-01 - Uncle ill . Rican w/Marco Polo
11-30-01 - JEWELS (RECORD RELEASE PARTY) & Fashion Show by: Nubian Soul
*Coming In December, B-Boy & DJ Contest
(See Jewels in the Basement for more info)
Andrew's Hall
10PM -2AM
AGES 18 +
FIFTH SUN PRODUCTIONS PRESENTS...
MIC CHECK
18 + EVERY TUESDAY
W/ Resident DJs:
www.5thsun.com
ALL EVENTS FOLLOWED BY AN OPEN MIC
D.J. LOS
E.Z.B.
Photography By Stewart Davis
E.Z.B.
& D.J. LOS

MUSIC, MUSIC, AND MORE MUSIC

JOEL PETERSON

The old narrative was that Detroit never recovered after the 1967 rebellion, and from the outside this seemed true. The city transformed from an acknowledged music capital—home to Motown, the largest black-owned business in the world, and dozens of other small but significant labels—to an industry ghost town in less than a decade. In reality, the adverse conditions made Detroit a prime location for significant music during the era of its "decline." As the A & R agents and coastal media stopped paying attention, the people making music in the city were freed to follow their own prerogatives. These artists churned out some of the most important work in the country, often with little commercial success or critical acclaim.

Principles of self-determination and self-reliance were ubiquitous in Detroit's African American community long before the rebellion, but it wasn't until '67 that they manifested in the broader cultural landscape and began to alter it. As these values crossed over to the New Left, they were transmitted to much of Detroit's music scene—via connections to the Detroit Artists Workshop (DAW) and its affiliates—inspiring an explosion of new sounds and approaches to every aspect of the music business. Conceived as a collaborative space for artists to develop and present work (ranging from poetry and photography to jazz), the DAW was formed in 1964 by poets John Sinclair, George Tysh, and Robin Eichele, musician Charles Moore, and several others. From the start, the group set a tone of creative autonomy, political engagement, self-reliance, and diversity that continued in many Detroit-area collectives in the coming decade. What is now known as the DIY aesthetic was already part of the ethos of post-rebellion Detroit and is perhaps the single unifying value that shaped the emerging Detroit aesthetic.

Of course, not everything following '67 was a musical declaration of a new society. First came the cathartic songs made explicitly in response to the rebellion. The best known, "Motor City is Burning," was written by Detroit Blues icon John Lee Hooker and first recorded, along with three other songs about the riot, in September 1967. The next year, lefty proto-punkers the MC5 began covering it, altering the lyrics to be more confrontational and adding references to the Black Panthers. Another early response was Essie Moss and Robert Grant's "The Detroit Riot." Released in 1968 on Detroit gospel label Bilessie Records (owned by Essie Moss and her husband Bill), this mournful gospel-soul classic begins with a recounting of the events of '67 and turns devastating as Moss' soaring voice testifies with the authority of a witness.

Motown also responded—at first tepidly, with the tune "I Care About Detroit" (sung by Smokey Robinson); but the real impact came in other 1968 releases, such as The Temptations' *Cloud Nine*, which eschewed the label's fabled wholesomeness for Barrett Strong and Norman Whitfield's topical lyrics accompanied by a psychedelic soul groove. Although Motown had dabbled in race issues and Vietnam protest songs on singles going back to 1963, from '68 forward, Strong and Whitfield—along with Marvin Gaye, Stevie Wonder, Edwin Starr, and others—made sure the most prominent black voices on American radio were singing about more than romance. From "Ball of Confusion" (another Whitfield / Strong protest classic for The Temptations) to Starr's anti-Vietnam War anthem "War" and Gaye's opus on the same theme *What's Going On?*—music about the times became the norm for Motown's marquée names. In tandem with these popular releases, Motown's imprint Black Forum (1970–73) solidified the label's contribution to black culture with music and spoken word releases by the likes of Martin Luther King, Langston Hughes, Amiri Baraka, Stokely Carmichael, and Elaine Brown.

Other sectors of life in the city were also shaking up the status quo. 1968 saw the exploitative labor conditions at the "Dodge Main" assembly plant give rise to the Dodge Revolutionary Union Movement, which coalesced with similar groups into The League of Revolutionary Black Workers. Besides using tactics like wildcat strikes and self-publishing to effect changes at the factories and within United Automobile Workers, The League embraced art as a force for change, as laid out in "An Open Letter to Black Artists." The League produced volumes of poetry and new labor songs for black workers, and they fostered a number of significant artists, including Aaron Ibn Pori Pitts, who read poetry with New York's free jazz greats and relentlessly promoted the work of his Detroit radical jazz collaborators.

FORCE

A fusion of music, art, and politics also birthed the White Panther Party, the far-left political collective formed by John Sinclair, photographer Leni Sinclair, and activist Pun Plamondon in 1968. The artists and musicians affiliated with the White Panthers were many, but among the most notable was the MC5, whose polemical, high-energy live shows galvanized a movement. Along with The Stooges, the MC5 was the anchor band at the Grande Ballroom, an old dance hall acquired by Detroit radio DJ Russ Gibb in the mid-1960s. As manager of the MC5, John Sinclair brought his experience running the Artists Workshop and White Panthers to radicalize a scene reaching a huge youth audience. Other Grande notables included SRC, mixing a bluesy vibe with heavy psychedelia; progressive rockers The Third Power; The Frost, a psychedelic band considered as intense as The Stooges and MC5 but whose output was plagued with distribution problems and bad cover art; and Savage Grace, another progressive group influenced by jazz artists such as John Coltrane and Sun Ra, both of whom played the Grande as well.

PUNK

This scene heralded a new type of rebellious rock, which spread to New York and London in the 1970s. One listen to the 1968 single version of the MC5's "Lookin' at You" and you can hear something more punk than anything NYC would produce for a decade. The band's influence on the New York Dolls and the Ramones has been widely cited, and anyone who saw Iggy Pop fronting The Stooges in this era could easily discern punk's two main archetypes—the idiot and the poet—already at their zenith. The early stages of punk could also be found in the mid-to-late '60s garage groups like The Index, The Rationals, and The Pleasure Seekers—the latter featuring a teenage Suzy Quatro, who is cited as rock's first female bassist and is an overlooked Detroit artist who has sold millions of records abroad. The Index never blew up, but they released one highly sought-after LP that presciently straddled garage and psychedelic rock. The Rationals was a transitional band that started as a successful garage and soul act and started headlining early Detroit energy rock bills with MC5 and The Bob Seger System.

Another band at the roots of punk was germinating in Detroit as well. Now known as the first Afropunk group, Death was formed in 1971. Initially, Detroit music impresario Clive Davis was onboard to produce a debut record, but he withdrew when the group refused to change its name to something more commercial. Death self-released a single from the session—the only official output during the band's initial existence. After several years of gigging and more unreleased recordings, Death disbanded in 1977. In 2009, Drag City Records released an LP version of the 1974 sessions and subsequent LPs of other recordings from the '70s. Now Death is performing again, and their music has been the subject of a feature-length documentary film.

The new sensibility of the 1970s continued to solidify across the spectrum of music in Detroit. In the North End, the polished, vocal harmony group Parliament transformed overnight into the liberation-freakout soundtrack known as Funkadelic. Driven by an Afrofuturist vision akin to Sun Ra's, frontman George Clinton is also an overlooked writer of topical songs. "Biological Speculation," from 1972's *America Eats its Young*, stands as one of the most poetic Civil Rights songs of its era, and 1975's "Chocolate City" celebrated the "browning of America" with good humor, decades before it became an alarmist news item.

Jazz harpist Dorothy Ashby and her husband, playwright John Ashby, ran the Dexter Theater on the west side, where they presented original work dealing with issues of specific concern to black Detroiters as well as feminist themes, including the musical *The Choice*. Shortly after the rebellion, Reverend Dan Aldridge of Mayflower Congregational Church invited Student Nonviolent Coordinating Committee Chairman H. Rap Brown to speak at the Dexter. The turnout overwhelmed the space, and Brown had to address the crowd from the theater's roof.

A graduate of Cass Technical High School's legendary music program, Dorothy Ashby was the first of several boundary-breaking female harpists to come out of the school. Known for extending the instrument's technical limitations as well as the contexts of its performance, Ashby became the first bebop harpist and a pioneer of world music. Ashby's junior, Alice Coltrane was another Cass Tech harpist who pushed her instrument even further into world music and the avant-garde, starting with the groups of her husband, saxophonist John Coltrane. After his death, she devoted herself to Indian spirituality, often working with saxophonist Pharoah Sanders, another John Coltrane alum. In the mid-seventies, she opened an ashram in California and made devotional music cassettes of electronics and voice that have finally been collected and issued on LP this year (2017). Both Ashby and Coltrane stand as two of jazz's most boundary-pushing artist ever, notably along analogous spiritual and transcendental lines.

Musical rebellions of other, familiar types from the era were happening too. From 1969–72, a folk-music commune in the Garwood mansion on Detroit's east side became the epicenter of protest music in the city and a hotspot for counter-culture celebrities. Raga-influenced folk guitarist Peter Walker took up residence for a time and cut an LP in the mansion. Across town, the Plum Street neighborhood was another hub for hippies, the anti-war movement, and street musicians, and was headquarters to the radical newspaper *Fifth Estate* and John Sinclair's production company, Trans-Love Energies.

This same span of time roughly covers Sixto Rodriguez's initial recording career as a protest-rock troubadour. Considered the "Bob Dylan" of the South African student anti-apartheid movement, it took 30 years for the Oscar award-winning documentary *Searching for Sugarman* to trigger the re-release of his classic records *Cold Fact* and *Coming From Reality*. These albums, reflecting a working-class perspective on themes of social disparity, street life, and relationships in conflict, are now recognized as major contributions to folk-rock protest music.

As Detroit's blues, rock, folk, and soul musicians brought stories of the era's struggles to mass audiences, the city's jazz and "creative music" artists (many of whom also worked in pop and soul acts) strategized new ways to engage in the city. In the early 1970s, two new collectives were explicitly conceived as responses to post-rebellion conditions. Launched in 1973, Tribe was a record label, artist collective, production house, and publishing company that put out the works of musicians Marcus Belgrave, Phil Ranelin, Wendell Harrison, Charles Moore, and Doug Hammond. *Tribe* magazine included interviews with African-American poets, musicians, and activists, as well as social and economic analysis and feature stories. The back pages listed black-owned businesses alongside the slogan "Don't buy until you check with *Tribe*." Although the label's overall sound was progressive jazz with a heavy dose of funky-soul, the core members were versatile, having recorded with Motown acts as well as Ray Charles (whose band was led by Belgrave for many years), B.B. King, and Chuck Jackson.

Tribe's contemporary was the Strata Corporation, a label, production company, and performance venue founded by Kenn Cox and his Contemporary Jazz Quintet cohorts. Along with Quintet bandmates Ron English, John Dana, Charles Moore, and Bud Spangler, Strata members included Lyman Woodard and Larry Nozero. Most of these artists participated in the Detroit Artists Workshop, and some Strata releases were produced by John Sinclair. The venue, Strata Gallery, programmed Detroit musicians alongside groundbreaking visitors like Charles Mingus, Ornette Coleman, and Sun Ra. Both Tribe's and Strata's records are now prized by collectors around the world, with originals commanding hundreds of dollars. In particular, the Lyman Woodard Organization's *Saturday Night Special* has had a second life as an influential record among DJs and hip hop producers and was reissued by the music magazine *Wax Poetics* in 2009. Adhering to self-determination and multiculturalism, at a time when such stances were often viewed as confrontational, the overall vibe of Tribe and Strata was one of positivity and consciousness.

Griot Galaxy leader, saxophonist Faruq Z. Bey, started the group when he "liberated" his first saxophone during the '67 Rebellion. Griot Galaxy stands out in the Free Jazz pantheon for the strength of its compositions (a rarity in a genre where improvisation rules the day) and the complexity of the metrical schemes and polyrhythms employed. Bey was a published poet as well as a musician, and his spoken word contributions imbued a literate analog to the group's polyrhythmic, poly-modal music. His wide range of interests included music from the archaic to the electronic, as well physics, etymology, and tonal linguistics. Despite a severe motorcycle accident in 1985 that effectively ended Griot Galaxy while he was in a coma, Bey gradually rehabilitated himself and continued to mentor and inspire Detroiters across several creative fields. After recuperating, he gigged regularly with many ensembles, releasing records and publishing books of poetry and music aesthetics until his passing in 2012.

Detroit jazz artist Roy Brooks was another musician with a commitment to activism. A master percussionist, Brooks made his early debut with The Four Tops, before jumping into the jazz world, first with eminent Detroit innovator Yusef Lateef and then with greats Horace Silver, Charles Mingus, Pharoah Sanders, Chet Baker, and Barry Harris. Brooks' titles *The Free Slave* and *Black Survival* reflected his politics, as did his ensemble names, such as Artistic Truth and The Aboriginal Percussion Choir. He brought many unusual elements into his percussion battery—squeaky toys, musical saw, found objects—and invented a system of breath-controlled tubing that allowed him to change the pitch of his tam-tam drums with air pressure. In 1976, Brooks joined up with Kenn Cox and pianist Harold McKinney to create Musicians United to Save Indigenous Culture, a jazz education center and presenting organization that also provided aid to ailing musicians. Brooks died under tragic circumstances in 2005, but a revelatory, posthumous release by his group The Improvisational Sphere was produced in 2011.

By the end of the 70s, there arose again the need for an organization to carry on the examples of self-determination, positivity, and experimentation set by Detroit Artists Workshop, Tribe, and Strata. The Creative Arts Collective (CAC) presented avant-garde jazz at the Detroit Institute of Arts from 1979–1992, and it remains an active entity today. CAC concerts showcased the city's vanguard best: Danny Spencer, CAC founder Spencer Barefield, Griot Galaxy, and up-and-comers like James Carter and Gerald Cleaver, performing their own work and collaborating with such guest artists as Roscoe Mitchell, Lester Bowie, and Leroy Jenkins. While Free Jazz and "Fire Music" was fading from the scene around the world, the CAC kept it burning in Detroit right through the music's international resurgence beginning in the 1990s.

Braininess mixed with an earthy groove is a part of the Detroit aesthetic that found expression through The Electrifying Mojo, the most influential non-musician in Detroit music in the later 20th Century. From the late-1970s through the 1990s, Mojo's midnight radio show was hugely popular and broke Prince, Kraftwerk, and The B-52s on Midwest radio. Arguably, his biggest contribution to music was being the first to play Detroit techno on air. "Sharevari" by A Number of Names—widely regarded the first techno track—was already a Detroit club hit before its release thanks to Mojo's airplay of an advance copy. A young Juan Atkins also received the Mojo stamp of approval when fellow techno pioneer Derrick May slipped Mojo "Alleys of Your Mind" by Atkins' project Cybotron. A few years later, Mojo changed his show's format to art music by African-American composers, from the 19th-century work of William Grant Still to the Anthony Davis's contemporary opera *Malcolm X*. Unsurprisingly, the commercial stations that hired him did not appreciate this programming, and Mojo, the only DJ in America who could get an interview with Prince, quietly disappeared from radio by the late-'90s.

Although the earliest techno artists were creating boutique releases with limited distribution, two collectives formed that would bring Detroit's electronic sensibility to broader audiences, both founded by artists Jeff Mills and Mike Banks. Music collective Underground Resistance (UR) injected radical politics and activism into their low-fi production, a combination that has made them one of techno's longest-running institutions. Rejecting the commercialization that flooded techno near the end of its first decade, UR deliberately geared their releases to poor, urban youth and kept their messages as gritty as the production, with the stated goal of raising consciousness to break the cycle of poverty. On the dissemination end, Submerge Records began as a vehicle for Banks and Mills' music before expanding into a clearinghouse for Detroit's other "urban electronic" labels. It was largely due to Submerge that techno became available in Europe— a crucial factor in the music's international success—and today Submerge remains the world's leading distributor of Detroit techno and related sub-genres, like ghetto-tech and electrofunk.

Artist collective Destroy All Monsters (DAM) was formed in 1973 by Mike Kelly, Niagara, Jim Shaw, and Cary Loren, but the group's underground notoriety has obtained a new visibility in recent years. The collective produced cassettes, films, and *Destroy All Monsters Magazine* with a proto-punk, DIY aesthetic using homemade instruments, tape machines, screen printing, etc. The original collective only lasted about two years, but each of the members continued making work under the DAM moniker. The middle incarnation brought onboard Laurence and Benjamin Miller who, as teenagers in 1969, recorded a private-label, proto-punk LP as Sproton Layer, also featuring their brother Roger (guitarist for Boston-based post-punk band Mission of Burma). The final version of DAM added Ron Asheton of The Stooges and Michael Davis of the MC5, but the group disbanded before releasing its first LP. In 1994, Sonic Youth guitarist Thurston Moore released the original DAM's collected early recordings on his label Ecstatic Peace!, and major international institutions subsequently held retrospectives of the group's films and visual artwork. The original Destroy All Monsters reformed and, like the Tribe and Strata collectives, found the world catching up with their achievements.

Although the explicit politics of Detroit music waned in the 1980s and '90s, the spirit of defying both the status quo and the odds still informed artists in the city. One Detroit group would aptly sum up the new, nihilistic "hardcore" punk style both in name and sound: Negative Approach. Formed in 1981, Negative Approach—along with The Necros (from Maumee, Oh) and Lansing's Meatmen—made one of the earliest hardcore scenes in the country. These bands issued a brutal sonic assault, and many aficionados cite Negative Approach as the hardest of hardcore. A new generation of fans is now buying their records, and the newly-reconstituted group is more famous than at any point during their original career.

Detroit rock in the 1990s, which may have been the last scene with a regional identity, made almost everything else happening in rock at the time sound trite and safe. Though dominated by the garage revival started by The Gories, the '90s scene was expansive and diverse, gaining steam with an explosion of new bands around 1992. The Hentchmen, Rocket 455, and The Detroit Cobras were among the first to follow the return to rock abandon, and ex-Gories members Danny Kroha and Mick Collins formed new bands, Demolition Doll Rods and The Dirtbombs. These band exuded a love of raw music and excelled as live acts. Yet it was often other, less-explicitly garage groups, like The Witches, Outrageous Cherry, and The Volebeats that were making timeless records among the best American rock produced since the '80s. Other diverse groups, like minimalist space-rockers Windy & Carl, ultra-eclectic pop-rock outfit His Name is Alive, and avant-songsters Only a Mother also steadily put out records that achieved degrees of national and international critical notice and cult-followings.

Oddly, Detroit didn't seem to produce any major early rap/hip-hop artists—with the exception of David Nelson (Dahveed Ben Israel), a founding member of The Last Poets. Considered the direct progenitor of hip hop, and one of the most radical Black acts ever, the Harlem-based group's themes of historical awareness and self-determination influenced Gil Scott-Heron, Grandmaster Flash, Public Enemy, Mutabaruka, KRS-1, and Afrika Bambaataa. Although often absent from cursory histories of the group—because he didn't perform on the 1971 hit record *This is Madness*—Nelson's peers consider him among the greatest of them all, and Last Poet Abiodun Oyewole has called him "one of my true teachers." Critics have called his contributions to records like *Right On!* the group's most poetically sophisticated, intellectual material.

By the mid-nineties, the career of one of the most quietly influential hip-hop artists ever was underway in the city. J Dilla was set on his music-making path when Parliament/Funkadelic alum Amp Fiddler gave him his sampling drum machine upon discovering the young Dilla's adeptness at building tracks with it. Dilla first showed his skills in the short-lived group 1st Down, subsequently forming the now-legendary Slum Village in 1996. Slum Village remained a regional sensation at the time, but Dilla's career took off when Fiddler introduced him to Q-Tip of Tribe Called Quest in 1997. Dilla's work on the group's singles and remixes and Q-Tip's solo recordings made him a hot commodity in the world of hip hop production and led to his collaborations with Janet Jackson, De La Soul, and Pharcyde.

Initially uncredited on most records, Dilla remained invisible to the public, even as he worked behind the scenes with Erykah Badu, Poe, Talib Kweli, and Common. MCA Records finally signed Dilla to a solo deal but then shelved two planned releases—including one where Dilla only raps and leaves the production to special guests, including Madlib, Kanye West, and fellow Detroiter Waajeed. The MCA debacle led to further collaborations with producer Madlib, however, with the two artist/producers forming Jay Lib in 2002 and releasing the album *Champion Sound* a year later. Dilla was still far from a household name when he released his final album, *Doughnuts*, in 2006. Three days later he passed from a rare blood disease. His inclusion as the only inaugural rap/hip hop artist in the Smithsonian's National Museum of African American History and Culture testifies to his achievements and legacy.

In the hip hop/digital generation, one of the best efforts to continue Detroit's progressive music legacy comes from a non-profit centered on access to technology and digital media as a means of advocacy and activism. Allied Media Projects doesn't create music as an organization, but the annual Allied Media conferences, and other special events sponsored by AMP, expose audiences to socially-conscious and demographically-marginalized performers from Detroit who have come of age in the 21st century. Artists like Tunde Olaniran, Invincible, and Monica Blair have all received the AMP bump, as have some of their elders whose careers didn't take off until the 2000s, like Jessica Care More—poet, performance artist, publisher, and founder of Black WOMEN Rock!—and the aforementioned Amp Fiddler, whose résumé extends to working with George Clinton, Prince, Moodyman, and The Brand New Heavies.

The examples covered here, however few among the innumerable possibilities they may be, they demonstrate that the events of 1967 changed Detroit's cultural landscape, and the city's music-makers responded to the challenges with new types of music and new ways of working. So many traveled this path, in fact, that it is deceptive to highlight individuals. We could find similar arguments to be made for Wolf Eyes' electronic noise populism; the psychedelic biker music of Nicodemus; the decades-old anarchist punk collective Trumbullplex; the largely-undocumented musical experiments of Chris Gerard; or the cottage industries of DAS' home recordings or American Tapes. The question that remains is whether Detroit's current creative community, inundated with transplanted artists less connected to the city's specific cultural identity, will preserve the singular place Detroit has held in American music.

A VIEW OF RESISTANCE, FROM A RECORD SHOP LIFE...

MARSHA MUSIC

In 1945, Joe Von Battle, my father, opened a record store on Hastings Street in Detroit. He got his start recording blues and gospel singers in the neighborhood and later went up the street to record the pastor of New Bethel Baptist Church, the Reverend C.L. Franklin, called "the man with the million-dollar voice." Franklin's sermons and songs offered messages of perseverance and hope in the era when Southern Jim Crow permeated the North. Soon, my father became the first person to record Reverend Franklin's daughter Aretha, whose singing, even at age fourteen, was extraordinary and would one day command R-E-S-P-E-C-T during the height of the Civil Rights Movement.

The sixties and the Motown years saw the continuation of non-violent protest in the South, and the struggle for equality in the North intensified, too. Today, many look at the buttoned-up suits and bouffants of the Motown stars as hopelessly uptight and conservative, but they, and the music they made, were symbols of an existential resistance. The intense discrimination they faced, both on tour and at home in Detroit, was a challenge to their very personhood. The men's skinny, razor-sharp suits were a form of uniform, their choreography an expression of order and discipline—with finesse. The women's garments—fitted, spangled, glamorous—were born of the high style of Black Detroiters then evolving into the country's largest Black middle class. At the annual Motown Revue at the Fox Theatre, Gordy's stars were hailed not just for their hit songs but also for their return from far-off travels. Folks knew what a trip to the South could mean for any Black American, and these elegant ambassadors of Detroit appeared as triumphant soldiers, back home after battles with Jim Crow.

12th Street in Detroit was exhilarating. It was a one-way thoroughfare before 1967, not the two-way street it is between the Boulevard and Clairmount today, and cars as long as boats drove by in a flotilla of steel, color, and chrome. The crowded neighborhood had inherited a population displaced from Detroit's demolished Black Bottom neighborhood, replaced by modernist Lafayette Park, and old Hastings Street, razed to build the Chrysler Freeway. The migration to the West Side packed 12th Street sidewalks in the daytime with bustling commerce, and at night with a never-ending theatre of Detroit style, musicality, and drama.

In the months and weeks before July 1967, things were the same, but different. All over the country, upheavals and unrest had exploded in cities where large populations of Blacks resided—there would be more than 159 eruptions across the country that year. In 1966, activists on Kercheval Street on the East Side rose up, but they were quelled by the police—and a heavy rainstorm. On Saturdays, I would run from behind the counter of the record shop and look out onto the sidewalk, at the Black militants swaggin' down 12th Street—and I knew something new was happening.

James Brown was never on a Detroit label, but we kids loved him, with his irresistible, often indecipherable lyrics—singsong conundrums

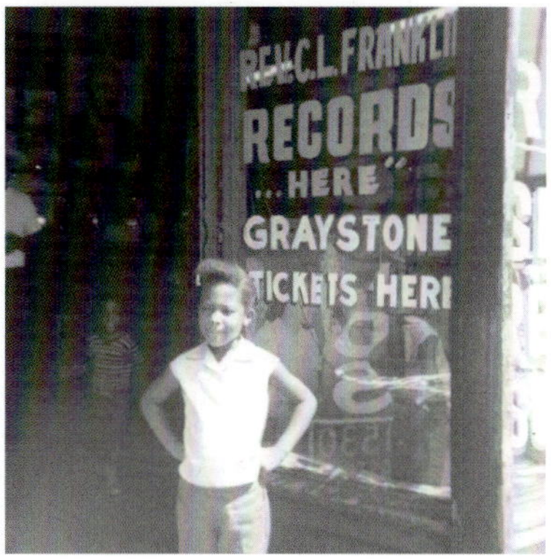

Marsha Music in the doorway of Joe Von Battle's Hasting's Street shop, circa 1959. Photographer unknown.

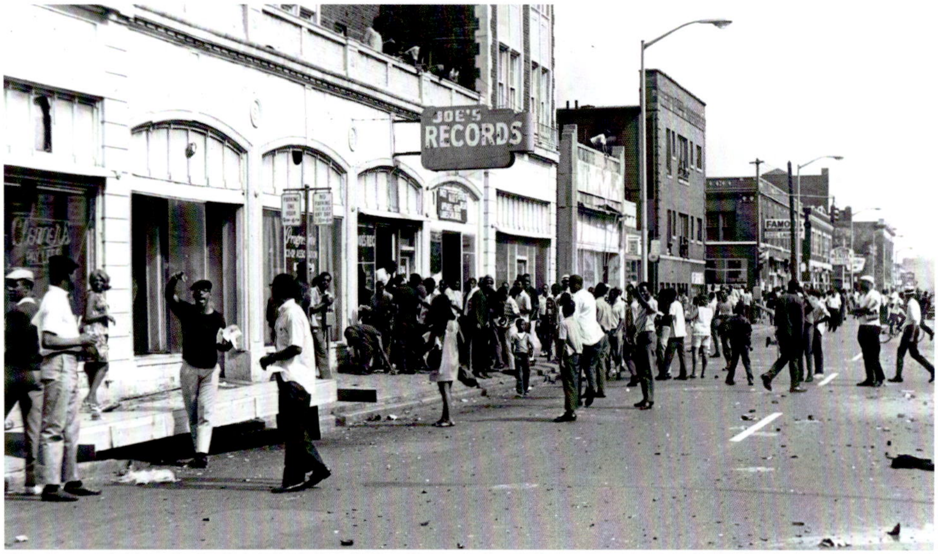

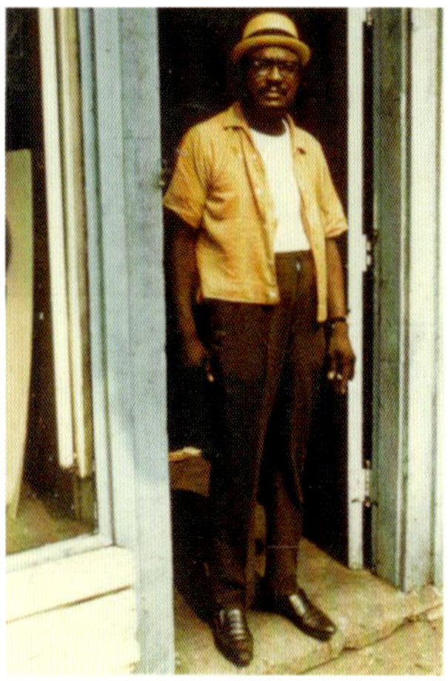

The looting of Joe's Record Shop on 12th Street, July 1967. Photo by Detroit photographer, Diggs.

Joe Von Battle in the doorway of his 12th Street record shop, early to mid-1960s. Photo by Mike Rowe.

in the secret lives of Blacks. We'd stare at his 45s on the turntable, his smiling jib going round-and-round, and follow his every dance command. He had been popular for years, but his old, slow songs, like "Try Me" and "Please, Please, Please" were anachronistic ballads of an earlier time—old fashioned songs the grown folks played when their parties got late and boozy, with some Dinah Washington and Ray Charles. But the late-sixties arrived and James Brown made a sharp turn to a tight rhythm sound, articulating the intensity of the social conflicts nationwide.

On the eve of the Detroit Rebellion, the new James Brown materialized—with "Cold Sweat," ostensibly a love-song but, in reality, a taut, brassy release that was less a song than an exhortation to tighten up for the coming hot summer. On a Saturday night, July 23, 1967, the Rebellion began, and six blocks away, my father's store was in its path—and that was the end of Joe's Record Shop.

In post-'67 Detroit, residents struggled to return to normalcy; and despite baseball (the '68 Tiger's pennant race) and increased access to houses and jobs, social upheaval permeated the culture. A year after the Rebellion, I was awash in its aftermath, distressed about the demise of my family's means of support and my father's alcoholic despair—yet I gravitated toward the resistance. I was awaiting something, but didn't know what it was. One day, on our kitchen radio, I heard it: "UH! Wit yo' BAD self! Say it LOUD! I'm BLACK and I'm PROUD!"

Don't let anyone tell you that James Brown was universally loved back in the day. A whole lot of Black folks detested him. They were ashamed of his deep, black Southern-ness, his processed hair and his raw, undiluted Black African-ness. He annoyed them like a loud, unruly cousin, an unwelcome visitor from back home; a reminder of all they felt ashamed of—and, of course, many Whites hated him too. He was not the light-skinned, light-eyed Smokey, the handsome, operatic Chuck Jackson, or the smooth, sexy Marvin Gaye. No, Brotha James was wiry and dark, with his carved Benin features, country-slick slang, and mile-high pompadour swapped for a thick, sixties Afro. He was a reminder of unruly Black men, the brothas on the street, the chain gang, the hard South folks left behind and didn't want to be—or see.

But "Black and Proud," released a year after July '67, was something else again. I wanted to sing it all day long, but to a lot of our elders, "Black" was just this side of obscenity. With this electrifying record, I learned much about the subtle protocols of race—that mixture of pride, fear, and self-hated that swirled within the world of Black grown-ups, especially when we were all supposed to be ashamed of what happened in '67.

My father, bereft and adrift after the loss of his shop, and angry at all militant exhortations, was secretly proud of Brown and his shout-outs about their mutual Georgia origins, "in Augusta, G.A." Daddy, born and raised in Macon, was surrounded by Northern voices, including my mother's, that dripped contempt for his Southern roots and all from which he'd come. James Brown spoke a language of a South that countless Northern Blacks had tried to disavow. At the same time, they were homesick with his odes to down home, on records whose only lyrics were Southern foodstuffs. While our capri-wearing mothers watched Mary Tyler Moore and mastered her fondues and soufflés, James Brown evoked our national cuisine below the Mason-Dixon line: "Smothered Steak!" "Grits and Gravy!" "Candied Yams!" "Cracklin' Bread!"

Though Black Nationalism increased after '67, it was hardly the dominant thought in the everyday world of Detroiters. Brown's pride in his blackness was a defiant statement of sustenance for his people, and we devoured it like manna. His politics were simplistic exhortations to Black entrepreneurial power, distained by many activists of the time; a mishmash of Horatio Algerisms we in the Northern movement endlessly criticized. But most of us in the struggle admired Brown's uncompromising calls for his people to rise up from discrimination and dependency, and regardless of critics, he was a griot of both the Black bourgeois and the masses.

James Brown led a historic shift in a people's consciousness. He took African-American music and turned it inside out to reveal its rhythmic skeleton—and even his shouts to the band were sufficient to create a new genus of music, unembellished by lyricism and melody. James Brown changed the way that Black people moved, shifted the axis of black dance from the feet to the torso and back again. Before long, adults who had despised him were dancing the Camel Walk and, like my mom and aunties, they started wearing Afros too. Detroit fell in love with James Brown.

The destruction in the city was formidable, not just on 12th, 14th, Linwood, and Dexter—the commercial avenues of the formerly Jewish community on the West Side. There was also serious damage to retail areas along the other spokes emanating from Downtown. There were—and are today—vociferous aspersions cast upon Detroiters for "burning down their own businesses and neighborhoods"—with little mention, however, of the authorities' decisions to allow homes and commercial structures to burn—and some people have long accused the authorities themselves of creating damages.

The shock of the rebellion was so great, to Black and White Detroiter's alike, that a kind of revisionist history developed as a way to explain, vilify, and cope with the trauma. The idea that "all the Whites left Detroit after '67" is a common cliché, easily debunked by facts. For one, the "flight" actually began just after World War II, more than two decades prior. There is a well-promulgated falsity—especially by those who have little or no experience in the city—that Detroit "burned down" in '67. Yet, a recently available video, shot from a helicopter flying over the city during the aftermath of the rebellion, presents startling visual evidence confirming many Detroiters' common knowledge that, in fact, the city remained overwhelmingly intact after the conflagration, even in neighborhoods that suffered much destruction.

[1] Many suburbanites and outsiders attribute the vast devastation evident in the city today to "the riots," when the most significant part of the city's residential destruction stems from the foreclosure crisis two decades later. Most of the neighborhoods currently decimated were intact after the unrest in 1967—some even in the last few years.[2]

After the Rebellion, a new police unit sprung to life—STRESS (Stop The Robberies Restore Safe Streets)—which amounted to increased aggression in the Black community, a battering ram of retaliation for '67. In 1968, a group of Black workers at the Dodge Main Plant in Hamtramck formed DRUM—Dodge Revolutionary Union Movement—as a force against the entrenched discrimination in both the auto factories *and* United Automobile Workers. Before long, DRUM amalgamated with workers in other plants and folks in the community to form The League of Revolutionary Black workers (LRBW)—and I joined up with them. The '67 unrest was like a cork burst from a bottle, allowing long-suppressed frustrations and resistance to explode in Detroit. But many Black leaders and grassroots folks in the community also broadly condemned the outrage and vilified the destruction of the uprising.

Eventually, Motown left for Los Angeles, but the music that permeated and defined the city did not die. The years after the Rebellion saw an explosion of protest music, mixed with popular sounds. My father's old friend John Lee Hooker sang a mournful elegy to the Rebellion, "The Motor City Is Burning," and the airwaves were a steady stream of the Staple Singers, the Isley Brothers and Curtis Mayfield—their songs formed a bedrock of resistance music in continuous play on

1 "Detroit Riots," YouTube video, 22:34, posted by the U.S. National Archives, March 14, 2016, https://www.youtube.com/watch?v=TqPVsSNudHs. This video documents Detroit, using ample aerial footage, from July 26, 1967 to August 1, 1967.

2 For more on this, see my essay "The Kidnapped Children of Detroit," in *A Detroit Anthology*, edited by Anna Clark (Cleveland: Rust Belt Chic Press, 2014); available on my website, marshamusic.wordpress.com.

Black radio in Detroit. White stations CKLW, WKNR, and Robin Seymour's TV dance show, *Swingin' Time*, engaged in a defacto resistance to the intense segregation of the time. Blacks and Whites, who largely lived in apartheid-like separation, often listened to the same Detroit radio sounds. WABX was musically radical "underground radio"—the first album-oriented rock station in Detroit and, in its earliest days, a center of cultural resistance.

Though Motown's music was not typically expressly political, Edwin Starr's explicit single "WAR" reflected the growing popular resistance to the conflict in Vietnam. The Temptations tried on a new, psychedelic sound in "Ball of Confusion," with its kaleidoscopic poesy of social turmoil; Marvin Gaye asked "What's Going On?"; the cover of Stevie Wonder's album *Where I'm Coming From* depicted him as a soldier in the Vietnam War; and in "The Devil is Dope," the quintessentially-Detroit group The Dramatics sang about the enemy Detroiters watched grow ever closer to home.

Black Arts activist Aaron Ibn Pori Pitts, another founder of the LRBW, was a working union rep who got me my first job in the factory and who was experimenting with avant-garde piano and sax in local performances. In the League's Highland Park offices we listened to the Last Poets, Abbey Lincoln, John Coltrane, Les McCann, and Nina Simone. Jazz singer Terry Collier personified a cerebral, conscious artistry and Isaac Hayes was an exemplar of the New Black Man, with his persona of a chained, bare-chested Black Moses. With anti-war protest and rebellion at every turn, the Parliaments morphed from Temptation-like yeomen, suited and slick-haired, into George Clinton's free-style funk group Parliament-Funkadelic. In the sun-porch library of the League, I read about the MC5, John Sinclair, and the White Panthers in the radical newspapers *Fifth Estate* and *South End*. And whether we were fans or not, White artists' music of protest—Bob Dylan, Joan Baez, and Buffalo Springfield's "For What It's Worth"—dominated our aural landscape in the end days of the war in Vietnam. Sweet Honey in the Rock also had a solid core of fans among Detroit's activists and freedom movement fighters.

FUNK

By the '80s, The Electrifyin' Mojo spun a multi-genre collage of albums and records in opposition to the growing corporatization of music and the encroaching loss of the local radio DJ. His variegated sets were where I first heard Rap and Hip-Hop; I'm old school, and even I knew this was fast becoming the new Detroit sound. On the East Side, in the '90s, despite eyes on Eminem, the prodigy J Dilla was a master craftsman of the genre; his roots in Conant Gardens—the historic community of the city's first Black middle-class homeowners—nurtured his intense musical inventiveness and enterprise, with his voluminous production of both music and artists.

In the west side suburb of Belleville, Juan Atkins, Kevin Saunderson, and Derrick May made electronic sounds out of innumerable streams of modern music, rebuking clichés of Black music as an expression of destitution and poverty. These creators of Techno Music also arose from the Black middle class, toward the end of Detroit's age of prosperity. Yet their music—a new, aural assemblage art, born in Detroit—crossed the ocean to fundamentally alter the musical atmosphere of Europe—and then the United States.

Today, as development returns to the city, there is increased recognition of the historical importance of Detroit's music and the need to illuminate its past and present sounds—for Detroiters as well as our many visitors. The multi-disciplinary arts collective ONE Mile re-energizes the legacy of Detroit's music and Afro-futurism on a newly reconstituted Oakland Avenue, in the city's North End, where John Lee Hooker once played. Fans the world over flock to the Techno museum, Exhibit 3000, at the Submerge Records headquarters on East Grand Boulevard, and forces are aligning to create an "all-night music zone" in the city's abandoned factories. The Rhythm and Blues Hall of Fame celebrates Detroit's roots music; Detroit Sound Conservancy preserves our musical artifacts; United Sound Systems continues its recording legacy; and both Bert's Warehouse and Baker's Keyboard Lounge thrive among the city's most-iconic and longstanding music venues. Through social and economic maelstroms, reconstruction, and, gentrification, Detroit and its music persist—and I still Say It Loud, I'm Black and I'm Proud.

THE EXHIBITION

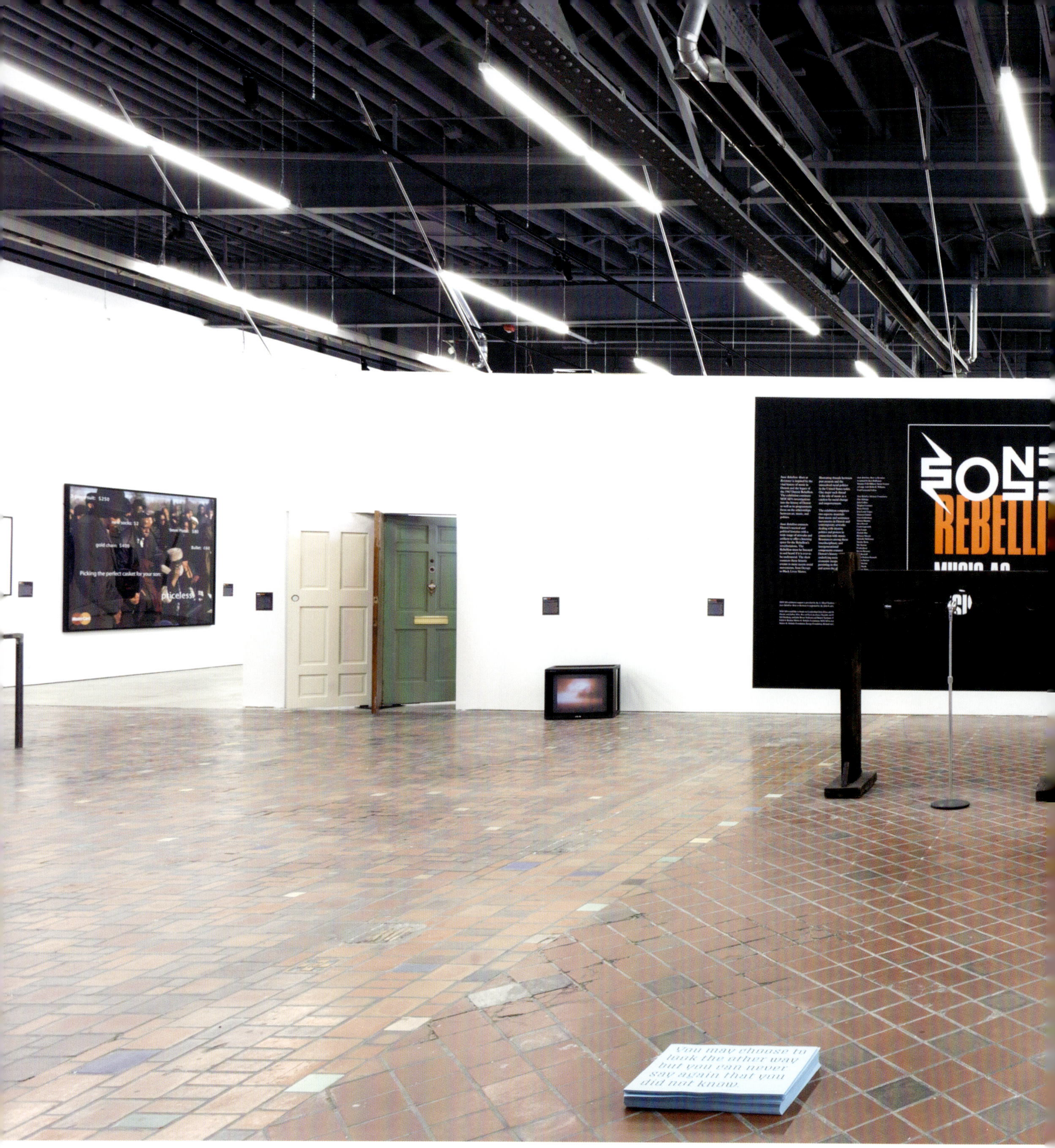
Picking the perfect casket for your son:
priceless
You may choose to
look the other way
but you can never
say again that you
did not know.

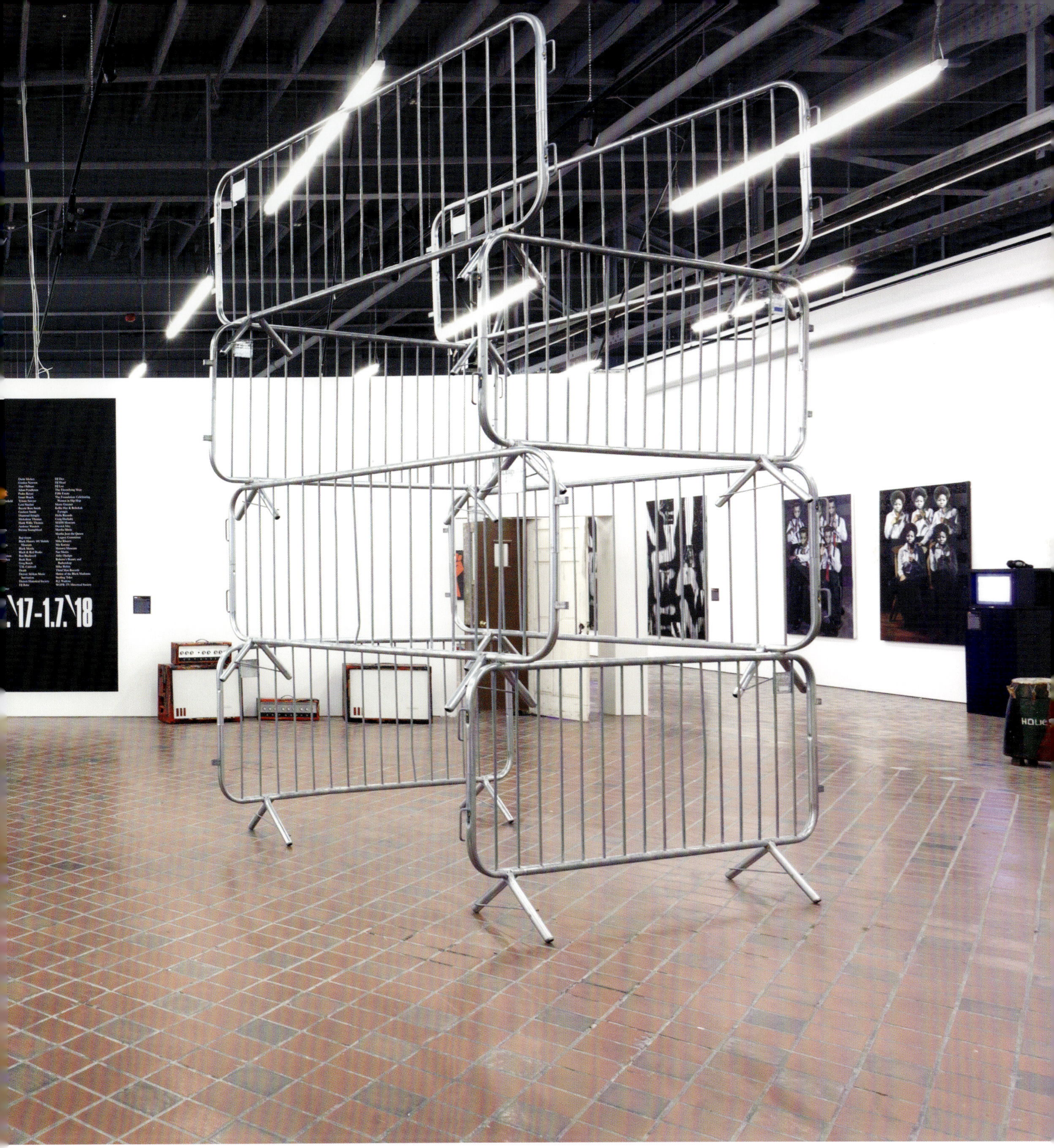

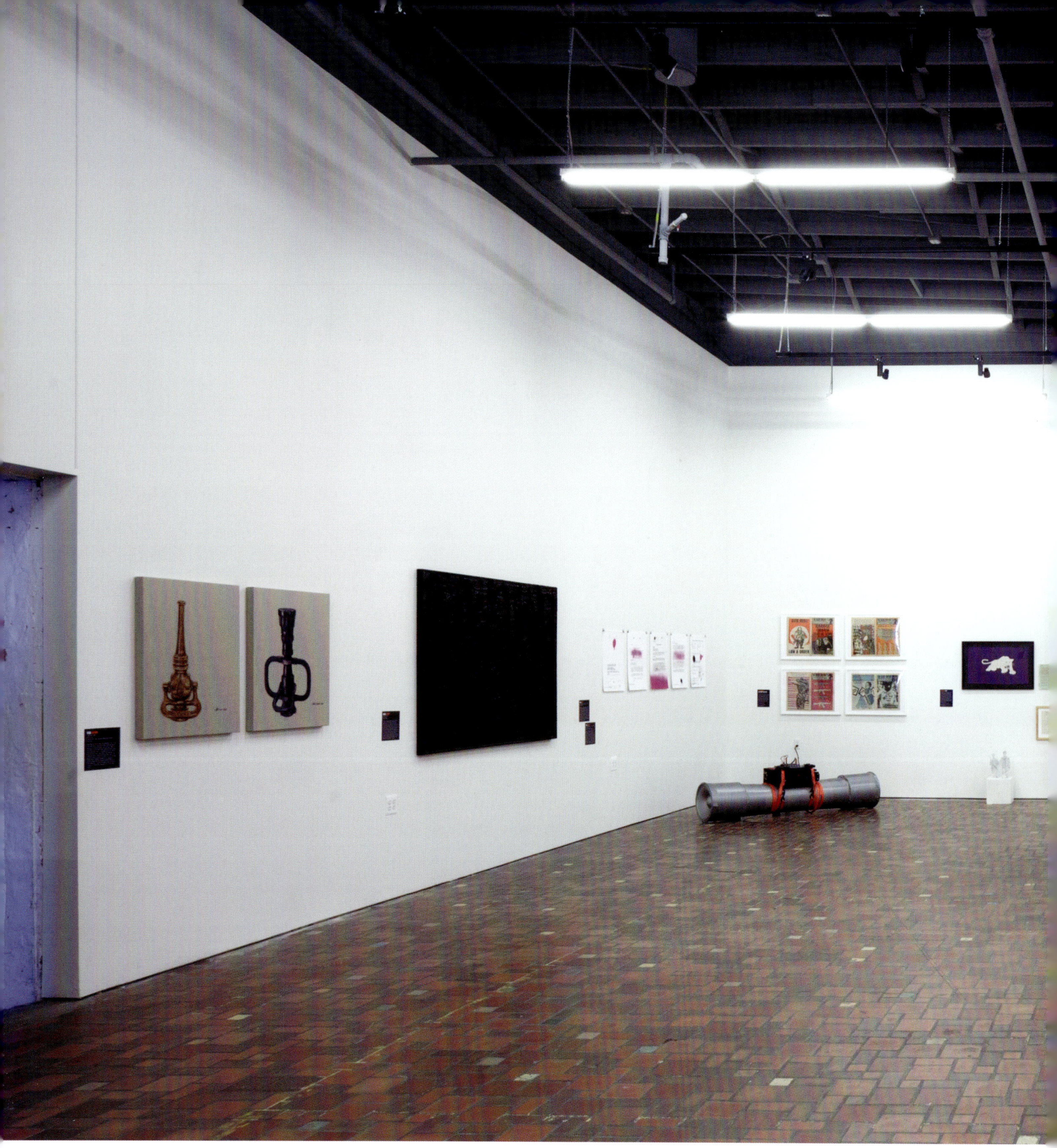

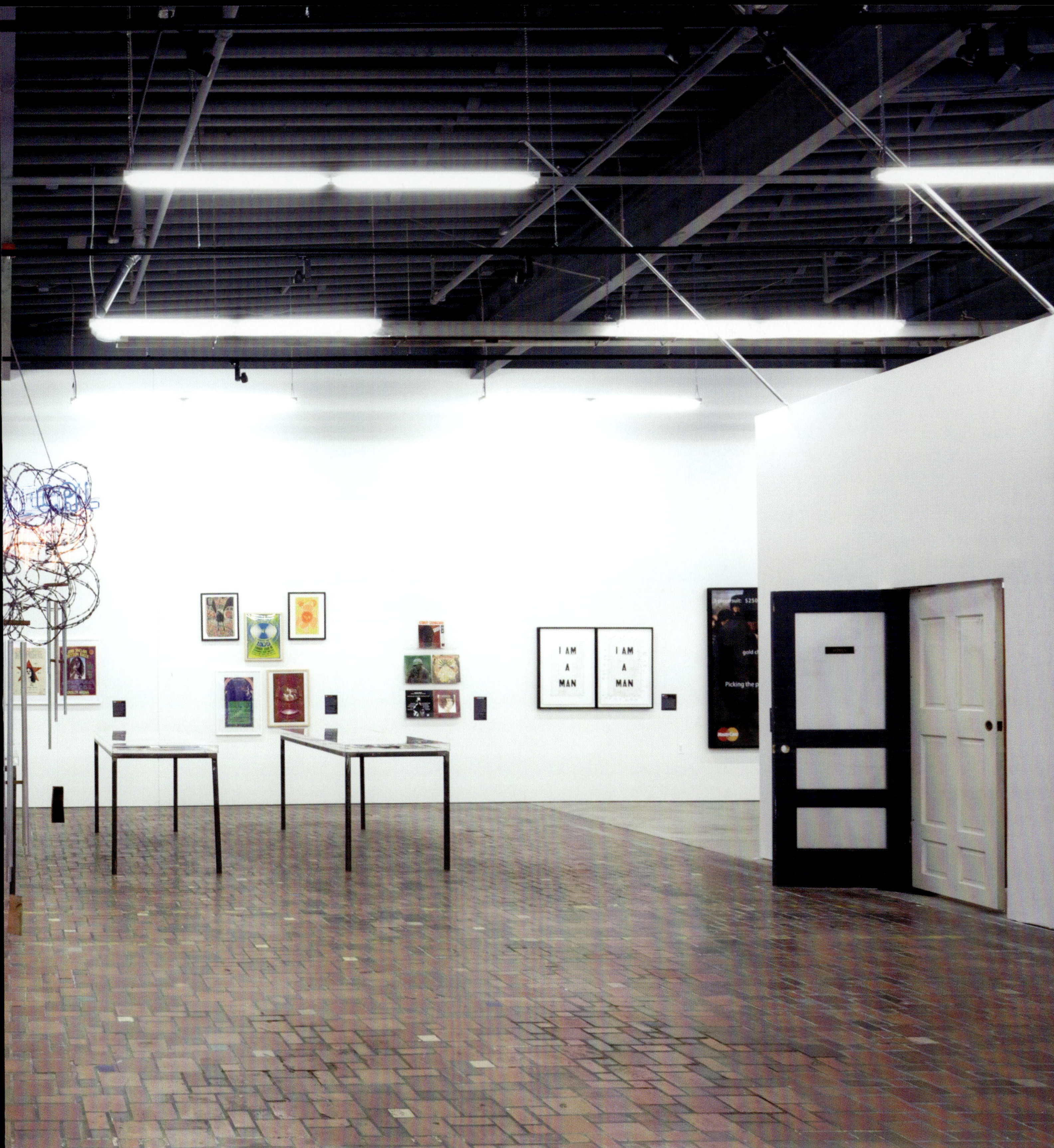
I AM
A
MAN
I AM
A
MAN

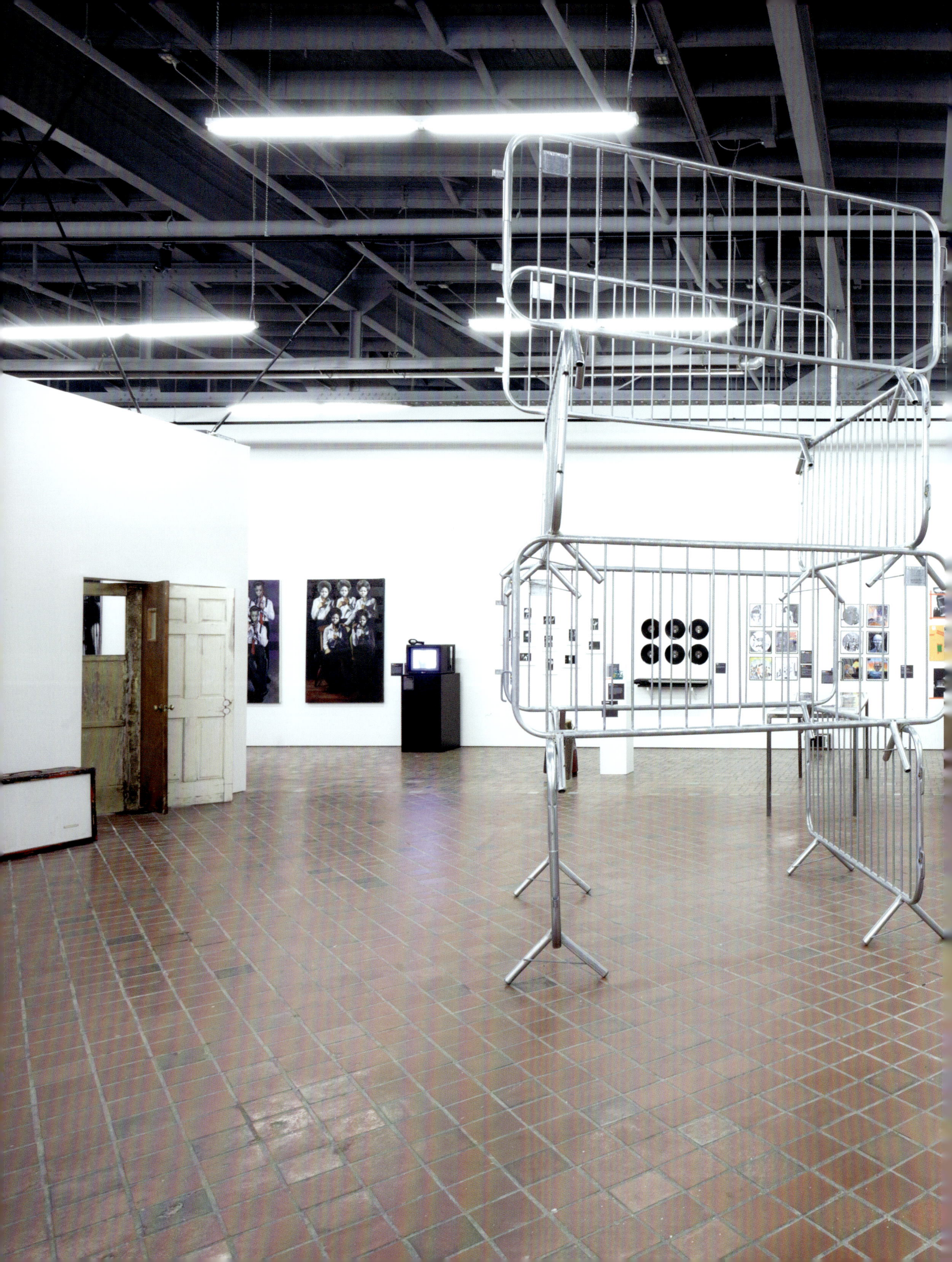

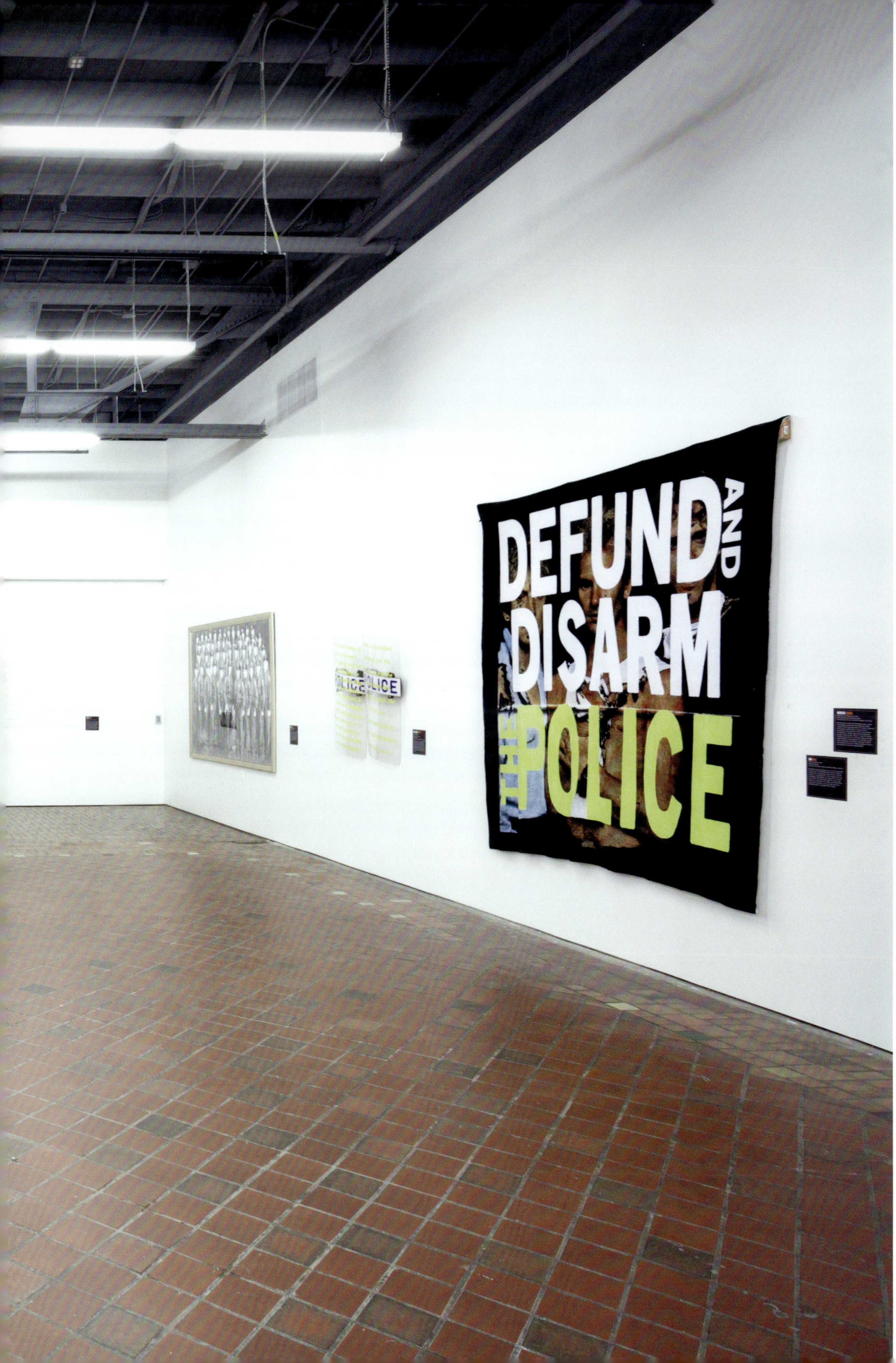
DEFUND
AND
DISARM
THE
POLICE

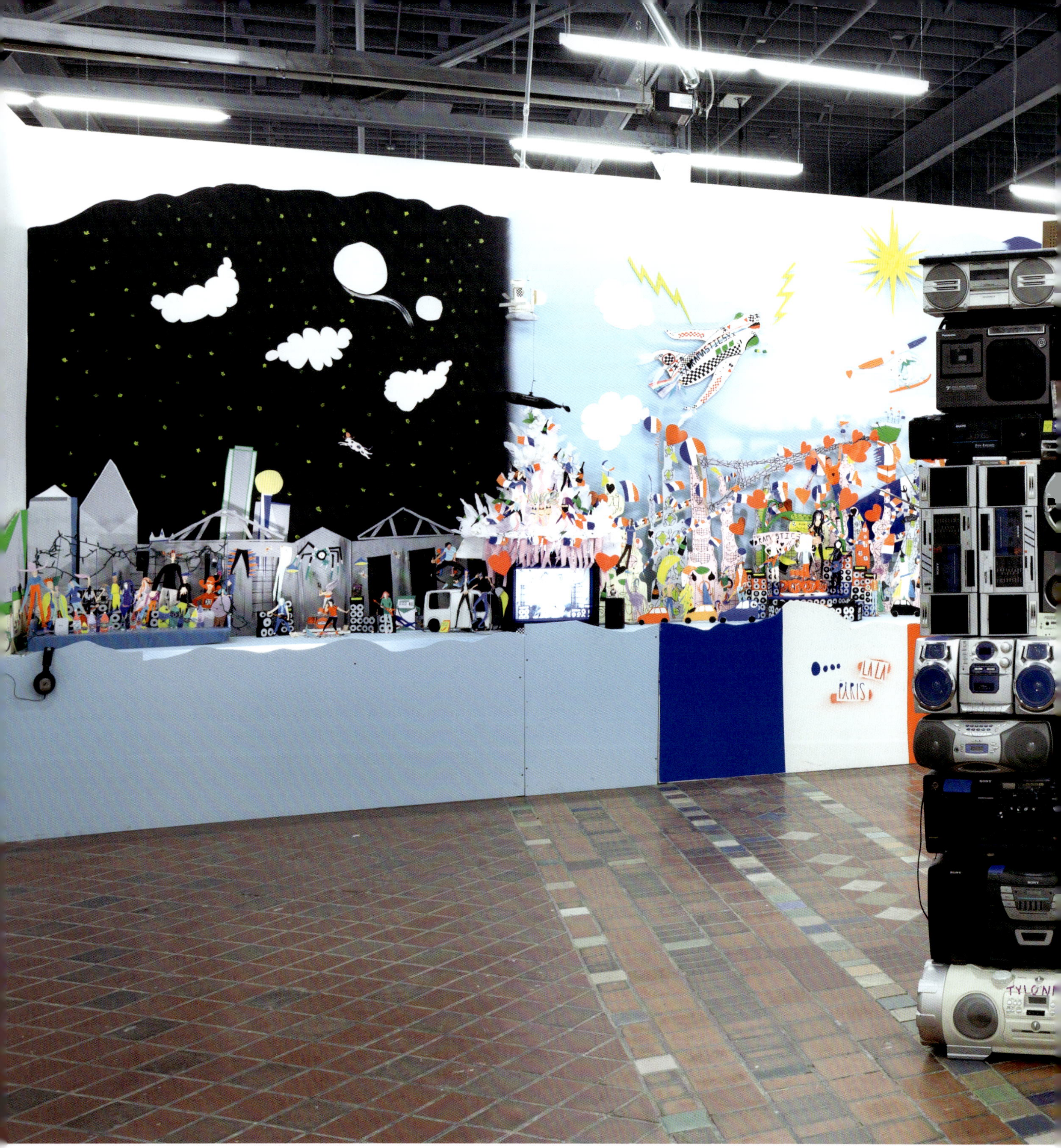
LA LA
PARIS

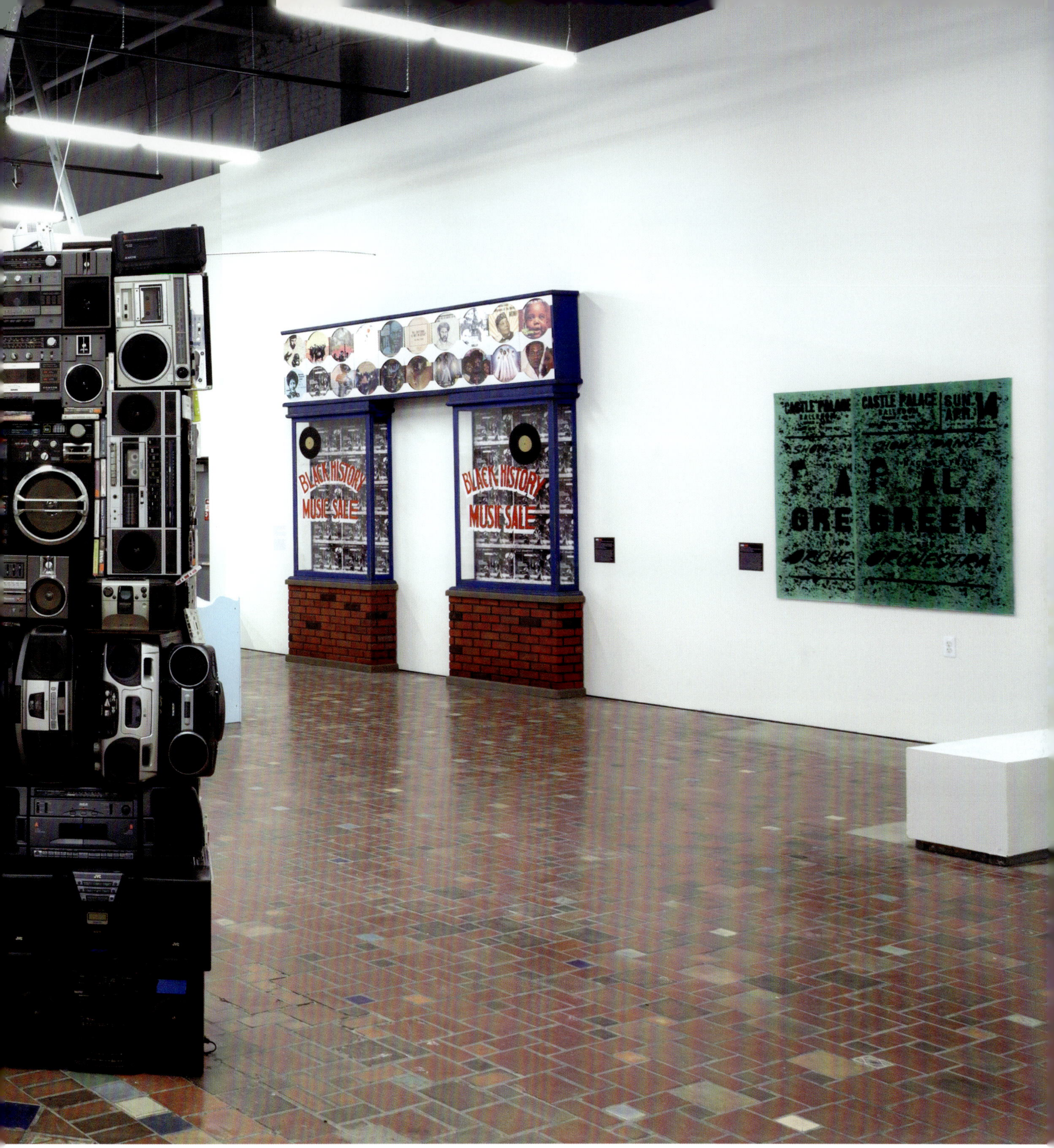
BLACK HISTORY
MUSIC SALE
BLACK HISTORY
MUSIC SALE
CASTLE PALACE
GREEN

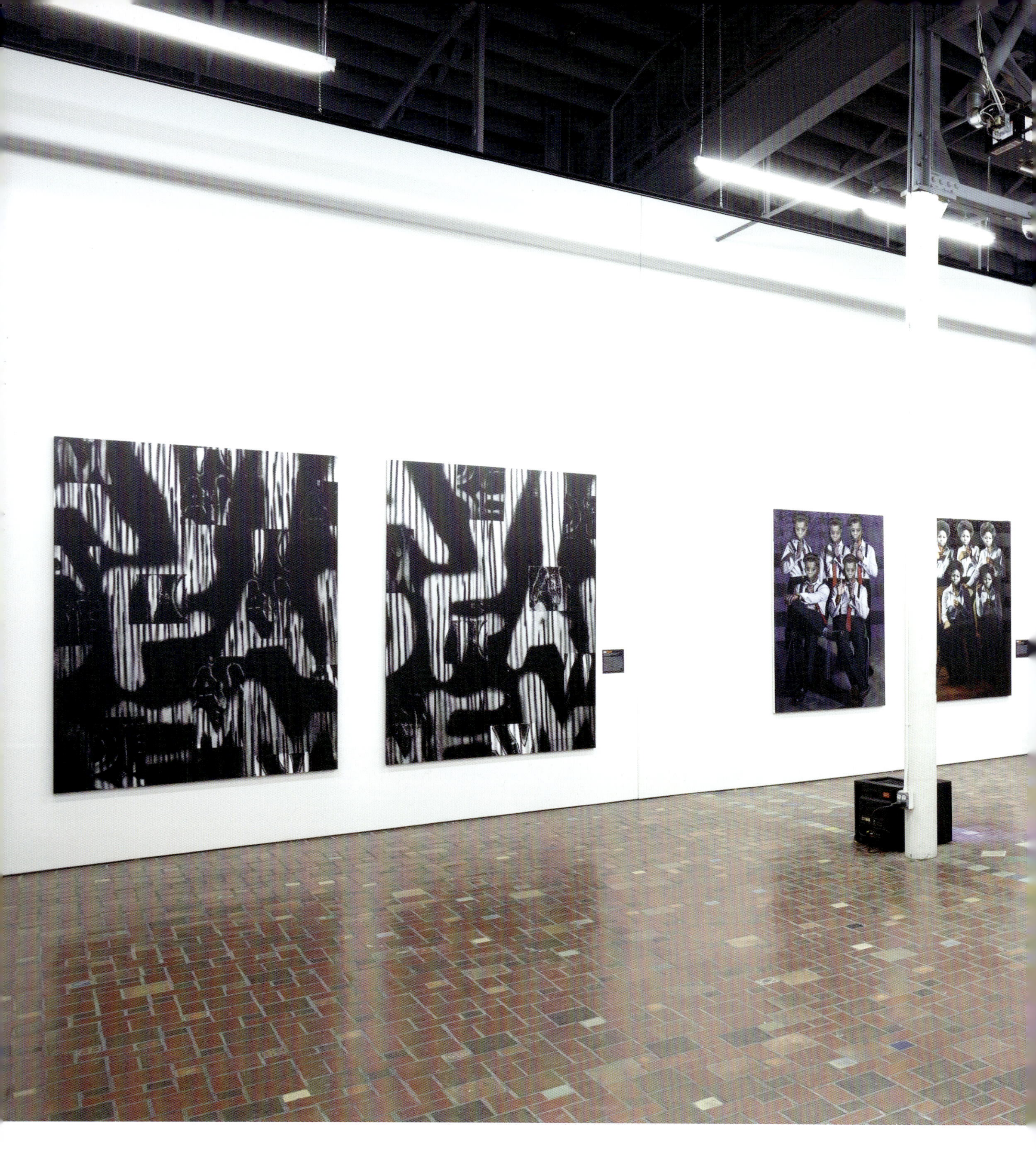

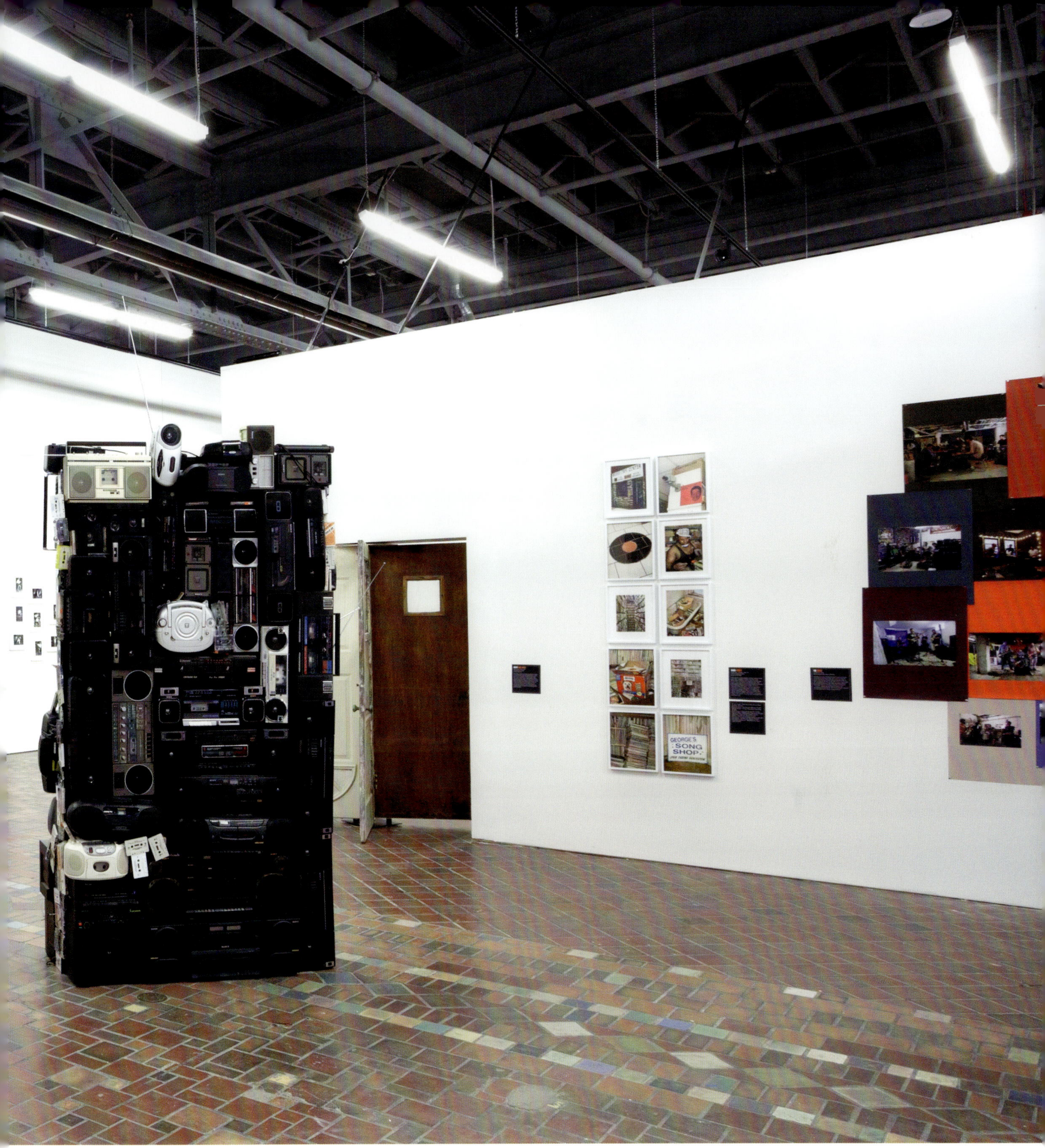
GEORGE'S
SONG
SHOP

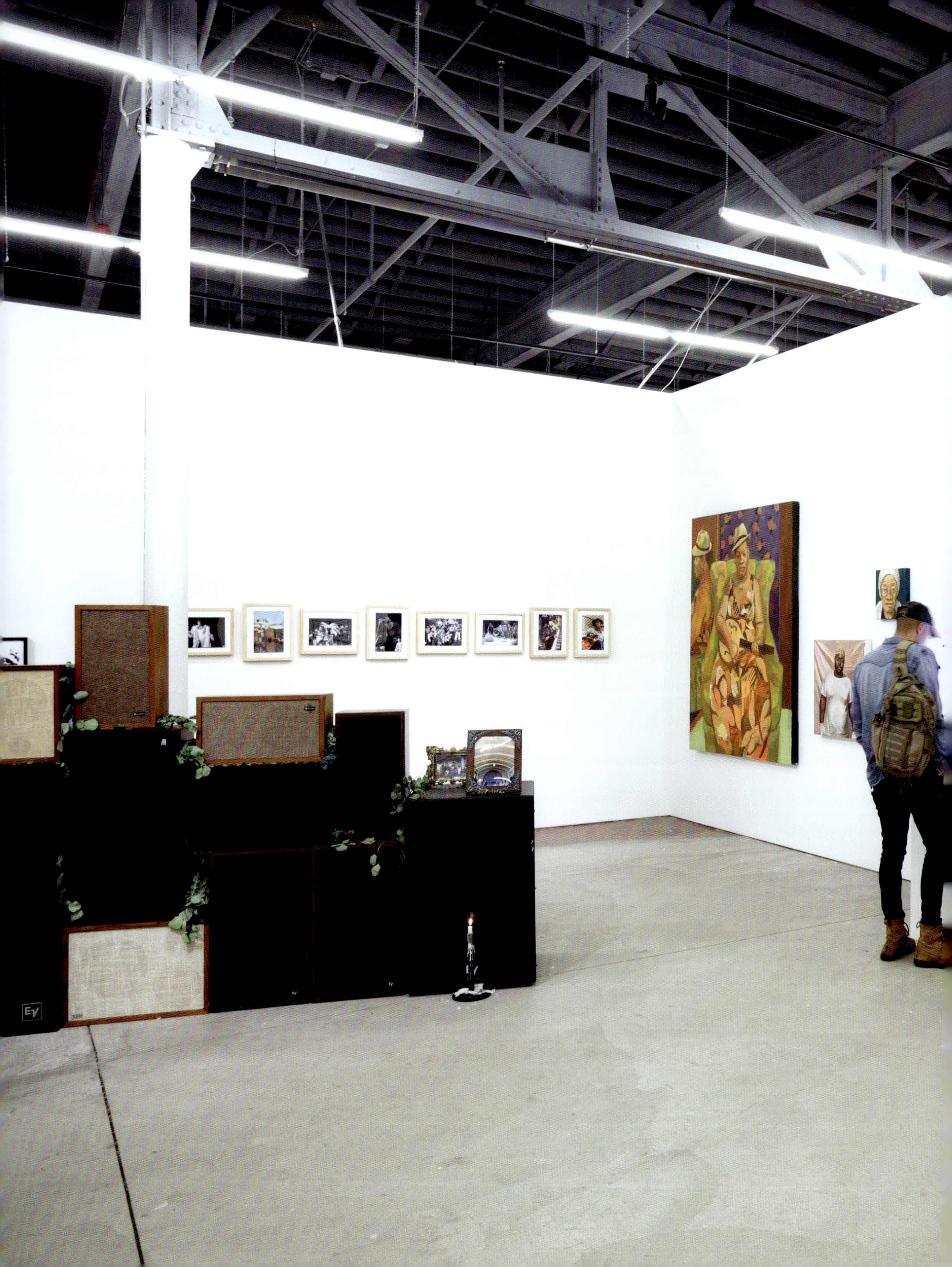

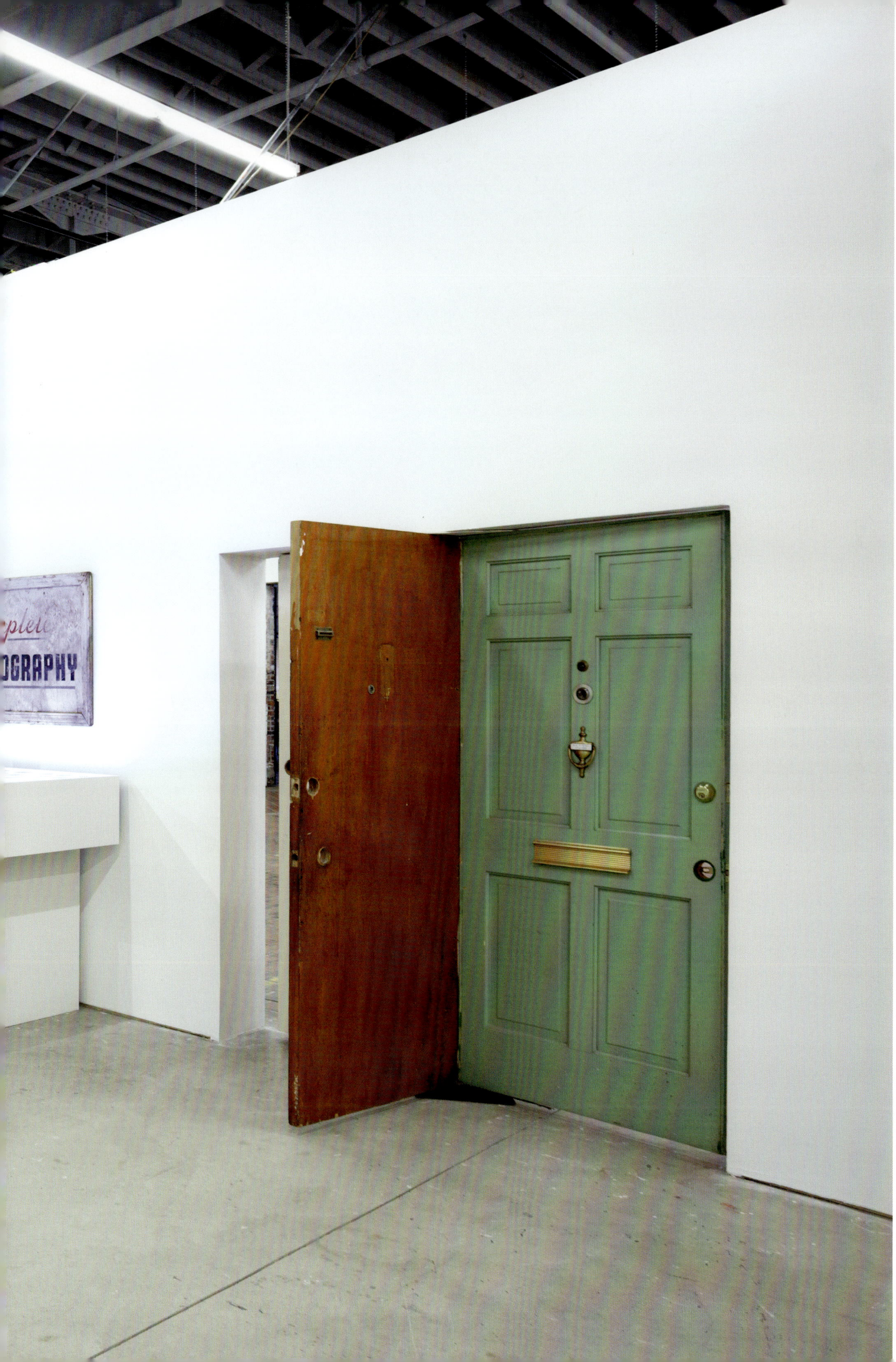
OGRAPHY

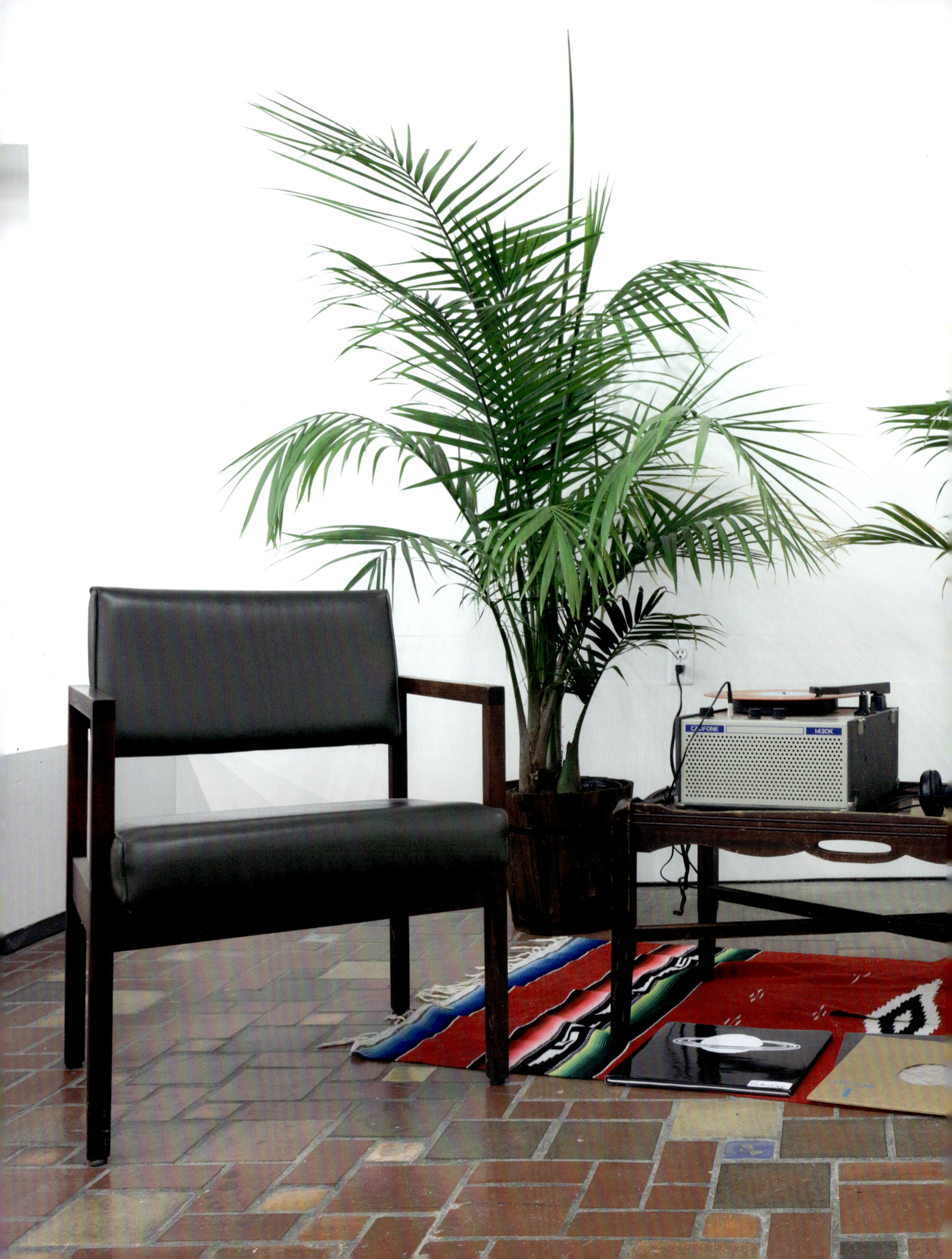
1430K

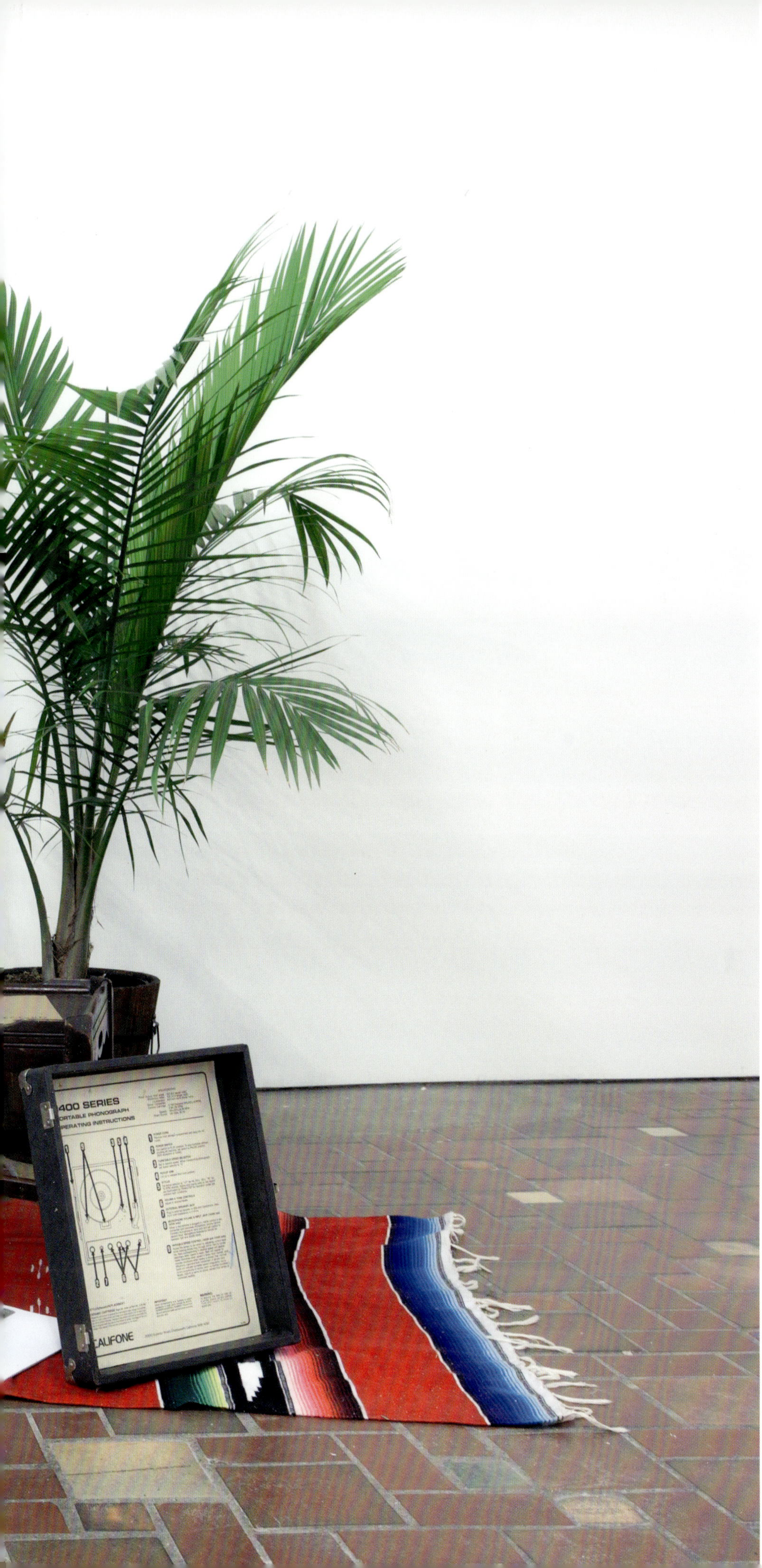
400 SERIES
CALIFONE

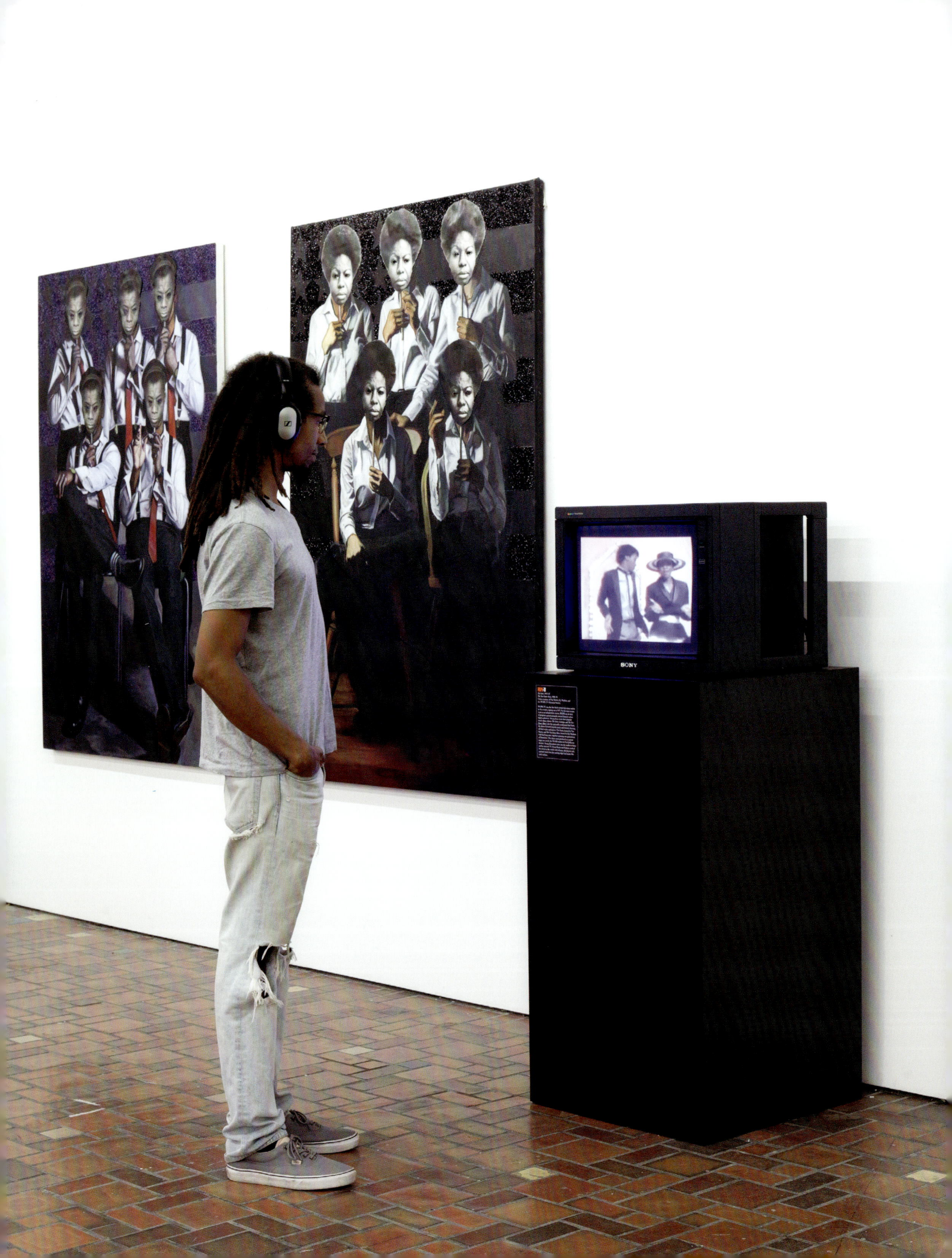
SONY

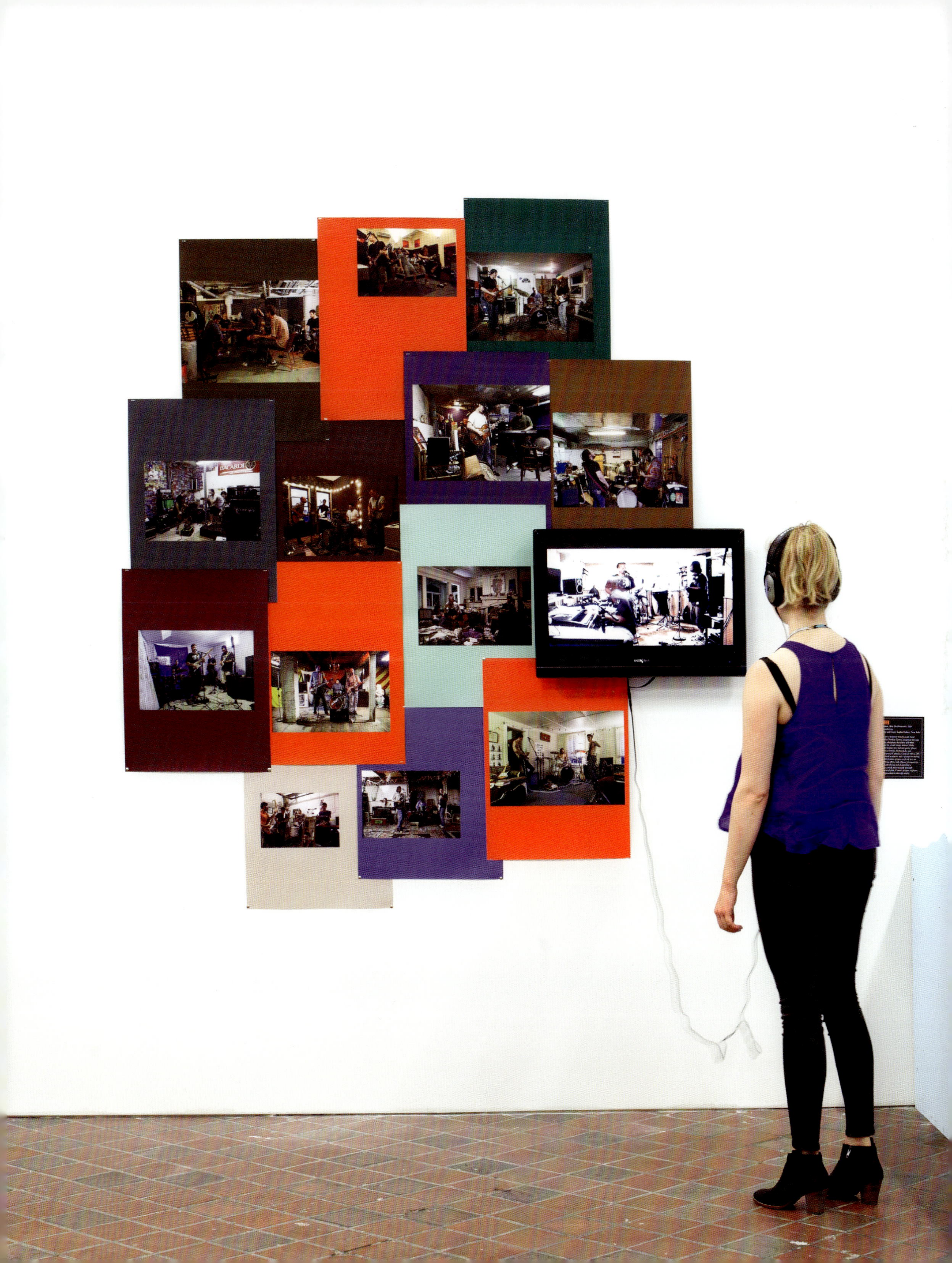

DETROIT'S SONIC REBELLION PLAYLISTS

MIKE RUBIN

Writer and expatriate Detroiter Mike Rubin has compiled several playlists of homegrown music, with a focus not only on landmark recordings in the evolution of each different genre, but also an ear for expressions of dissonant dissent, caustic comment, and sociopolitical subtext, their messages disseminating from concert stages and DJ booths to mosh pits and dance floors.

SONIC REBELLION VOLUME 1
SHOCK WAVE: DETROIT DISSONANCE, FROM PROTO-PUNK TO PROTOMARTYR

Title	Time	Artist, Year
Shock Wave	3:30	Index, 1967
2+2=?	2:49	Bob Seger System, 1968
Kick Out the Jams (Uncensored)	3:02	MC5, 1968
American Ruse	2:32	MC5, 1970
Skunk (Sonically Speaking)	5:15	MC5, 1971
Future/Now	3:06	MC5, 1971
I Wanna Be Your Dog	3:10	Stooges, 1969
1970	5:14	Stooges, 1970
Search and Destroy	3:26	Iggy & the Stooges, 1973
I Got A Right	3:22	Iggy & the Stooges, 1977
Politicians In My Eyes	5:51	Death, 1976
Freakin Out	2:49	Death, 1976
You Can't Kill Kill	2:05	Destroy All Monsters, 1974
City Slang	5:16	Sonic's Rendezvous Band, 1978
Strawberry Cheesecake	2:50	A-Moms (Algebra Mothers), 1979
Insanity	1:40	L-Seven, 1982
Sex Drive	0:55	Necros, 1981
Police Brutality	1:10	Necros, 1983
Pressure	0:16	Negative Approach, 1982
Tied Down	1:35	Negative Approach, 1983
Dead Stop	2:43	Negative Approach, 1983
To Label Is to Limit	1:22	Bored Youth, 1981
Vengeance	1:27	Fix, 1981
The Next Big Thing	1:07	Born Without A Face, 1986
Undertow	2:09	Born Without A Face, 1987
Spanish Bubblegum (live on WCBN)	2:16	Tom Gemp, 1987
Underfed (live on WCBN)	2:45	Tom Gemp, 1987
Feral	2:09	Gories, 1989
I Think I've Had It	2:13	Gories, 1989
The Big Three Killed My Baby	2:29	White Stripes, 1999
Fell In Love With A Girl	1:50	White Stripes, 2001
Get It While You Can	2:27	Dirtbombs, 2003
Don't Break My Heart	1:46	Dirtbombs, 2003
Wayne County Roads	4:16	Tyvek, 2012
Come & See	3:57	Protomartyr, 2014
A Private Understanding	5:19	Protomartyr, 2017

SONIC REBELLION VOLUME 2
FREE YOUR MIND AND YOUR ASS WILL FOLLOW: FUNKADELIC'S SATIRIC SOCIAL COMMENTARY

Title	Time	Artist, Year
Music For My Mother	5:39	Funkadelic, 1969
I Got A Thing, You Got A Thing, Everybody's Got A Thing	3:54	Funkadelic, 1970
Free Your Mind And Your Ass Will Follow	10:07	Funkadelic, 1970
Funky Dollar Bill	3:17	Funkadelic, 1970
Eulogy And Light	3:36	Funkadelic, 1970
Can You Get To That	2:50	Funkadelic, 1971
You And Your Folks, Me And My Folks	3:37	Funkadelic, 1971
Super Stupid	3:57	Funkadelic, 1971
A Whole Lot of BS	2:14	Funkadelic, 1972
If You Don't Like The Effects, Don't Produce The Cause	3:48	Funkadelic, 1972
Everybody Is Going To Make It This Time	5:57	Funkadelic, 1972
America Eats Its Young	5:54	Funkadelic, 1972
Biological Speculation	3:10	Funkadelic, 1972
Wake Up	6:28	Funkadelic, 1972
March To The Witch's Castle	6:02	Funkadelic, 1973
Cosmic Slop	5:20	Funkadelic, 1973
Standing On The Verge Of Getting It On	5:10	Funkadelic, 1974
Better By The Pound	2:44	Funkadelic, 1975
Who Says A Funk Band Can't Play Rock?	6:18	Funkadelic, 1978
Lunchmeataphobia (Think, It Ain't Illegal Yet)	4:12	Funkadelic, 1978

SONIC REBELLION VOLUME 3
INNER CITY BLUES: SOCIALLY CONSCIOUS SOUL (& SOULFUL FOLK-ROCK)

Track	Time	Artist, Year
Cloud Nine	3:38	Temptations, 1969
Runaway Child, Running Wild	4:50	Temptations, 1969
Ball of Confusion	4:10	Temptations, 1970
Papa Was A Rollin' Stone	7:02	Temptations, 1972
Love Child	3:03	Diana Ross & the Supremes, 1970
War	3:29	Edwin Starr, 1970
What's Going On	3:55	Marvin Gaye, 971
Save the Children	4:03	Marvin Gaye, 1971
Inner City Blues (Make Me Wanna Holler)	3:07	Marvin Gaye, 1971
Mercy Mercy Me (The Ecology)	2:31	Marvin Gaye, 1971
Higher Ground	3:14	Stevie Wonder, 1973
Living For the City	7:25	Stevie Wonder, 1973
You Haven't Done Nothin'	3:26	Stevie Wonder, 1974
Village Ghetto Land	3:25	Stevie Wonder, 1976
Pastime Paradise	3:28	Stevie Wonder, 1976
Black Man	8:30	Stevie Wonder, 1976
Sugar Man	3:49	Rodriguez, 1970
This Is Not A Song, It's An Outburst: Or, The Establishment Blues	2:07	Rodriguez, 970
Hate Street Dialogue	2:34	Rodriguez, 1970
Inner City Blues	3:27	Rodriguez, 1970
Rich Folks Hoax	3:06	Rodriguez, 1970
Gommorah (A Nursery Rhyme)	2:21	Rodriguez, 1970
Cause	5:30	Rodriguez, 1971

SONIC REBELLION VOLUME 4
ALLEYS OF YOUR MIND: INNOVATIONS IN ELECTRONIC MUSIC

Track	Time	Artist, Year
Intro: Midnight Funk Association	1:18	Electrifying Mojo, 1977-1985
Methane Sea - Aftermath	5:32	Richard Davis, 1978
Alleys Of Your Mind	3:33	Cybotron, 1981
Clear	4:48	Cybotron, 1983
No UFOs	7:02	Model 500, 1985
Night Drive	6:10	Model 500, 1985
Off To Battle (Remix)	6:07	Model 500, 1987
Strings of Life	8:25	Rhythim Is Rhythim, 1987
Nude Photo	5:40	Rhythim Is Rhythim, 1987
It Is What It Is	6:28	Rhythim Is Rhythim, 1988
Good Life	4:05	Inner City, 1988
Force Field	5:11	Reese & Santonio, 1988
Pump the Move	4:20	E-Dancer, 1991
The Art of Stalking	6:19	Suburban Knight, 1990
Oscillator	6:25	Paperclip People, 1991
Paperclip Man	5:00	Paperclip People, 1991

SONIC REBELLION VOLUME 5
FOR THOSE WHO KNOW: UNDERGROUND RESISTANCE AND BEYOND

Riot	4:55	Underground Resistance, 1991
Punisher	5:38	Underground Resistance, 1991
Code Of Honor	4:04	Underground Resistance, 1992
Sonic Destroyer	5:00	X-101, 1992
Groundzero (The Planet)	7:33	X-102, 1992
Changes of Life	4:54	Jeff Mills, 1992
The Seawolf	5:49	Underground Resistance, 1992
Nocturbulous	5:42	Dark Energy, 1993
Mind of a Panther	3:17	Dark Energy, 1994
Sea Quake	4:35	Drexciya, 1992
Positron Island	4:08	Drexciya, 1993
Living On The Edge	3:35	Drexciya, 1994
Take Your Mind	2:44	Drexciya, 1994
Water Walker	3:40	Drexciya, 1994
The Countdown Has Begun	3:09	Drexciya, 1995
Minus	5:13	Robert Hood, 1994
Jupiter Jazz	4:31	Underground Resistance, 1992
Hi-Tech Jazz	5:36	Galaxy 2 Galaxy, 1993
First Galactic Baptist Church	7:12	Galaxy 2 Galaxy, 1997
Daystar Rising	3:44	Octave One, 1998
Jaguar (Original Mix)	6:37	Aztec Mystic A.K.A. DJ Rolando, 1999
Transition	6:25	UR, 2002
Kill My Radio Station	4:24	UR, 2007

SONIC REBELLION VOLUME 6
DETROIT STATE OF MIND: FURTHER STRATAGEMS OF ELECTRONIC WARFARE

Technarchy	5:59	Cybersonik, 1990
Spastik	9:21	Plastikman, 1993
Losing Control	6:57	DBX, 1994
Parallax View	5:03	Ectomorph, 1995
Master Organism	3:06	Dopplereffekt, 1995
Sterilization	2:30	Dopplereffekt, 1997
Detroit State of Mind	5:48	Anthony "Shake" Shakir, 1998
Instant Insanity	12:10	Theo Parrish, 2001
Welcome Back	3:01	Theo Parrish, 2014
Make No War	7:33	Theo Parrish, 2014
U Can Dance If U Want 2 (Mix 5)	6:34	Moodymann, 1997
Det.riot	2:48	Moodymann, 2008
Solely Supported	5:52	Omar-S, 2010
Hell On Earth	3:52	Omar-S, 2017
Dr Crunch	5:53	KMFH, 2013
Paradise Valley	4:42	Jay Daniel, 2016

CHECKLIST OF ARTWORKS AND OBJECTS IN THE EXHIBITION

BARBARA WEINBERG BAREFIELD

Selected photographs, 1973–81
Digital prints, 2017
Courtesy the artist
Aretha Franklin, Ford Auditorium, 1977
Faruq Z. Bey on the roof of the Kean Building, Detroit, 1979
Patti LaBelle, Masonic Temple, Detroit, 1975
James Brown, Ann Arbor Blues and Jazz Festival in exile in Windsor, 1974
Creative Arts Collective Ensemble at Detroit Institute of Arts, Detroit, 1981
Sun Ra Arkestra, Ann Arbor Blues and Jazz Festival, Ann Arbor, 1973
Sippie Wallace with her great grand-niece, Detroit, 1979
John Lee Hooker, Ann Arbor Blues and Jazz Festival in exile in Windsor, 1974

SADIE BARNETTE

Government Employees from *My Father's FBI File*
2017
Archival pigment prints on archival paper
22 x 17 inches each (5 prints)
Courtesy the artist

ANDREA BOWERS

Radical Hospitality
2015
Stainless steel, aluminum tubes, wood, chain, 4 neon signs with cable and 2 power sources
118 1/8 H x 39 3/8 W x 39 3/8 D inches
Courtesy KADIST, Paris and San Francisco

VIVIAN CACCURI

High Fidelity
2017
Vintage loudspeakers, custom soundtrack, tallow candles, framed photographs, foliage
Dimensions variable
Courtesy the artist and A Gentil Carioca, Rio de Janeiro

JUAN CAPISTRÁN

We Like the Cars That Go Boom... the roar of the people could be farts
2011
Cardboard, stereo amp, speakers, sound file
14 x 24 x 84 inches
Courtesy the artist and Artists Pension Trust

NATHAN CARTER

Ladies and Gentlemen, Meet the Dramastics
2016
Mixed Media Installation
Dimensions variable
Courtesy the artist and Casey Kaplan, New York

MARCELO CIDADE

Monumento ao Monumento
2010
Galvanized iron containment gates
236 7/32 x 78 ¾ x 78 ¾ inches
Courtesy the artist and Galeria Vermelho, São Paulo

MINERVA CUEVAS

Disidencia v. 2.0
2008–10
HD video, 25:43 minutes, color, sound
Courtesy the artist and Kurimazutto, Mexico City

CHRISTOPHER CUSHMAN

Heaven / House of Charles, FIERCE! Collection, 1994
Digital prints, 2017
Courtesy the artist

JAMAL CYRUS

Transformation Green
2016
Graphite, wax, vinyl records, grits and gel medium on dyed canvas mounted on styrene
54 × 59 inches each
Courtesy Inman Gallery, Houston

Pride Frieze - Jerry White's Record Shop, Central Avenue, Los Angeles
2017
Record sleeves, digital prints, ink, watercolor, tape, masonite, Golden Gac 100, gesso, acrylic paint, Russian Birch plywood, Golden Fine Pumice Gel, wax, Plexiglass, reclaimed salvage wood
121 ¼ x 126 ½ x 12 inches
Courtesy Inman Gallery, Houston

BEN HALL

Orwell in Burma
2017
Stretched Fleece
90 x 90 inches
Courtesy the artist and Young World, Detroit

A. QADIM HAQQ

Digital prints, 2017
Courtesy the artist and Techno Art Gallery, Detroit
Analog Assassin (Underground Resistance, Underground Resistance), 2002
Knights of the Jaguar EP (The Aztec Mystic, Underground Resistance), 1999
Night Vision Records concept art, 2006
Classics (Model 500, R&S Records), 1993
Muse of Silence (Orlando Voorn), 2008
Divine Intervention (Orlando Voorn), 2013

MATTHEW HARRISON AND CORINE VERMEULEN

Benign Violations
2017
HD video, 11:18 minutes, color, sound
Courtesy the artists and Jessica Silverman Gallery, San Francisco

DAVID HARTT

The Republic
2014
HD video, 16:08 minutes with score by Sam Prekop
Courtesy the artist and David Nolan Gallery, New York

JIBADE-KAHLIL HUFFMAN
Yesterday (Our Love Went into a Coma)
2011–ongoing
Video, monitor, microphone, love poem
Color, 3:51 minutes, silent
Courtesy the artist and Anat Ebgi, Los Angeles

JULIANA HUXTABLE
Untitled (Faceless)
2017
Vinyl text
Dimensions variable
Courtesy the artist and Reena Spaulding Fine Arts, New York
Rashid Johnson
Birth of Cool
2014
Black soap, wax
48 ½ x 72 ½ x 2 ½ inches
Courtesy the artist

TITUS KAPHAR
2016/1963
2016
Oil on Canvas
30 x 20 inches each panel
Courtesy the artist and Jack Shainman Gallery, New York

RICHARD LEWIS
Tracey With Mandolin
2013
Oil on canvas
72 x 60 inches

Self-Portrait as a Muslim
1999
Oil on canvas
24 x 24 inches

My Mother
2010
Oil on canvas
12 x 12 inches
Courtesy the artist

GLENN LIGON
Condition Report
2000
Iris print and Iris print with serigraph, 2 parts
Edition of 20, 7 Aps and 2 PPs
Published by Jean Noblet Studio
32 x 22 3/4 inches each
Collection of KADIST, San Francisco and Paris
© Glenn Ligon; Courtesy of the artist, Luhring Augustine, New York, Regen Projects, Los Angeles, and Thomas Dane Gallery, London.

DANIEL JOSEPH MARTINEZ
Riot Shield (Butter)
Riot Shield (Cherry Blossom)
2012
Riot shields with paint
39 3/8 x 19 1/8 x 5 3/4 inches each
Courtesy the artist and Roberts and Tilton, Los Angeles

A Meditation on the Possibility of Romantic Love; or, Where You Goin' with That Gun in Your Hand: Bobby Seale and Huey Newton Discuss the Relationships between Expressionism and Social Reality Present in Hitler's Paintings
2005
White Carrara marble
11 x 4 1/2 x 1 inches each
Courtesy of the artist and Roberts and Tilton, Los Angeles

DARIN MICKEY
Death Takes a Holiday
Archival pigment prints, 2014–15
Dimensions variable
Courtesy the artist
"5th Ave Façade," Fifth Avenue Records and Tapes, Brooklyn, NY 2014
"Basement Stack," Attic Records, Millvale, PA 2015
"Bathtub Storage," George's Song Shop, Johnstown, PA 2015
"Dusty Fingers," Platter World, Garfield, NJ 2015
"Floor to Ceiling," R&B Records, Upper Darby, PA 2014
"Milk Bone," Platter World, Garfield, NJ 2015
"Mosaic," Attic Records, Millvale, PA 2015
"Renovations," George's Song Shop, Johnstown, PA 2015
"Surveillance," Attic Records, Millvale, PA 2015
"Trespassers & Survivors," R&B Records, Upper Darby, PA 2014

GORDON NEWTON
Deconstructed Amplifiers
2003
Wood, electrical components, paint, resin, cardboard, cloth
Courtesy Third Man Records, Cass Corridor

ALAN OLDHAM
Digital prints, 2017
Courtesy the artist and Techno Art Gallery, Detroit
Illuminati Child (Alan Oldham, Final Sessions), 2016
Expressed (Erik van den Broek, De:Tuned), 2016
Social Housing (MArquisHawkes, Houndstouth), 2016
Rhythim Is Rhythim, Beyond the Dance (Derrick May, Transmat), 1989
Rhythim Is Rhythim, Nude Photo (Derrick May, Transmat), 1989
The Detroit People Mover EP — iRobots Remix (Derrick May, Juan Atkins, Orlando Voorn, Opilec), 2013

ADAM PENDLETON
Untitled (A Victim of American Democracy)
2017
Silkscreen ink and spray paint on canvas
84 x 60 inches
Courtesy of the artist

PEDRO REYES
Armas (Destruction)
2012
HD video 3:50 minutes, sound

Armas (Taller)
2012
HD video 4:25 minutes, sound

Armas (Conceierto)
2012
HD video 4:58 minutes, sound
Courtesy the artist and Lisson Gallery, London and New York

IMANI ROACH
Good to Me as I Am to You (After Aretha)
2017
Paraffin wax
18 sculptures
5 x 4 x 3 inches each
Courtesy the artist

TYLONN SAWYER
Class Photo #3: Black Convening
Class Photo #4: Black Convening
2017
Oil, collage, and glitter on canvas
70 x 46 inches each
Courtesy the artist

Cabal: Class of 2016
2016
Charcoal drawing and mixed media on canvas
60 x 96 inches
Courtesy the DeAndre and Desiré Levy Collection

LENI SINCLAIR
Selected photographs, 1968–92
Pigment prints, 2017
Courtesy the artist
John Sinclair, 1968
MC5, 1969
White Panthers in Ann Arbor, 1970
Fred Smith—MC5, 1969
Fred Smith—MC5, 1969
Fred "Sonic" Smith—MC5, 1969
Sign of the Times, 1992
Wayne Kramer—MC5, 1969
Black Panthers in Detroit, 1969

BAYETÉ ROSS SMITH
Got the Power: Detroit
2017
Dimensions variable
Vintage boom boxes, custom mixtape
Courtesy the artist

CAULEEN SMITH
Black Utopia: Rehearsal Tapes and Lectures Selected from the Alton Abraham / Sun Ra Audio Archives
2012
Double LP
Courtesy the artist and Corbett vs. Dempsey, Chicago

DIAMOND STINGILY
Dad is Byron
2017
Audio, vintage telephone
42:32 minutes
Courtesy the artist

MICKALENE THOMAS
Do I Look Like a Lady?
2016
Mixed media installation
Installation views, LA MOCA
© Mickalene Thomas / Artist Rights Society (ARS), New York.
Courtesy the artist and Lehmann Maupin, New York and Hong Kong

HANK WILLIS THOMAS
What Goes Without Saying
2012
Wooden pillory and microphone
64 x 66 x 36 inches installed
Courtesy the artist and Jack Shainman Gallery, New York

Priceless
2004
Lambda print
70 x 96 inches
Courtesy the artist and Jack Shainman Gallery, New York

KEVIN JEROME EVERSON
It Seems to Hang On
2015
HD video, 19:50 minutes, sound, color and B&W
Courtesy the artist and Picture Palace Pictures, New York

STERLING TOLES
Resurget Cineribus
2017
LP Cover Layouts
12 x 12 inches
Courtesy the artist

ANTHONY WARNICK
You May Choose
2017
Prisoner-produced offset prints
12 x 18 inches each
Courtesy the artist

BRENNA YOUNGBLOOD
Revolver
2013
Mixed media
60 x 60 x 60 inches each
Courtesy Honor Fraser Gallery, Los Angeles

1960S CONCERT POSTERS AND POLITICAL CONCERT POSTERS
Archival posters, 1966–71
Courtesy Greg Bosch, Detroit
Gary Grimshaw, MC5, The Chosen Few, Grande Ballroom, October 6–7, 1966
Gary Grimshaw, Sun Ra, MC5, Community Arts Auditorium, Wayne State, June 18, 1967
Donny Dope, Tim Buckley, Grande Ballroom, July 21–22, 1967
Gary Grimshaw, Chambers Brothers, MC5, Thyme, Grande Ballroom, September 1–2, 1967
Carl Lundgren, Lyman Woodard Trio, The Woolies, John Lee Hooker, December 26, 28–30, 1967
Gary Grimshaw, Steering Committee's Guerrilla Lovefare, Grande Ballroom, January 29, 1967
J. & S. Stoddard, International Solidarity Day, Grande Ballroom, October 2, 1970
Gary Grimshaw, John Sinclair Freedom Rally, Crisler Arena, Ann Arbor, December 10, 1971

ONYX ASHANTI
3D-printed glove and beatjazz icon
2016
Courtesy the artist

EFE BES
Modified drum from Ghana and mask
Wood, acrylic paint, beads, yarn, duct tape
Courtesy the artist

BLACK FORUM LABEL
1970–73
Records courtesy Motown Museum
Stokely Carmichael, *Free Huey!*, October 1970
Guess Who's Coming Home: Black Men Fighting Recorded Live in Vietnam, narrated by Wallace Terry, February 1972
Imamu Amiri Baraka and The Original Last Poets, *Black Spirits*, April 1972
Imamu Amiri Baraka, *It's Nation Time: African Visionary Music*, April 1972
Elaine Brown, *Elaine Brown*, April 1973

THE BLACK PANTHER: BLACK COMMUNITY NEW SERVICE
Founded by Huey Newton and Bobby Seale
Art direction and graphics by Emory Douglas
Vol. 3, no. 11 (January 5, 1969)
Vol. 5, no. 27 (January 2, 1971)
Courtesy Morry Greener, Detroit
Vol. 5, No. 20 (November 14, 1970)
Vol. 5, No. 25 (December 19, 1970)
Private collection, New York

EDWARD T. BRESLIN
Riot Film
1967
HD video transferred from 16mm film, 12:13 minutes, color, silent
Courtesy Detroit Historical Society

THE ELECTRIFYING MOJO
Radio program, WGPR-FM
1982
Courtesy The Electrifying Mojo and WGPR-TV Historical Society

DERRICK MAY
Ensoniq Mirage Sampler-Synth and Transmat Labels
Ca. 1986–88
Courtesy the artist

CARL PERRY
4x5 negatives from Perry's Photo Studio, Detroit
1960s–1970s
Courtesy T.M. Caldwell, Paul Lee, and Joseph Sopkowicz

WGPR-TV
The Scene, 1975–87
The New Dance Show, 1988–95
Videos courtesy Nat Morris, R.J. Watkins, and the WGPR-TV Historical Society

WHITE PANTHER PARTY FLAG
Circa 1968
Courtesy the Ben Blackwell Collection

ACKNOWLEDGMENTS

Sonic Rebellion: Music As Resistance

Organized by Museum of Contemporary Art Detroit

A rebellion by Jens Hoffmann with Robin K. Williams

Exhibitions Manager: Zeb Smith
General Coordinator: Naaman Rosen
Graphic Design: Judith Banham / Middlecott Design

We would like to direct our sincere thanks everyone who has participated in *Sonic Rebellion: Music As Resistance*: Onyx Ashanti, Sadie Barnette, Efe Bes, Andrea Bowers, Black History 101 Mobile Museum, Black Merda, Black & Red Books, Ben Blackwell, Book Beat, Greg Bosch, Vivian Caccuri, T.M. Caldwell, Juan Capistrán, Nathan Carter, Marcelo Cidade, Minerva Cuevas, Christopher Cushman, Jamal Cyrus, Tim Davis, Death, Detroit Historical Society, DJ Babe, DJ Dez, DJ Head, DJ Los, Emory Douglas, The Electrifying Mojo, Kevin Jerome Everson, Gary Grimshaw, Ben Hall, A. Qadim Haqq, Matthew Angelo Harrison and Corine Vermeulen, David Hartt, Kellie Hay and Rebekah Farrugia, Hello Records, Craig Huckaby, Jibade-Khalil Huffman, Juliana Huxtable, Rashid Johnson, Titus Kaphar, Mike Khoury, Miz Korona, Richard Lewis, Glenn Ligon, Daniel Joseph Martinez, Derrick May, Darin Mickey, MAHS Museum, Marsha Music, Martha Jean the Queen Legacy Committee, Nat Morris, Motown Museum, Gordon Newton, Abby Oladipo, Alan Oldham, Adam Pendleton, Pedro Reyes, Imani Roach, Mike Rubin, Tylonn Sawyer, Shrine of the Black Madonna, Leni Sinclair, Bayeté Ross Smith, Cauleen Smith, Diamond Stingily, Kathy Thayer, Third Man Records, Mickalene Thomas, Hank Willis Thomas, Sterling Toles, Anthony Warnick, R.J. Watkins, WGPR-TV Historical Society, Brenna Youngblood

Furthermore we would like to thank the following individuals who in various ways have helped to bring this exhibition together: Dashiell Arkenstone, Marc Arranaga, Amy Bark, Devon Bella, Fred Bidwell, Valentina Branchini, Joe Brittain, Rev. Sharion Ifetayo Brown, Dave Buick, Caroline Burghardt, Piper Carter, Lori Cassady, Federico Castro Debernardi, Bryce Detroit, Jeremy Dimick, Xander Dorr, Mike Dutkewych, Katie Edmunds, Teresa Eggers, Isabella Ellaheh Hughes, Khalid el-Hakim, David Ellis, Mattia Filippo Baldassarra, Alejandra Gaeta, Marcos Gallon, Maureen Gillis, Ingrid González Díaz, Claudia Gould, Michelle Grabner, Bobby Hackney, Brad Hales, Jamie Hardis, Cornelius Harris, Sami Hopkins, Karen Hudson Samuels, Kerry Inman, Tracy Irwin, Nathan Kelber, Nathan Kitch, Lisa Kurzner, Sophia Hoffmann Lambri, Isabelle Lauerman, Scott Lawrimore, Andrea Leal Montemayor, Emily Letourneau, Cary Loren, Liz Malarkey, Piper Marshall, Ariel Middlebrook, Liz Milnes, Madeleine Molyneaux, Jennifer Mora, Jessica Morgan, Marta de Movellan, George Newall, Amanda Nudelman, Michael O'Brien, Hans Ulrich Obrist, Devan Owens, Adriano Pedrosa, Lorraine Perlman, Roe Peterhans, Michael Plunkett, Loring Randolph, Coraleen Rawls, Martha Reta, Jazmine Rivera, Brendan Roney, Nicole Ruegsegger, Jamie Russell, Husain Salah, Nicole Sachs, Edward Schexnayder, Mia Serafini, Satori Shakoor, Jessica Silverman, Mary Skarbek, Trienere Steinberg, Emily Sundblad, Joanna Thornberry, Nina Tonga, Katherine Tuider, Valerio & Valerio, VC Lamont Veasey, Laura Watts, Peter Werbe, Anita Wilhelm, Vincent Worms

In addition we would like to thank the following galleries for their support: A Gentil Carioca, Rio de Janeiro; Anat Ebgi Gallery, Los Angeles; Artists Rights Society, New York; Artists Pension Trust; Casey Kaplan, New York; Corbett vs. Dempsey, Chicago; David Kordansky Gallery, Los Angeles; David Nolan Gallery, New York; Galeria Vermelho, São Paulo; Honor Fraser Gallery, Los Angeles; Inman Gallery, Houston; Jack Shainman Gallery, New York; KADIST, Paris and San Francisco; Kurimazutto, Mexico City; Lehmann Maupin, New York and Hong Kong; Luhring Augustine, New York; Picture Palace Pictures, New York; Reena Spaulding Fine Arts, New York; Regen Projects, Los Angeles; Roberts and Tilton, Los Angeles; Techno Art Gallery, Detroit; Thomas Dane Gallery, London; Young World, Detroit

Sonic Rebellion: Music As Resistance has been curated by Jens Hoffmann, Susanne Feld Hilberry Chief Curator at Large, with Robin K. Williams, Ford Curatorial Fellow.

Sonic Rebellion: Music As Resistance Advisory Committee: Dan Aldridge, Patrick Burton, John Collins, Meghan Courtney, Bryce Detroit, Jean Louis Farges, Dameon Gabriel, Oren Goldenberg, Marion Hayden, Shea Howell, Curtis Lipscomb, Cary Loren, Derrick May, Rebecca Mazzei, Michelle McKinney, Marsha Music, Miz Korona, Pirahnahead, Steven Reaume, Tim Retzloff, Karen Hudson- Samuels, Tylonn Sawyer, Leni Sinclair, Zana Smith, Sterling Toles

MOCAD exhibition support is provided by the A. Alfred Taubman Foundation. *Sonic Rebellion: Music as Resistance* is supported by the John S. and James L. Knight Foundation. The Ford Curatorial Fellows are supported by the Ford Foundation.

KNIGHT FOUNDATION FORD FOUNDATION

COLOPHON

This publication accompanies the exhibition
Sonic Rebellion: Music As Resistance

Museum of Contemporary Art Detroit
September 8, 2017 – January 7, 2018

Published by the Museum of Contemporary Art Detroit
Distributed by ARTBOOK/DAP, New York

Editor: Jens Hoffmann

Texts: Jens Hoffmann, Marsha Music, Joel Peterson,
Robin K. Williams

Copy Editors: Robin K. Williams and Lindsey Westbrook

Publication Design: Judith Banham / Middlecott Design

Print: OFSET YAPIMEVI, Istanbul

Photos courtesy of MOCAD and Naaman Rosen

Cover image: Vivian Caccuri, *TabomBass*, 2016.
Image courtesy of Luiza Sigulem.

MOCAD MUSEUM OF CONTEMPORARY ART DETROIT